PRAISE FOR *CHEDDAR*

"In this witty and well-researched study of an iconic food, Gordon Edgar serves up a satisfying slice of Americana. More than any other cheese, cheddar evidences America's tradition of innovation and embodies the paradoxes of our food system. From mammoth, processed blocks to clothbound, lard-rubbed wheels, Edgar details how cheddar straddles the continuum of industrial and artisanal manufacture to safely nourish great numbers of people while reinforcing class distinctions marked by taste. This welcome book credits the labor and ingenuity of America's food makers, both past and present."

—HEATHER PAXSON, author of *The Life of Cheese*

"On the surface, it would be easy to dismiss a book about a cheese so integral to the gustatory fabric of the American experience that it's hardly noticed as much more than a standard hamburger's melted shroud. But this paean to America's cheese tells the journey of a food integrally linked to the rise of 'cultures' in America (cheese and manufacturing, both) and, no less, to our value system. In Gordon's eminently capable hands, what could be a staid single-subject book is blithely entertaining, peppered with laugh-out-loud, respectful, and occasionally irreverent anecdotes, and ultimately a story chock-full of historical and contextual references that come together to create a newfound understanding and respect for a cheese that, because of this essential book, will never be 'just cheddar' again."

—LAURA WERLIN, author of *Laura Werlin's Cheese Essentials*

"Kudos to Gordon Edgar for his comprehensive history and contemporary analysis of America's iconic cheese. For any lover of cheddar, Edgar crafts the story of its unique place—from early farm-based, handmade products to standardized, industrial cheese to its renaissance over the past twenty to twenty-five years. A book to savor, it helps us understand how cheddar evolved over four centuries. He stirs an entertaining vat of literature, science, poetry, and sociology to reflect broad changes in American agriculture and our connections to food and place. Make sure to have a piece of cheddar, and perhaps a glass of beer, to accompany your journey!"

—JEFFREY ROBERTS, author of *The Atlas of American Artisan Cheese*

"Over the years I have read many thought-provoking works on cheddar cheese, mostly dealing with cheese science and technology, but rarely have such texts been 'fun' to read. Gordon Edgar's exploration of cheddar is both thought-provoking *and* fun, and has given me a fresh perspective on a cheese that I have studied for years and cherished all my life."

—PAUL KINDSTEDT, author of *Cheese and Culture*

"Gordon Edgar's latest work, *Cheddar*, is a lively story of this much-maligned but iconic cheese. No longer will I quickly pass over the large blocks of golden cheddar. Edgar has traveled the country unearthing the historic roots of cheddar, from the artisan clothbound wheels to the mass-produced blocks of commodity cheese, and writes with wit and humor. His passion and experience as a cheesemonger are evident, and the reader can't help but love cheddar by the end of this spirited book."

—KURT TIMMERMEISTER, author of *Growing a Farmer*

"*Cheddar* by Gordon Edgar is a book of vignettes, ripened from the author's wanderings around the country, milled with both large and small cheese-making experiences, peppered throughout with Gordon's political views, and aged to perfection.

Edgar shares his knowledge in sometimes smooth, sometimes sharp, and sometimes bitter ways, coming up with an overview that is tried, ripened, and ready to read."

—RICKI CARROLL, owner, New England
Cheesemaking Supply Company

Cheddar

Cheddar

A JOURNEY TO THE HEART OF
AMERICA'S MOST ICONIC CHEESE

GORDON EDGAR

Chelsea Green Publishing
White River Junction, Vermont

Project Manager: Alexander Bullett
Project Editor: Benjamin Watson
Copy Editor: Eileen M. Clawson
Proofreader: Laura Jorstad
Indexer: Linda Hallinger
Designer: Melissa Jacobson

Printed in the United States of America.
First printing September, 2015.
10 9 8 7 6 5 4 3 2 1   15 16 17 18

Our Commitment to Green Publishing
Chelsea Green sees publishing as a tool for cultural change and ecological stewardship. We strive
to align our book manufacturing practices with our editorial mission and to reduce the impact
of our business enterprise in the environment. We print our books and catalogs on chlorine-free
recycled paper, using vegetable-based inks whenever possible. This book may cost slightly more
because it was printed on paper that contains recycled fiber, and we hope you'll agree that it's
worth it. Chelsea Green is a member of the Green Press Initiative (www.greenpressinitiative.org),
a nonprofit coalition of publishers, manufacturers, and authors working to protect the world's
endangered forests and conserve natural resources. *Cheddar* was printed on paper supplied by
Edwards Brothers Malloy that contains 100% postconsumer recycled fiber.

Library of Congress Cataloging-in-Publication Data
Edgar, Gordon.
    Cheddar : a journey to the heart of America's most iconic cheese / Gordon Edgar.
        pages cm
    ISBN 978-1-60358-565-1 (hardcover)—ISBN 978-1-60358-566-8 (ebook)
1. Cheddar cheese—United States. 2. Cheese—Social aspects—United States. I. Title.

    SF272.C5E34 2015
    637'.354—dc23

                                                                        2015023765

Chelsea Green Publishing
85 North Main Street, Suite 120
White River Junction, VT 05001
(802) 295-6300
www.chelseagreen.com

This book is dedicated to my mother,
the person who first inspired me to write.

CONTENTS

ACKNOWLEDGMENTS

One of the saddest things for me in writing this book is that Ignazio Vella died before I really started working on it. Ig, of the Vella Cheese Company and Rogue Creamery, was one of the few people who managed to be part of the history of cheesemaking that I am writing about but also a great source of help and advice to the generation of cheesemakers who have made the American artisan cheese movement of the last forty years happen. I had many conversations with Ig over the years, as well as hearing him talk in public about the history of California cheese. Unfortunately, I was soaking it in but not taking notes. While I treasured those off-the-record times with Ig, I now regret that I didn't have a small recorder in my pocket.

Another acknowledgment I'd like to make is that, though this book has the grand title of *Cheddar*, obviously there is a lot of cheddar left out. I had to concentrate on just a few producers to make this work more succinct. There are literally hundreds of cheddar-makers whom I didn't mention in this book that are worthy of your attention. Check 'em out!

I really want to thank all the folks who let me interview them or who gave me tours: Kate Arding, Ricki Carroll, Sid Cook, Craig Gile, Ellen Fox, Tony Hook, Julie Hook, Dane Huebner, Mariano Gonzalez, Andy Kehler, Willi Lehner, Kelly McNamera, Neville McNaughton, Vince Razionale, Chris Roelli, Meri Spicer, Ari Weinzweig, Joe Widmer, and Rick Woods.

I also want to thank all the folks who put up with my obscure e-mail questions that must have seemed really random: Marc Bates, Tori Harms, Jason Hinds, Mark Johnson, Tami Parr, Mary Quicke, and Marianne Smukowski. Jeanne Carpenter, Paul Kindstedt, and Daniel Utano deserve extra appreciation for this by fielding numerous off-the-wall requests.

I am indebted to the following folks for letting me read something they wrote or hear something they said and agreeing to let me quote them later: Jane Burns, Lissa Howe, Rebecca King, Emiliano Lee, and Patty Peterson.

Cheddar might not have been as complete without the following specific people: Kathleen Shannon Finn for the inspiration early on, Mariah Sparks for the constant encouragement, Andrea London for introducing me to Ig Vella, Sheana Davis for inviting me to hang out with her and Ig so many times, Kelly Parrott for making me buy Tilly in 40-pound blocks, Reno Rossi for pushing me to buy that mammoth cheddar, Anna Muraco for putting up with me wanting to visit the World's Largest Cheddar, Christine Hyatt for sharing her knowledge and old ACS presentation, Heather Paxson for the concept of "post-pastoral," the Rome New York Historical Society for letting me look at their archives, Vicki at the Erie Canal Village for the hospitality, Debra Dickerson for the book loan, Ben Watson for the editing, Alexander Bullett for shepherding this book through the publishing process, Eileen Clawson and Angela Boyle for copy editing, Chelsea Green for believing in this book, Elizabeth Wales for helping me focus the concept, *Culture Magazine* (especially the Skinner sisters) for publishing five hundred words that later became part of the first chapter, my dad for always asking how it was going, and Megan Beene, Michelle Bruton-Delgado, Cary Bryant, Brad Dubé, David Gremmels, Matt Hart, Tim Healy, Jen Lopez, Lenny Rice Moonsammy, Julianna Uruburu, Christina Fleming, Mateo Kehler, and the whole Creighton family for encouragement at just the right moments.

All the folks in the Rainbow cheese department [Mariah, Pete, Andreas, Elizabeth, Kirsten, Myles, Seblé, Samantha, Megan, Anna (emeritus), Kelly (emeritus), and Jenny (emeritus)] and all the other Rainbow Grocery Cooperative worker-owners.

Lastly, I want to thank Laurie Jones Neighbors, my favorite person in the whole world. Laurie reads my terrible sentences, suggests great ideas (like the original idea for this book), and keeps me honest. I don't know that this book, or the last, would have happened without her. I am just so happy we, and Hermann Schnitzel, have such a great little life together.

Chapter 1

Mac and Cheese, Class War, and the Many Meanings of Cheddar

I walked in early with my judge-privilege. I could hear echoes from my footsteps. It sounded like I was walking into a cop-show trap set in a post-industrial warehouse, or—if I want to be less dramatic—stepping through a cheese make-room in the afternoon, when the work for the day was done. Soon, however, the space filled faster than I would have thought possible. Doors opened, food prep clattered, and the crowd rhubarbed as everyone hurried in to get their money's worth. The expected smells competed with each other to dominate the room: cheese, pasta, meat . . . dairy, doughy, dead. And presumably delicious.

Who would have thought that being invited to judge a macaroni and cheese cook-off would send me on a journey to see what cheddar can tell us about America?

Growing up, I thought that there were two things that were quintessentially American: casseroles and road trips. Though as I got older I developed a more nuanced view of the concept of "American," what transpired at this contest would send me on a series of road trips to look for deeper meaning found within a main casserole ingredient.

Being a cheesemonger has brought me many tremendous experiences. My first trip to France was an all-expenses-paid cheese tour. I have stayed at the houses and visited the farms and creameries of many of the best cheesemakers in the United States. I have an incredibly small niche of local fame that leads to people yelling things like, "Hey! Cheese Guy!" from moving cars instead of throwing things at me. My crowning local achievement, however, was being chosen to be a judge at this macaroni and cheese cook-off.

I am from a casserole culture. And while mac and cheese is not always casserole based, it is pretty much the only meal I never get tired of in any form. So being asked to judge a competition gave justification to my career choice of milk, mold, and fermentation. And I love pretty much any mac and cheese: love making it, love eating it, love emptying out the cheese bin in my fridge with so many scraps of samples that the portion cost would be prohibitive if done at a restaurant. Love.

I was excited about this event from the moment I was tapped for service. To heighten the anticipation even further, the event was not a country-fair-style cook-off. No, this was a hipster foodie event, so I expected to taste a lot of experimental dishes. Would there be a PBR-infused mac and cheese? Mac and cheese with grassfed beef formed into faux Vienna sausages? Locally sourced, artisanal, gluten-free, cruelty-free, ancient grain pasta topped with locally sourced, artisanal, gluten-free, cruelty-free, grassfed, rBGH-free, raw milk cheese? While I would often prefer a traditional version at home, I couldn't wait to see what the contestants would come up with.

Also, word of mouth had made this a hot ticket. As a monger, I am prone to exaggeration, but I am telling the truth here: the event sold out in under three minutes. The San Francisco–based online foodie hubs were filled with hate from those jealous that they could not attend. The Internet, like an overripe Brie, tends toward bitterness.

The cook-off was held in an old warehouse called Public Works right under the freeway, a venue that had been recently converted to an art space, dance club, and cottage-food market, though not usually all at the same time. It was a familiar setting because my workplace, Rainbow Grocery Cooperative, is also in an old warehouse and under the same freeway just two blocks away. In fact, this event was on Erie Street, which dead-ends across the street from our store. Down by us it's more of an alley, curving just enough that you can't see all the way down it to the next street. Once the loading dock for sausage factories and a lumberyard, it is now more often a homeless encampment, a place to score drugs, or a place to get mugged. Often, someone[1] adds an extra "E" at the start of the street sign to better introduce the alley to the unknowing pedestrian. The end of the street, where the contest was being held, dead-ends into weedy city land, sits next door to a women's health center, is down the street from the old armory that is now a porn studio, and is across the street from a couple of high-end restaurants.

Which means it is a perfect place to hold a fancy hipster mac and cheese cook-off.

I walk by this area every day on my way to work, but I had never actually walked down this part of Erie Street before I arrived to judge the event. Even though I was early, there was already a line down the block. Clearly I was not the only one who felt there was something special about mac and cheese.

SF Food Wars, a mostly one-woman organization that started having cooking contests to raise money for the San Francisco Food Bank while having foodie fun, put on this event, and no one entered to get rich or famous. The top prizes were one hundred dollars and a few gift certificates from local businesses. Still, bragging rights were at stake, and the competition figured to be fierce. During its short-lived three years of putting on events, SF Food Wars' cook-offs had garnered much attention and given winners local fame far greater than one might expect from two hundred people standing around eating the iconic American food of the day.

Public Works, pre-event, was a big, empty, postindustrial space. I was escorted up to the judging platform, where I met up with my fellow judges: food writer Tamara Palmer (who also acted as the resident judge at all Food Wars events), and Heidi Gibson (who had just won a nationwide grilled cheese contest and opened a grilled cheese restaurant in San Francisco). We were on partial display, easier to see than the actual contestants, who were frantically serving up plates to growing lines of eaters. Many of the entries were from culinary school grads, caterers, and local restaurants, so I figured we were going to taste some crazy, fancy-ass, *Top Chef*–y, ingredients-no-normal-person-would-use kind of stuff.

Attendees were also judges in their own right since there was a People's Choice Award given to the audience favorite. The ballot box sat right below our raised judging area. On two walls of the room, contestants served up their dishes. On a third wall there was a bar. We were on the last wall, sitting behind and slightly above the huge tower of prizes. The space was packed to—and possibly past—capacity. As the attendees started to settle in to their eating, the clatter gave way to discussion-hum and the muted sound of compostable potato forks hitting recycled paper plates. The atmosphere was young, excited, and, given the way tickets were sold, trending toward cliques of the Internet-savvy and urban food geeks, which of course overlap somewhat. Ironic T-shirts and trucker hats? Sure, there were some, but the Food War was more Google Bus than the newest drunken Ping-Pong[2] event.

Insulated from the surges of the crowd, we judges had a runner who would go and fetch us our judging portions of mac, as well as free beer. "Hmmm," I thought, "we don't *usually* get free beer at cheese judgings." "Free beer" is still a magic phrase for me, and it was actually effective on that day in helping me remember my place. Though I have judged a number of national cheese competitions, I am not really a professional mac and cheese judge. Palmer, Gibson, and I discussed the ground rules, and I realized immediately that our role was a lot more relaxed than everything about official cheese judging. No score sheets, no specific criteria—and we could talk to each other. Oh, and did I mention free beer? I know mac and cheese is comfort food, but I didn't expect to feel so much at home.

The good feelings kept coming: there was an announcement that the vegan entry had dropped out. While I am the "fake cheese" buyer at our store as well as the cheesemonger, and I can appreciate the utility of ersatz mozz for the right person at the right time, I really didn't feel the need to eat it or judge it against the other fifteen entries made with real cheese.

When the macs started arriving, I was not disappointed. There was a mac with habanero-infused olive oil and topped with chiles; a hearty whole wheat mac with butternut squash and hazelnuts; and classic mac with pork belly. We were treated to "Quack and Cheese" with duck confit; a non-casserole mac that consisted of crusty little balls of mac emphasizing the traditional bread-crumb/hard-cooked-cheese top; and mini-macs nested into tiny cups of maple-smoked bacon. The chefs threw in every amazing ingredient you could think of: greens, prosciutto, handmade chorizo, and so on. Expensive cheeses were used liberally, often in regional themes. One entry used all local cheeses; others employed Asiago, goat cheese, truffle cheeses, triple creams, and Parmigiano Reggiano. Clearly, what differentiated these macs from the recipes you can find on the Internet, on the back of a pasta box, or in your grandma's recipe file was, for the most part, a lack of reliance on cheddar.

My fellow judges and I discussed, dismissed, and deliberated. As we ate and debated, person after person pushed through the crowd to vote. It was as tough a decision as one can have: judging a bragging-rights contest of one's favorite food, and the argument and enthusiasm were infectious. Of course, I am not the only one who thinks of mac and cheese as a favorite. Jeannie Choe, the organizer of SF Food Wars, said that the mac and cheese contests were always their most popular events: "Mac and cheese is definitely an iconic American dish, but I think the appeal nowadays has a lot to do with customization, elevation, and, here in San Francisco, Californization. . . . Mac and cheese is a food that makes people irrational, unpredictable, and irresponsible. In other words, they will drop everything and trample a baby kitten for good-quality mac."[3]

I can say that we, as judges, rewarded creativity and classic style, balance of flavor and texture, and all-around good flavor—you know, all those things that food judges say at every county fair or reality TV show. But for me in this kind of judging, it's often about which one just *feels* right in the end when you are considering all the ones you have tasted. We picked the mac and cheese nested in bacon. It was also the one that was Vermont based and whose star ingredient was an aged cheddar.

The People's Choice winner was also one of our favorites, but the People's runner-up, which did not place in the judges' rankings, caused consternation. When that entry's chef accepted the award, he dropped a bombshell. His recipe was mostly Velveeta, the "pasteurized prepared cheese product" that—to lovers of cheese, tradition, and small family farms—symbolizes everything that's wrong with the American food system. Serious foodies in the audience looked embarrassed. Numerically speaking, many of them must have eaten, enjoyed, and voted for the evil anti-cheese! Was this entry an act of mockery and sabotage? Performance art attempting to deflate the foodieness that often barges in—entitled and unaware—in neighborhoods such as this one without regard to its effect on the community? A call to think about trendy repurposing of a cheap filling meal as another out-of-reach fancy food?

Up on the judging perch, I hadn't noticed that a skirmish in the class war had been raging below me. I thought back to a drunken party I had attended years before. It was at a large collective house (since evicted) right next to the San Francisco Tenants Union in the Mission District a few blocks from where we sat. I knew folks there from activist politics and the not-for-profit punk rock record store collective (not there anymore) where we volunteered. It was a party, but it wasn't very festive. One person there, a fixture of the local music scene and main coordinator of a collective venue (on that night, recently evicted), announced he was leaving the city. He was being evicted from his longtime apartment to make way for people who could pay more, and he couldn't find another place he could afford.

It's hard to explain to non–San Franciscans how under siege you feel in this city if you don't make a lot of money. We all live in fear of eviction for profit—not for nonpayment of rent—of losing friends who need to move to a more affordable city, of losing every cheap diner or neighborhood bar that we love so that someone can replace it with a high-end concept business.

As people got drunker at that party, some bitterness took hold, focusing on a super-fancy restaurant that had opened recently. "Did you see that place?" the about-to-move musician asked the room. "Fish tacos for twenty dollars. Fucking fish tacos! You can walk two blocks and get fish tacos for a couple of bucks. I guess it's worth an extra eighteen dollars for some people so they don't have to talk to brown folks. Damn. These people don't even know good food. We could probably serve them shit tacos for twenty dollars, and they'd be happy. SHIT TACOS!"

Among a small group of people the phrase "shit tacos" has lived on to this day. When one of us sees a new expensive restaurant displacing a taqueria or other cheap eatery, our first question is always, no matter what the food style, "How much are the shit tacos?"

There's irony here, too, though. Farmers in this country, who have often been on their land longer than we urban dwellers have been in our apartments and neighborhoods, face many of the same issues as renters in a gentrifying city. There are many pressures that force people off the land and out of the cheese business, and especially, until recently, out of the cheddar business. One of the solutions proposed by many foodies, of course, is that people need to pay more for their food. High-end restaurants that serve twenty-dollar tacos—whether fish or shit—are posited as part of the "solution" because, theoretically at least, they pay small-scale, local farmers a premium for quality, which in turn enables these food producers to stay on the land. What these restaurants do in the neighborhoods where they open varies, of course, and their effect is open to debate.

The restaurant that was the source of the twenty-dollar fish taco rant? It sat within about a football field's length from the mac and cheese judging. The judging—with the division of the judges' choices and the People's Choice Award—had become an unexpected battleground. Both winners were cheddar based, but which cheddar could really be called "the people's cheese": one aged for over two years in Vermont, produced by one of the most respected makers of cheddar in the country, or processed cheese food based on cheddar flavor? A Velveeta mac and cheese—normal to so much of the country—dramatically brought these often unspoken questions of authenticity, mode of production, flavor, class, and food justice to the surface, much like rennet does to whey in a cheese vat.

I like journeys. Predating my "career" as a cheesemonger, I had a teen obsession with a book on roadside attractions. I had the opportunity to visit quite a few in California growing up, then many more in some cross-country drives in the mid-eighties, but for some reason (one might call it fate) the page featuring "The World's Largest Cheese" called to me—but it just didn't fit into any of the routes I took. Even as I later visited Wisconsin on cheese business, I could never quite accomplish my quest. So finally, about ten years ago, when a friend needed help in driving across the country, I volunteered, with one condition. We had to take one extra day to see the cheese monument.

Since my friend is a sociologist by trade, she didn't flinch at this request. I have never been to grad school, but I am sure it must be part of the training of sociologists to not show emotion when people demonstrate odd cultural obsessions. I have never asked her, but perhaps she shifted from friendly conversation to research mode at that moment. Whatever the case, she agreed, even though it added a couple of hundred extra miles to a twenty-five-hundred-mile trip.

I have visited a lot of roadside attractions. Crazy roadside art may just be my favorite part of being an American. Not many—actually, surprisingly few, as far as I'm concerned—are cheese or dairy related, although I did get my picture taken with the enormously accurate veiny udders of Salem Sue, the World's Largest Holstein Cow, while passing through North Dakota. Over a few years of my life, I spent an inordinate amount of time driving from one end of the country to another, and while I have seen the important sights—the Washington Monument, Mount Rushmore, and so on—I always enjoyed what I considered "the real American monuments" more: places built by obsessed and otherwise frustrated but extremely talented people. Places such as the Garden of Eden, Nitt Witt Ridge, Watts Towers, the House on the Rock, the Winchester Mystery House, and the Forestiere Underground Gardens.

Unexpectedly on this journey, in fact, my sociologist friend and I had stopped at the amazing Porter Sculpture Park in South Dakota. We hadn't planned it; we were just driving on I-90, and there it was. While wandering

around the welded scrap metal art in the insane Midwest summer humidity, I asked the creator if he lived there year-round. No, he replied, he lived
on a farm and raised sheep the rest of the year.

"For meat or milk?" I asked.

He looked at me as though I was yet another stupid city person. "People
milk sheep?" he said. He wasn't really asking.

Clearly, if someone who works with livestock for a living has never
heard of a traditional and common way that many people in the world
use that same animal, there is a need for cheese history to be more widely
taught. In France (and, true, one would expect this of France) cheese is
so important to the culture that it has been argued that Camembert is a
national symbol. One of the best cheese books ever written argues that one
can glimpse centuries of change in France's national character by looking
at the history of Camembert.[4] In fact, one of the most enduring battles
in Normandy is over who really invented Camembert. The statue com-
memorating Marie Harel as the inventor of Camembert is undoubtedly the
reason that she is remembered today, perhaps at the expense of others who
were just as influential, and certainly at the expense of the concept of farm
recipes as a community effort and a part of oral tradition. Commemoration
is not a trivial thing.

The fact that her statue was funded by an American doctor who believed
in the medicinal benefits of the mold, cultures, and milk in Camembert
shows that cheese love has been crossing borders for a very long time.
However, many cheese practices have never been translated into "American." That a sheep farmer didn't know that much of the world milks ewes
doesn't reflect ignorance as much as it illuminates the history of dairy in the
United States. Until very recently, it was mostly all cows and all cheddar.

The real World's Largest Cheese, to which our cheese-seeking detour
was dedicated, was a 34,951-pound cheddar. Made in Wisconsin, it was
transported to New York and displayed in a large trailer during the 1964
World's Fair. I knew that the cheese—nicknamed "the Golden Giant"—was
eaten at the fair, but I also knew from my reading that a monument to the
Giant still stood in Neillsville, Wisconsin. Finally, I thought at the time, my
search will be over soon.

We got in late on that Midwest-humid summer night. Still, I was eager. I
asked the woman at the motel desk how I could find the big cheddar.

She replied, "You mean the big cheddar *replica*?"

For a moment I thought over the attractions I had visited previously. Why did the World's Largest Talking Cow get to be just "a cow" but the World's Largest Cheese had to be a "replica"? But I didn't dwell on it. The motel worker's semantic twist and lack of enthusiasm should have been a red flag, I realized later. If I'd been reading a cheese mystery, and I saw that response on the written page, I would think it was an obvious bit of foreshadowing, and I would have looked for the important clue to take with me.

However, I was too wrapped up in cheese reverence to notice. After all, while driving through the miles of small-town highways, I daydreamed that we would arrive and be warmly welcomed by local Wisconsinites with family histories related to the mammoth cheddar. Such stories as, "My cousin got married in front of it four years ago because she felt like it was more relevant than the church they grew up in." Or, "My grandfather lost an arm during the milling of the curds that made the original cheese. But the finished block was so beautiful that he never regretted it for a minute." I expected excitement, pageantry, and civic pride to be evident around a commemoration of the world's biggest cheddar.

In retrospect, I may have had unreasonably high expectations.

I approached—breath held—anxious to see the monument to cheese that American cheesemakers deserve, ready to see small-town civic pride on display. Residents of the state of Wisconsin go all out on their roadside attractions. Huge replicas of farm animals and wild beasts litter the highways. I didn't expect majestic. I was hoping for actual sculpture but would have been happy with a campy Styrofoam mass painted orange. Really, anything that showed the local love for cheese would have satisfied.

Unfortunately, this was not to be. No, what was housed in a beautiful, glass-sided trailer, painted with ORIGINAL WORLD'S LARGEST CHEESE, was not a replica of a cheese at all. It was a replica of the *large crate* that was used to transport the Golden Giant to the World's Fair.

It was a wooden box. ⟵

My sociologist friend looked at me. I could almost see her taking notes in her head. I spent the next couple of hundred miles in the car apologizing for taking us so far out of the way for *that*, but truly, I was disappointed not for our wasted day, but for cheese people everywhere.

I knew that cheddar was more important than this. I knew it deserved a better monument. I didn't know it at the time, but I think that was the moment this journey was born. Clearly cheddar was underappreciated, even though—or maybe because—it is ubiquitous. Cheddar has something to tell us, and I guess I'm the one who is going to try to interpret its story. That's what happens when you are a cheesemonger at an urban grocery store in a working-class neighborhood instead of a monger at an upscale cheese shop. Cheddar is not just something I can take for granted—unlike the makers of America's roadside monuments.

Driving away from the World's Largest Cheese Replica, I started to wonder, what would a monument to American cheese look like? And what does cheddar have to tell us about America?

An argument could be made that a monument to American cheesemaking should be a replica of, well, American cheese: an individually wrapped processed cheese single. In terms of importance in the world of food production, it's not so silly, really. Processed cheese food holds an important—if somewhat dubious to foodies—place and has a silent majority of support among eaters. And it does bear the name "American cheese."

Perhaps it's appropriate that the Henry Fordism of American food production brought us something called "American cheese." After all, the mass popularity of processed cheese is a culmination of much of the history and emblematic of the tensions inherent in both the new "artisan" food movement and the plight of farming and food-making in this country today.

Cheddar is a cheese that Americans eat without shame. More mozzarella may be produced and sold, and the image of Swiss cheese may be more visually recognizable, but no cheese is more loved than cheddar. Though it has historic importance and tradition, it's a cheese that spans the gamut of eaters. Some like it mild and cheap, some like it sharp and bitey, some like it traditionally made and rubbed with lard. But it's a cheese of comfort, and it is largely bereft of snobbery. It's *eating* cheese—not cheese you need to serve *just so*, or explain too much.

Unlike Camembert, there is no popular founding myth or partisan debate about cheddar's heroes or origins. In fact, the history of cheddar is largely untold outside an academic audience. That a cheese originally from England became America's favorite cheese is not entirely surprising. It certainly has been Americanized to the extent that most people have never even tried a traditional version. That there is a lack of oral history regarding how it came to be is not surprising, either, given how many changes it has gone through and given that there is a great regional diversity in the way people want their cheddars to taste.

In fact, through my cheese travels I have found that in some places there actually are *local* oral histories regarding regional cheddars or specific makers, not just all-encompassing ones. People swear allegiance to their home state versions, especially if they are from Vermont, New York, or Wisconsin. Even within those areas, cheese eaters will align themselves with the makers in particular counties or towns in a way that reflects the origins of cheesemaking in the world. There once was a time when milk could not travel very far without going bad, and if there wasn't a local cheesemaker, there probably was no great local love for cheese.

From farm-made varieties to local producers and co-ops to large factories and incredibly long shelf lives, the story of cheddar-making in this country reflects the shift of the U.S. population from the land to the urban areas, and the shift of food production from family farms to large-scale industrial agriculture. Cheddar-making, once a career choice that seemed like a wise financial move and a good escape from farming, now is an extremely hard way to make a living for a small-timer.

At a time when food politics is becoming more of a political issue—for increasingly militant urban shoppers "voting with their dollars"; for working people who chafe at the elitism of being told that "food should be more expensive"; for practical-joking home chefs who want to stick a fork in the foodie pretension that may help gentrify them out of their city—cheddar is an interesting food because it has fans on all sides of the food debate.

Every cheese eater in the country appreciates cheddar, though he or she may love completely different cheddars for completely different reasons. Cheddar has regional differences, subjective (but strongly held) beliefs by followers and makers from all over the world. It also, in the cheese-positive foodie wave that has highlighted more obscure and "new" cheeses, has gotten a little lost in recent years. While in no danger of extinction—indeed, more nuanced and traditionally influenced cheddars are probably being produced now in the United States more than at any time in the last hundred years—cheddar does get snubbed or forgotten at times, from both sides of the cheese counter.

Rarely is the snubbing malicious. It's more the idea that everyone knows cheddar. Cheddar does not necessarily create a buzz at a party or the excitement of a new food trend. But, I would argue, we—as cheesemongers, as cheese lovers—don't really know cheddar. It's everywhere, but why is that? A cheese that is used in Big Macs, mousetraps, and mac and cheese, yet is still served in mansions, is a cheese that calls out for more attention.

As for the World's Largest Cheese Replica in Neillsville, it's no longer there. Rumor has it that it was sold because someone wanted the refrigerated trailer. The wooden box, I assume, was used to heat someone's home in a cold Wisconsin winter, which probably was a better use for it anyway.

I shouldn't have been looking for what cheddar has to tell us in a monument. There's no perfect food to study to tell us about ourselves. America is too big and too diverse for that. But some of the answers can be found in a food that came to the United States as an immigrant and was transformed, not always for the better, by that process. Cheddar spans the regional and class differences in the United States, encompassing everything from traditionally made cheese crafted by hand and covered lovingly in lard, as it has been for centuries, to Kraft processed singles that are extruded by machines absent the human touch beyond the push of a button. Any cheese that appeals to that many people has a story to tell. There is a lot to say about cheddar, I think, and it also has something to tell us about ourselves.

Chapter 2

The Idea of Wisconsin and the Wisconsin Idea

After I decided that I wanted to search for the meaning of cheddar, I had to figure out where to start. Besides spending way too much money on obscure, out-of-print cheese books and reading them—arguably the best kind of journey possible—the first destination seemed obvious: Wisconsin, a state that roots its identity in dairy.

Not only does Wisconsin wear its cheese pride on its head, it also has a particular pride in cheddar. The only state with an official Master Cheese-maker program, Wisconsin boasts twenty-three master cheesemakers proficient in cheddar[1] and probably the most cheddar-makers of any state in the Union. Almost a full third of all cheese made in the state is cheddar.[2]

Jeanne Carpenter, Wisconsin cheesemonger, writer, and fourth-generation Wisconsinite, puts the Wisconsin love affair with cheddar this way:

> To most Wisconsinites, cheddar is our state symbol. It is the very meaning of our state slogan, America's Dairyland. We wear it on our heads at Green Bay Packer games (albeit in a foam version with holes—not sure about that), we debate which age we like best at dinner parties, and we swear that orange cheddar still tastes better than white, when we all know they taste the same. Cheddar is truly Wisconsin's identity. Of the 129 cheese plants in the state, 60 make cheddar—producing 561 million pounds of just this one type of cheese every single year. That's a lot of cheddar.[3]

Cheddar-making is also still rooted in community. I have witnessed—in my many visits to the state on official cheese business—fierce debate over whose region has the best cheddar, which producer makes the best cheddar curds, how a certain cheddar no longer in existence was the best cheddar ever and you just will never know how good it was because you didn't live it.

I don't want to give the wrong impression. The arguments—while intense—never got violent or anything. Wisconsinites are far too unified in their belief that their cheese is far superior to anyone else's in the country. They will always fall back on that unity before, say, a gang brawl between Widmer's Warriors and Henning's Hellcats can break out.

Yes, Wisconsin—home of the disappointing packing crate memorial to cheddar—was the obvious point to start my journey in earnest. When Chris Roelli, of the Roelli Cheese Company, invited me to attend the gathering of cheddar-makers he was hosting, I had to go. Even so, I was not quite prepared for what I had gotten myself into.

My first day in Wisconsin was all about transportation. I got a direct flight from San Francisco to Milwaukee, and my trip was fast and pleasant. I picked up my rental car in my after-flight daze, said no to all the scare-tactic extras, and was on my way. Very soon after landing I was driving out of Milwaukee, listening to a punk show on the left of the radio dial, and heading west to Shullsburg, which is in the southwest corner of the state, closer to Illinois and Iowa than to Madison or Milwaukee. Driving through small-town Wisconsin was a great way to acclimate to a few days of cheese talk.

Unfortunately, as I got to Darlington, where I was staying, I realized my big-city ways had not prepared me for small-town life. It was 9:15 p.m. Wisconsin time; I hadn't eaten, and nothing was open. Well, nothing except the gas station McDonald's, and it was about to close, too. I had to think fast . . . cobble together a meal of Pringles, powdered donuts, and cookies from the gas station mini-mart or get my first McDonald's meal in about twenty years.

I'm an American. I did what I had to do. Oddly, or perhaps not oddly at all, the Big Mac tasted exactly the same as I'd remembered; the same as the hundreds of Big Macs I had eaten growing up. There is an irony in this. Here I was, traveling halfway around the country simply to be in the presence of some of the best cheesemakers in the world, and I was eating food that is the polar opposite of what they make or I sell. For even as makers strive for consistency in their cheese, the object of a great cheesemaker—due to seasonality, maturation, or whim—is not to make the same-*tasting* cheese every time.

The mini-mart did carry New Glarus beer, so I bought a six-pack of Spotted Cow, a brand that's not available outside Wisconsin, to pair with my Big Mac, just to prove I really was a snobby urbanite. It was, in a word, *terroirific*.

While I started my physical journey in Wisconsin, I began the educational part before I left home, by making a list. I soon realized, though, that I would have to unlearn some of what I thought I knew. On that list, long since scribbled over and recycled, were a lot of mistruths and half understandings of how cheddar reigned as America's most popular cheese for about 150 years:

"Cheddar is the most popular cheese in the land."
False, though true for a long time.

"England invented it, and America cheapened it."
Kind of true, but not totally.

"Certainly America never exported it, except maybe recently to Asia."
False. Totally and completely false.

"Today's 40-pound block was a precursor of Velveeta."
False.

"Traditional clothbound cheddar went extinct in America."
True, but more complicated than I thought.

"Vermont cheddar and Wisconsin cheddar are very different."
True, but more out of tradition than necessity.

"'Cheddaring' defines cheddar. Always has, always will."
False.

"The cheddar factory built in New York in 1851 was the country's first cheese factory."
Controversial, and depends on the definition of "factory."

"There would be controversies about what could be called 'true cheddar.'"
True, but duh.

"Cheddar will tell us something about our food system."
Well, geez, I hope so, since I decided to spend a couple of years figuring out what it has to say.

Now, while I have no one to blame but myself for a lot of these misunderstandings, the fact that I have worked for over twenty years in the cheese business and didn't really have a working knowledge of how today's cheddar came to be tells me that most other people probably don't either. Many of these assumptions that I thought would provide my base of knowledge turned out not to be true, and I'm a big cheese expert, right?

That I bulked out my list with a couple of gimmes at the end didn't even keep my batting average from being pretty sad. To spare you, Dear Reader, from the same fate, let's go over a little cheddar history so that you don't feel the way I did walking into a room of some of the most experienced cheddar-makers in the country: like I just walked into an exam I forgot to study for.

It's difficult to pinpoint when any food practice began. Certainly historically—for survival—people borrowed whatever was useful from wherever they could so they could keep from starving. Some innovations or changes to traditional cultural practice became commonplace because people were trying to improve their lives by working less hard or making more money from the food they produced.

Most cheese, historically speaking, can be seen as simply an attempt to extend the life of milk. Especially in the days before refrigeration and pasteurization, the shelf life of milk was very short. Its transformation into cheese could literally mean the difference between life and death, a chance to have food that could last beyond today's immediate hunger. It also, later on in history, provided an opportunity to earn an income, something that could potentially put some distance between a farmer and poverty.

The debate about where cheddar fits into the food system has raged for centuries, not only from before cheddar's introduction to America, but before there even was an America. Made by peasants, it was often eaten by kings, which demonstrates that the problem of artisan producers not being able to sell their products in their own communities is something that has been with us a very long time.

Like many well-known cheeses, cheddar has its own particular history. Like those other cheeses, it has its origin stories, its moments of transformation, and its heroes, but unlike other cheeses, cheddar also has—to many at least—its villains as well. Cheeses with long histories have been transformed from small-town sustenance food to sought-after delicacy, and many eventually became what we think of as staples. Cheddar paved the way to the commoditization of cheese. But that comes a lot later in our story.

Many sources mention cheddar as having Roman roots. It makes sense, because Romans spent some time in what is now England, and they had learned and improved cheese skills from the Greeks, who had done the same with the Egyptians. Pliny the Elder in his 1st-century CE writings mentioned French Cantal—a majestic, 80- to 100-pound cylinder that is still produced today—and the Romans would certainly have been familiar with it. A big wheel of traditional cheddar is not so very far off from Cantal, relatively speaking, in terms of size, shape, flavor, and relative make process.

What we call cheddar today, even the name-controlled West Country Farmhouse Cheddars, is linked, but not identical, to the cheese made in that region in the 12th century,[4] when history begins to record it. Until the process was standardized closer to our present time, it was more cheese *from Cheddar* than what we would think of as cheddar cheese. After all, lack of a unified make process is a trait of food production in the era of *actual* artisans. By the way, chef and food writer Clifford A. Wright cites the first record of what we would now call "macaroni and cheese" appearing near the end of the 13th century in southern Italy.[5] Cheddar, England, is more than a thousand miles away, and in that era's much less global economy, it took a while for cheddar to become associated with the dish. Thomas Jefferson and his daughter Mary are often mentioned as popularizers of macaroni and cheese in America even though, when they served it at the White House, they preferred parmesan as the cheese.

As with many cheeses, cheddar acquired its name from the village where it was sold, and it was made in outlying areas of the immediate region in southwest England. Since farmers of those days could not directship orders made through the Internet, they had to bring the cheese to market on a periodic basis. These markets were kind of like today's farmers markets but without the cell phones, certifications, or health inspectors. Like many of the other cheeses that we think of as classics now, at first cheddar was strictly regional and rarely found outside its area of production. However, it was soon discovered that this cheese traveled better than soft cheeses, such as Camembert, so it was sought out by the foodies of the day: kings, queens, rich merchants, and so on.

There was variation in the size and shape of cheddar—a practice that actually continues with its modern-day equivalents to this day—because different-size farms produced different-size wheels based on how large their herds of cows were. In the days before milk was commonly pooled, the size of the cheese depended simply on the amount of milk on hand. In the Elizabethan period, according to the great cheese writer and cheesemonger Patrick Rance, some villages were producing wheels of 120 pounds[6] that took up to five years to mature. But these monster wheels differed in many ways from what even the most traditional producer of cheddar makes today. As well as other technical differences, they were rubbed with a thick layer of salt. This rubbing created cheddars with very thick rinds to prevent cracks, rot, and maggots.

In America cheese was produced from the earliest days of English colonization. This was a farm-based industry for the first hundred years or so, mostly done by the farm wife or, on bigger farms, overseen by her. However, production methods changed in the 1850s, and cheddar became the dominant cheese, surpassing Cheshire, a similar cheese but one that is almost forgotten today in the United States.

Indeed, it wasn't until the mid-1800s that what we think of now as the "traditional" cheddar came of age; that is, a cheese where the whey is scalded and the curd is salted and milled, then "cheddared": slabs of curd piled on top of each other, over and over, expelling more whey from the cheese. The curds are then put into tall cylindrical forms, pressed, wrapped in cheesecloth, and larded to seal the cheese. These big greasy wheels began to be covered in naturally occurring mold and bacteria, wrapped in cheesecloth, and rotated to ensure even aging.

The late 1800s was a time of cross-pollination among cheesemakers in the United States, as well as between the United States and England, as well as other English-speaking countries. Indeed, it's not too far a stretch to consider Roelli's 2011 Gathering of Cheddarmakers a continuation of that tradition. In fact, I am capitalizing "Gathering of Cheddarmakers" from now on, because the closer I got to the Roelli event, the more I started thinking of it as the cheddar equivalent of a stadium rock show, such as Monsters of Metal! In your head please add reverb when you see those words.

The mid-19th century is also the part of history when people's names, not just their regions, began to be associated with cheddar, and we'll visit some of those later in the journey. Probably not so coincidentally, this is also the period when cheddar-making went from being a female-dominated, farm-based cheese (especially in America) to a male-dominated, factory-made one.

If this were an English book, I would spend a lot more time talking about Joseph Harding, who is often referred to as the "Father of Cheddar." From a cheese-oriented family, Harding was all about improving cheddar and sharing information. He improved a tool to mill the cheddar curds in 1856, making the production more uniform and easier for everyone involved. He also was an early adopter of hygiene, which meant that there was less chance of cheddar's causing mass death to those who ate it. Safety, generally regarded as a positive step in food production, tends to increase a food's popularity. Harding shared his techniques widely, and his influence helped bring what we think of now as "traditional cheddar" to America and other English-speaking countries.

Harding's main bequest to the world of cheese was standardization. He studied cheesemaking methods, selected the best, then spread the word through individual makers and dairymen and cheesemakers' associations. And it was around this time that ordinary folks started eating cheddar on a regular basis. In the words of English food writer Horace Annesley Vachell, cheddar became known as a retailer-friendly "everyday, cut-and-come-again cheese."[7]

This standardization sparked the rise of cheddar-making factories, which changed the face of rural America over the late 1800s. In the 1900s these factories further refined the process, waxing their cheese after bandaging it and making what is called "rindless" cheddar. The precursor of the natural cheddar sold in most grocery stores today, the waxed cheddars led to a maximization of profit per gallon of milk since the sealing process was more effective than wrapping the wheels with cheesecloth. The seal allowed less loss of weight during the aging process, even if there also was an accompanying loss of some of cheddar's dynamic flavors. Since cheese is a food that is sold by the pound, and since aged cheeses lose (water) weight as they age, trying to retain the poundage that you have left when the cheese is put into the aging room has always been a top priority for the factory cheesemaker and often the target of innovative food technology, for good or ill.

Eventually this process gave way to further advances in the maximization of profit from milk by making cheddar in rectangular blocks—40- or 640-pounders—and covering them in plastic, not wax. These blocks, of course, are compact, store nicely on pallets, and can age a long time when vacuum-sealed in state-of-the-art plastic. Makers were experimenting with rectangular cheeses as early as the 1890s, but the plastic-covered

40-pounders would not come into vogue until after World War II, when technology tested in war was used to keep cheese from molding and profit from evaporating, literally. By the end of the 20th century, cheddar factories would be working on a scale unimaginable to a farmstead[8] or early factory cheddar-maker in the 1800s.

Rindless waxed cheddar was the ultimate factory cheese product until Joseph Kraft—yes, *that* Kraft, as in Kraft Foods, later owned by Philip Morris—came along. Though the Swiss had invented the concept of processed cheese a few years earlier, the Americans, particularly Kraft, ran with it after the end of World War I. Processed cheese differs from rindless cheddar in an important way. Originally made from rindless cheddar, it was heated and emulsified and formed into a "homogeneous plastic mass" to extend its life indefinitely. Later inventions of processed sliced cheese and processed cheese food (fewer dairy ingredients needed) came as the years followed, including the ubiquitous Velveeta, which not only was my favorite cheese growing up but which, in the form of a Velveeta mac and cheese entered in a fancy foodie contest, became a working-class flag of honor.

Which brings us back to the SF Food Wars macaroni and cheese cook-off. We judges recognized the Vermont-style mac and cheese as classic, even though it is really more reflective of cheddar's midlife crisis—an aged block cheddar with regional-based flavor. When I watched the crowd react to the Velveeta Betrayal, some eaters rejoiced, but many more were angered by their own unwitting choice of faceless factory production methods over the comforting, white-garbed, artisan cheese, smelling of milk and sweat. It was as if they had betrayed their own chosen cultural identity.

I woke up the day of the Wisconsin Gathering of Cheddarmakers a little nervous. Who was I to hang out with all these great cheesemakers? I mean, yeah, I sell the cheese of some of these folks, but I wasn't bringing anything to the table. I was grateful to Chris Roelli for inviting me, but not only was the Gathering a not-open-to-the-public event, it really wasn't even an open-to-the-profession event if you weren't an actual cheddar-maker. I wasn't the only guest invited, but I was the only one from outside the region and therefore also the only Californian.

Being a California cheese person traveling to Wisconsin to be with Wisconsin cheese people made me a little paranoid. The California mega-dairy model took the U.S. milk production title away from Wisconsin and helped drive many family farm operations out of business, until the Wisconsinites reinvented their smallness as a marketable attribute. And those "Happy Cow" commercials put out by the California Milk Advisory Board? Wisconsinites really, really hate those commercials. Really. Hate.

Which makes sense because they see themselves, for the most part, as the true dairy farmers, the ones who have smaller herds that actually graze outside, at least when it is not winter in Wisconsin. While there are plenty of cows in California that have million-dollar views of the ocean, cool breezes, and fog-fed grass for much of the year, to most dairy farmers outside the state, the image of a California dairy farm is a mega-dairy. They picture an enormous brown dirt feedlot full of flies and stench.

Statistics show why. The average dairy farm size in Wisconsin is still under 100 cows.[9] In the United States as a whole it is 172.[10] California? We average 850 cows per dairy farm.[11]

That's a lot of cows per farm!

I decided to embrace my role as a Californian in a different way. Since everyone was asked to bring 5 pounds of cheddar to share, I brought a half wheel of cheese from Central Coast Creamery in Paso Robles. When it came time to share the cheese during an awesome lunch of steak sandwiches and beer, it certainly stood out, being the only cheddar in the room made with goat milk. This was a room full of traditionalists. They were polite. They all treated me extremely nicely, and though the goat cheddar I brought wasn't exactly treated like a turd in the punch bowl, only a few very courteous or curious folks actually tried it. The goat cheddar beamed brightly, shining white as goat cheese does, while the others disappeared. For the record, the cheese was not at fault. Central Coast Creamery makes one of the best goat-milk cheddars available. It's just that for a lot of the traditionalists in the room not only do "goat" and "cheddar" not go together, it is likely that "goat" and "cheese" don't either.

The day lived up to its promise of "cheesemaking, fellowship, and education." There were over 350 years of experience in the make-room and some of the biggest names in the cheddar world. Some producers, such as Hook's and Henning's, are literally household names in Wisconsin because people's fridges hold packages of cheese that bear their names. Other cheesemakers—Willi Lehner, Andy Hatch, Bruce Workman, Chris Roelli—were famous in the cheese world for their creations (Bleu Mont Cheddar, Pleasant Ridge Reserve, Edelweiss Emmental, and Dunbarton

Blue, respectively). Also in attendance among the twenty-five or so folks there was John Jaeggi, coordinator of the Cheese Industry and Application Program at the Wisconsin Center for Dairy Research.

This Gathering of the Cheddarmakers was actually a follow-up to the visit of a bunch of folks from Neal's Yard Dairy the previous year. Neal's Yard is an English company that makes, ages, sells, and distributes most of the best handmade cheese from the United Kingdom. While my focus is on American cheddars, it should be noted that Neal's Yard owner Randolph Hodgson, who recently won a lifetime achievement award at the BBC Food and Farming Awards, is often credited with saving and reviving British farmhouse cheesemaking, including traditional English Cheddar. Neal's Yard also has directly helped improve cheesemaking in the United States, inspiring the Gathering of the Cheddarmakers being just one small example of encouragement among many. A few months after Neal's Yard's visit, someone floated the idea of setting up another gathering where a couple of different vats of cheese—one clothbound, traditional-style cheddar and one 40-pound block-style cheddar—would be made so everyone could taste the differences. The cultures and recipes would be as similar as possible, and the milk would be the same.

Jaeggi and Roelli were the two "vat captains" for this all-star team of cheesemakers at the Gathering I attended. The make-room was serious, as the leaders in their craft exchanged information. However, there was also the joking and mocking you'd expect from those same people when they are in a room full of peers making cheese that they are not actually trying to sell.

Watching people make cheese is awesome. Actually making the cheese, though, is hard work. Cheddar is especially hard work if one does it the way it is traditionally done, cutting up the coagulated curds into slabs and piling them on top of one another to press out more whey to give the cheese the texture we expect. The cheese room is humid, and there is a lot of lifting, cutting, and pushing that needs to be done from nonoptimal ergonomic positions.

I was lounging off to the side with my camera and notebook. Not only was I planning to take advantage of a week off from my own nonergonomic lifting, I didn't want to get in the way. If I haven't given you the picture clearly enough, my grabbing a loaf of curd would have been like asking Willie Mays to sit so I could take a couple of swings or asking Patti Smith to hand me the mic for a sec so I could read my slam poetry.

> Clearly it was a privilege to share that day with these folks. The thing that struck me the hardest, being in a room with so much experience and mastery of craft, is how California lacks this kind of hands-on knowledge, passed down from generation to generation. With the passing of Ig Vella (of Vella Cheese and Rogue Creamery) in 2011, this issue is even more acute. Ig was *the* resource and connection to cheesemaking history in California for many, many people. In Wisconsin being a third-generation cheesemaker isn't common, but it's not like finding a raw milk Brie either. Widmer's Cellars, Roelli Cheese, Carr Valley, and Henning's Cheese all come to mind right away, but there are even more with whom I'm less familiar, their cheese not getting out west regularly.

Wisconsin really has cheesemaking rooted in community. It showed at the Gathering of Cheddarmakers with the exchange of jokes and information, with the camaraderie of the shared meal—and more New Glarus beer—and with the fact that so many people took time off from their own work to travel across the state and spend the day working for nothing besides shared community knowledge, experience, and connection.

Wisconsin's dairy tradition is deep and unlike that in the rest of the country. This tradition is integral to the way Wisconsinites see themselves and also no historical accident. There is an idea of what Wisconsin has been and should be, and it comes from a political movement—largely led by farmers—that developed a philosophy called "the Wisconsin Idea."

How does this relate to today's reality and the modern cheddar-maker? In early 2015 it was as if Wisconsin governor Scott Walker knew the country needed a reminder of why the Progressivism of over one hundred years ago is still important today. Walker's proposed 2015–17 budget for the state of Wisconsin gutted the funding for the state's Extension programs and rewrote the mission of the state universities to dramatically change what Wisconsin residents see as something that makes their state special. In particular, Walker attempted to cut out parts of the document that mandated that the university educate "to extend knowledge and its application beyond the boundaries of its campuses"[12] and attempt to improve "the human condition."

Massive backlash by outraged Wisconsinites stopped Walker's plan in its tracks. An official statement was released within hours that confirmed, "The Wisconsin Idea will continue to thrive. This was a drafting error. The final version of the budget will include the Wisconsin Idea."[13] The crisis was short-lived because so many Wisconsinites mobilized so quickly.

The Wisconsin Idea is not a mere historical event in Wisconsin. As writer Jane Burns of the *Wisconsin State Journal* explains:

> That cheddar cheese you love, that milk you put in your coffee, that ice cream dripping off your chin in the summer—that's the Wisconsin Idea. The university's knowledge was spread throughout the state—well beyond the classroom and to the citizens. The first big beneficiary of the Wisconsin Idea was the state's agriculture, particularly the dairy industry.[14]

There are a lot of dairy trade publications out there, but I have always been intrigued by *Hoard's Dairyman*. I will admit that for a long time after I first saw it I just assumed it was some kind of fringe hippie dairy farmer publication because of its frequent use of the term "progressive dairy farmer." It's hard to remember, from my vantage point as an urban, politically active person a decade and a half into the 21st century, what the classic definition of "Progressivism" is, and what that definition has to do with dairy. I hear the term "progressive" bandied about all the time in my city, including at the worker-owned cooperative where I work. But in that context "progressive" usually just means left-of-center reformist ideas, as differentiated from the larger, more powerful body of corporate Democrats.[15]

I couldn't square that definition with the articles *Hoard's* published, which were not concerned with politics as much as developments in milk testing, breeding, or the total mix ratio of feed. *Hoard's* is named after W. D. Hoard, a founder of the Wisconsin Dairyman's Association in 1872 and governor of the state from 1889 to 1891. He founded the newspaper in 1885, and it continues today as a main source of information and inspiration for the "progressive dairy farmer."

It's beyond my ability in this journey to delve into all the nuances of the history of Progressivism (Wisconsin's senator Robert La Follette Sr., one of the Progressive Era's most well-known heroes, wrote a ten-volume series on the topic himself while serving as governor, and you can probably find it in your library), but progressive thought as it relates to farmers is crucial to understanding Wisconsin and the trajectory of cheddar. In fact, the famous

La Follette is often considered a beneficiary and advocate of the Wisconsin agriculturalist movement that helped bring him to power.

Wisconsin's pride in cheese was born of disaster and desperation. Before cheese began to take root as much more than a supplemental hobby for most farmers, Wisconsin was all about wheat. While New York was forming factories, setting up dairy cooperatives, and exporting large amounts of cheese to England, land speculation and wheat growing were the specialties of Wisconsin. It was among the first states to go all out for wheat production, and this crop brought enormous wealth—at first. However, within about thirty years the expense of land (because of a level of speculation that sounds as much like present-day San Francisco as 19th-century Wisconsin) and monoculture farming took its toll on farm acreage. By the 1870s most wheat yields were "spiraling downward,"[16] and farmers were going broke.

With the soil incapable of growing crops, animal husbandry seemed like the only choice for survival. Concurrently, the national "Better Grass Movement" had begun a push to reenergize America's soil with pasture. After a flirtation with sheep, cows became the choice of most Wisconsin farmers, despite cattle's association with "women's work."[17] Indeed, in Richland County, where the land had always been considered the least suitable for wheat because of its terrain, dairy farmers were already producing almost half a million pounds of, yes, cheddar by the end of the 1860s.[18] Richland County's cheddar production would become a model for the rest of Wisconsin as crops began to fail across the state. And this was the beginning of Wisconsin's fascination with cheddar.

In Edward Janus's *Creating Dairyland*, a book that starts with the idea that "the dairy cow created Wisconsin,"[19] the word "progressive" is used almost as a synonym for "scientific" much of the time. Finally I had a rubric of sorts for understanding why *Hoard's Dairyman* still devotes most of its web page to scientific articles written for farmers, as well as an insight into the worldviews of the dairy farmers I had met over the years. Janus details the ways in which Wisconsin farmers, and especially the dairy farmers of the last part of the 19th and early part of the 20th century, were fighting a battle for science and against unexamined traditional ways.

Clearly, science did improve the lot of the farmer during these years. Tremendously, in fact. In terms of breeding stock, feed, and the science of cheesemaking—harking back to the best practices of Joseph Harding—this was an era of profound advancements of technology and an increased standard of living for the farmer. As Janus explains:

> Progressives built their program of social betterment on the Darwinian principle of selection through competition. . . . With the improvement of cows, soil, crops, machinery, markets, and especially men's [sic] minds, humanity as a whole will advance. In their hearts progressive dairy farmers believe that more protein at less costs benefits us all.[20]

The Wisconsin Idea pre-dates the national Progressive movement, and many of the practices and beliefs of the national Progressives took firmer root among the Wisconsin farmers. The Wisconsin Idea as legislative action supported farmers by helping them procure credit more easily, regulating unhealthy production practices,[21] and developing university Extensions throughout the state, which further demonstrated the practicality of combining science and farming. When these Wisconsin Idea wins were under threat by Governor Walker—even one hundred years later—Wisconsinites remembered and immediately fought back.

Folksinger Utah Phillips said, "The long memory is the most radical idea in America,"[22] and I tend to agree. In terms of cheese, while there are plenty of great cheesemaking newcomers, no place has a connection to the traditions of American cheese and cheddar-making like Wisconsin. Andy Kehler, a founder of Jasper Hill Farm in Vermont, in contrasting the two states that have an equally proud dairy tradition (Wisconsin and his own Vermont), says:

> Wisconsin is surprising. It's totally surprising. You still see the infrastructure that existed a hundred years ago. In Vermont it's virtually disappeared. Where every town once had its own creamery, once it was mandated that milk had to be refrigerated, that's when that really started to disappear. The economies of filling a railcar full of milk and shipping it to Springfield, Massachusetts, changed the dairy landscape here.[23]

Progressives managed to transform their ideas of the 1800s into legislation all over the United States in the first decades of the 20th century.

What actually became law differed in emphasis from what Wisconsin dairy farmers may have wanted, but they focused on three areas: regulation of corporations (antitrust laws), consumer protections (food safety acts), and conservation (national park creation). Ideologically similar to the experience of most Wisconsin dairy farmers, the national Progressives were driven by a belief in science.

A belief in science, in our present era, sometimes feels as though it is in decline. In an age in which some elected officials think that ignoring climate issues is okay because THE RAPTURE IS COMING or in which others believe that vaccines are evil,[24] it can be hard to remember that there was a time when invoking science was thought of, generally, as something smart people did. It's something Wisconsin dairy farmers and cheesemakers do every day.

As Janus puts it:

> Today's dairymen and -women are still waging the progressives' crusade against the past and those who think humanity happier there. For progressive dairy farmers, the past is not nearly as wonderful as the future will be. This faith in science, thinking, the future, competition and a rational plan to extend wealth to all is the Wisconsin Idea.[25]

Progressivism made Wisconsin what it is today. Without the vision of combining easier credit for farmers, science in the aid of the family farm, and the promise of prosperity, it's hard to see how Wisconsin would have become America's Dairyland. Indeed, Wisconsin has managed to maintain its cheese crown to this day, even after it was surpassed in fluid milk volume by the mega-dairies of California.

But when the Progressive Era begets the age of the "scientific" management principles of Taylorism—a concept well suited to cheddar production, and something that would change the very nature of agriculture in America forever (see chapter 11)—does it then sow the seeds for the destruction of the small farmer and cheesemaker?

We'll try to figure that out later in this journey. Let us first show appreciation to what these Wisconsin cheesemakers produce. →

Chapter 3

Of Bandages and Blocks

I am eating some Bleu Mont Cheddar as I write this. My keyboard is getting oily, but I don't care. Crystalline, dank, earthy, grassy, big, cellar-y, bright, meaty, shard-y . . . sweet, but not sweet like candy—sweet like a well-made pastry, the sweetness perfectly balanced with the other flavors. The Wisconsin Idea, yeah, sure . . . all I know right now is that eating this cheese is a great idea.

I have, many times, mocked the use of the term "cave" (or "caaaaaaaav," as some like to pronounce it). It's hard to resist mocking the pretension of using the word when "cave-aged" often means, "aged in a modern, strip-mall, temperature-controlled warehouse where the cheese may be stored in plastic anyway." While moderating a panel at the American Cheese Society conference one year, I even used it as a *Pee-wee Herman Show*–style word of the day, in which the audience was encouraged to scream every time a panelist used "cave" in a sentence. But caves—even ones built, not found, by cheese agers—do have a lot of value. Caves prevent excess airflow, thus maintaining the environment of beneficial microbes that help the cheese develop flavor, and they control the temperature and humidity efficiently.

Willi Lehner does not have cows. He doesn't even have a cheese room, vats, a cheddar mill, or a gang press. What Lehner does have, however, is a cave.

Lehner makes cheese with the milk of others at other people's cheese plants—well-known and respected cheesemakers such as Chris Roelli and Kerry Henning. He has a knack for making and aging amazing cheeses, and they sit in the cave he dug out of his hillside, which is perfect for developing their flavors.

And flavor is what this cheese is all about. The Bleu Mont is a bandage-wrapped (or clothbound) cheddar. Most cheddars aren't made like this any-more. After the cheese is formed, it is hooped and pressed in sheets of muslin. Rather than being aged in plastic, the cheddar is greased up with lard. Same concept—reduce cracking and moisture loss—just the old method. This is a cheese closer in look and flavor to the majority of cheddars being made 150 years ago than to those coming off a conveyor belt today. It needs to be cared for and rotated, tasted and potentially re-larded, examined for mites and cracks.

It's not an easy cheese to make. As Ari Weinzweig, longtime Zingerman's owner and food writer, puts it, "Clothbound [cheddar] had a lot of problems. Which it still does. You get a lot of cracks and molding. . . ." And the reason clothbound stopped being the cheddar style of choice? The "priority [for most cheddar-makers] was not complex, intricate flavor—it was yield."[1]

Any question why someone would go to the trouble of making a cheese like this is answered when you taste it. I described it above, down to the grease stains on my letter keys, but the most important taste characteristic in a clothbound cheddar—whatever its individual attributes—is depth. There's just a lot going on in good clothbound cheddar, and Lehner makes one of the best in the world. It's not an easy cheese to make or age, but it's also more challenging for the eater. You don't just stick this in a ziplock bag until you get around to it. It's appointment eating.

Why the flavor difference? The cheddar is a living, breathing, growing cheese under that layer of greasy cloth. Cheese aged in plastic is aging, too—don't get me wrong—but not in the same way, with the same speed, or with the same interaction with its environment. In 2015 Hook's Cheese Company released their twenty-year aged cheddar, which was a block, not a bandaged one. Twenty-year bandaged cheddar doesn't exist and never will. The bandage and lard do not stop all the airflow, and after twenty years there would be nothing left but a desiccated, concave wheel of woody inedible cheese and mites.

Clothbound cheddar is also more unpredictable than block cheddar. You might make the cheese pretty much the same way every time, but the goal of the end product is not standardization; it's to bring out the best flavors of the moment. Lehner's cheese does that; different batches I have tasted had the same flavors I wrote about above, but each one emphasized them differently, and some had other attributes: onion, apple, walnuts. That's the beauty of a traditional cheese. You don't know exactly what you will get, and sometimes it is an amazing surprise.

Willi Lehner's cave and Bleu Mont Dairy are witness to the best ideas of sustainability. A windmill towers over the field, solar panels dot the land,

and most of it was built by hand. This idyllic-looking farm is the kind of thing that really puts a city person to shame. When you see something like this, you kind of want to go back to the land, too; I mean, even if you've never really spent much time there before.

After traveling the world and making cheese in the Alps, Lehner realized that traditional cheese production didn't use stainless steel and massive warehouses, but wood boards and earth. Digging a cave into the hillside of his land was a better expense than building a cheese plant, especially in Wisconsin, where there were so many available to borrow or rent when he wanted to make a batch of cheese. Caves are the envy of other traditional cheddar-makers as well. Mariano Gonzalez of Fiscalini Farmstead Cheese—one of the most decorated traditional cheddar-makers in the world—still speaks about the cave he wanted to build at his old job at Shelburne Farms in Vermont, as well as the one he tried to build at Fiscalini. At Fiscalini they had actually dug a hole, which sat for years before they covered it back up, the expense of finishing being so high. "They buried my dream," Gonzalez said.[2] He said it with a laugh, but the kind of laugh that implies a "What are you going to do, eh?" at the end of the sentence.

The best word to describe the inside of the Bleu Mont caves is "peaceful." Even looking back at the pictures from my visit fills me with a sense of calm. "Lack of air exchange" is the technical phrase for one of the desirable aspects of a cave for aging cheese. Willi Lehner's cave had that for sure. It was peaceful and still, and there was nothing for a visitor to concentrate on but the earthy, humid, cooked milk, woodsy, slightly ammoniated smell of cheddars aging. And it's the only cheese-aging facility I've ever been to where Crocs are mandatory footwear.

A couple of years after I visited Lehner, I spent two days in Wisconsin holed up in the judging room of the Monona Terrace Convention Center in Madison, Wisconsin. I was judging some of the eighteen hundred or so cheeses at the American Cheese Society conference, but it was hard to tell I was in Wisconsin. It was a day and a half before I realized that I could open a door on the other side of the room, walk out into an architecturally distinct Frank Lloyd Wright lobby, and have an incredible panoramic view of Lake Monona. And I do mean incredible. Water-skiers were performing stunts and jumps. It felt more like a spaceship than a window. The view was so big that you could almost see the curvature of the earth. Wow.

My home county in California actually has a Frank Lloyd Wright build-ing as its Civic Center, so this building felt oddly homelike. I was surprised, two thousand miles away, at the memories the similar structure brought up. I'm not sure if that was a good or bad association: the Civic Center back home was where I made my first library visit but also where I paid my first traffic ticket and was the site where a friend of our family committed suicide. Later I was told that the Madison convention center had actually been delayed for years due to haters, but that was likely a blessing in disguise, since they were able to omit some Wright features that our Civic Center has, like the unplanned, rain-caused "fountains" that flowed inward and destroyed part of the library.[3]

I have written this before, but I will say it again: The thing I like the most about judging cheese at a competition is the purity of it. Just me, my teammate technical judge, our triers,[4] and our mouths. No packaging, no stories, no sales pitches, no loyalty, and no having to assess whether a cheese will sell. Just pure cheese appreciation and love.

After the numerical judging for each class of cheese is complete, all the judges get to taste the winners of each category to decide on Best of Show. I did what I usually do. I went around to each table, dutifully tasting every cheese, even the flavored cheeses, the fresh cheeses, and the butters that never win. I narrowed it down to about ten cheeses, then gathered a piece of each, sat in a corner of the room, and tasted them off against each other. While entries are anonymous, they have codes on them so we can place our votes. The secret cheese company code is always the first number. Imagine my shock when I realized that three of my top six cheeses were from the same company! I didn't know who it was. I didn't know any com-pany that was making such amazing cheeses in three distinct categories: alpine, grana (parmesan), and cheddar. I knew no one had entered all three categories before in my decade of judging cheese events.

When we found out the winners, I realized they were all Willi Lehner's. His cheddar and "Big Sky Grana," sweeter than I would have expected for the category but definitely the best U.S.-made hard Italian-style cheese I have ever tried, tied for third overall. The other cheese on my list was called "Alpine Renegade," and unfortunately, it hasn't been seen, at least outside Wisconsin, ever since. During the "Festival of Cheese" where all the cheeses entered into the competition are displayed and sampled, all three of Lehner's winners drew crowds. The (mostly) professional audience was fascinated by these traditional beauties, gathering around to see them, taste them, and take their photos for folks back home.

A 40-pound block of cheddar fascinates people as well.

Maybe not quite as much as a clothbound cheddar wheel, an 85-pound Italian Parmigiano Reggiano, or a 200-pound Swiss Emmental does, but when customers see us cutting one, they often stay and watch. When people have only seen cheese in consumer-size portions and we are cutting two 40-pound blocks for half the week's customers, they gather around and watch. Some cheese cutters even like to stack the blocks extra high to show off, piling up a mountain of consumer cuts, but just cutting them attracts stares. It's a lot of cheese.

Once you've worked in cheese awhile—at least in the kind of cheese environment that caters to a large, economically diverse crowd—40-pound blocks of cheddar are ubiquitous. They become not only a staple of one's workday, but a rote unit of measure. "My bag is so heavy I feel like I'm carrying half a cheddar." "Your kid is getting so big she's almost a full forty!" "We had to carry that old TV down three flight of stairs. It felt like two Commodity Blocks."

Actually, grocery store cheesemongers have their own measurement system. A small Brie is 2.2 pounds,[5] a large Brie is 7 pounds, a baby Swiss is 24, a cheddar block is 40, a Parmigiano Reggiano is 85 pounds, and an Emmental is 200 pounds. You can weigh almost anything using this system.

It's no surprise that cheddar is ubiquitous enough to be thought of this way; in fact, one of the "essential functions" of our job is the ability to repeatedly lift 40 pounds. The peculiar motion one needs to get them in the correct position for cutting has even Popeye-fied my forearms a little. I think his secret was not spinach, but cheese.

The sizes have pretty much consolidated at this point, but there used to be a real variety of cheddar sizes. A few old-time cheese companies still make some of the varieties, but old Kraft pamphlets celebrate a wide array of shapes and sizes: jems, midgets, flats, daisies, truckles, longhorns, young Americas, prints, and I'm sure others lost to history. It really was a complete weight system based only on cheddar.

Not only can cheeses be used for measurement comparisons more exact than, say, the ancient cubit, but they can also be used for art. Cheddar carving uses the 40-pound block as a medium, and I have seen some beauties: Mount

Rushmore, the Chicago skyline, even (online) a SpongeBob SquarePants that really called his whole essential nature into question. I once bought, at an auction after the annual American Cheese Society conference, a cheese head made out of low-fat cheddar that I scared friends with by sneaking it into their house. Eventually, since cheese carving is truly ephemeral art, it made it to show-and-tell at their kid's school and was then eaten for lunch.

This large block of cheese, so common in the world of the grocery store cheese professional, is never seen this way by most consumers. Even I, who must have been involved in the selling of over half a million pounds of block cheddar by now, had never seen the 640-pound monster blocks reputed to be made in some large factories until this cheese journey began.

The first time I ever saw block cheddar being made was, fittingly, in Wisconsin. California doesn't have the same kind of cheddar tradition as the Badger State, so while I had seen dry jack, blue, and a million kinds of goat cheese being made, I had to travel to watch cheddar being made in a small cheese room.

When I walked into Widmer's Cheese Cellars, I thought I had gone in the wrong door. You walk in off the street and you can practically touch the cheese vat. Widmer's Cheese Cellars is an old-school, no-frills, multigenerational, grandfathered-in (actually great-grandfathered in this case) cheese factory. The cheese factory, until this present generation, doubled as a home for the cheesemaker and his family, who lived above the vats, the forms, the presses, and the aging cheese.

I was used to cheese make-rooms being set a little farther away from the front door. It's not like the street outside in Theresa, Wisconsin, was extremely busy or anything. I've been there twice, and I don't remember any traffic jams or crowds. Heck, I live on what is considered a very quiet street in San Francisco, and at 4:00 a.m. there is probably more going on outside than on the average cheesemaking morning at Widmer. You park outside in one of the abundant parking spots, find the building with the wooden representations of the cantons of Switzerland, go in the front door, and boom, you are almost making cheese yourself.

Joe Widmer, master cheesemaker and third-generation owner of Widmer's Cheese Cellars, is also famous for brick cheese, an American original made mostly in Wisconsin for well over a century. It got its name not from the shape of the cheese, but from the fact that actual bricks are used to expel moisture from the cheese. The first thing you notice inside the factory, after the lactic, dairy air, is all the bricks piled up on shelves supported by chains. The shelves are bowed and look like they could give way any second. The decorating theme of the Cellars is stainless steel, as it is in almost every cheese make-room, but the bricks lend an air of tradition and permanence. Living in a city where the dominant businesses are computer related, I find a place where people make tangible and historic things very refreshing. Sometimes a San Franciscan longs for bricks and mortar.

It's probably a cliché to say that visiting the Widmer's Cheese Cellars in Theresa, Wisconsin, is like taking a step back in time. I mean, when don't we say that about a factory that has remained pretty much the same for three generations? Still, looking around the make-room and seeing real bricks for brick cheese stacked on a long drooping wooden shelf across one wall makes you feel as though you could be there at any time since the late 1800s—if you can ignore yourself taking pictures of those bricks with your cell phone to show your coworkers back home, since they've probably never seen anything like this.

Vermont has companies with older roots—Crowley Cheese, 1824, and Plymouth Artisan Cheese (open in 1890, but closed from 1934 to 2009)—and California has a couple of multigeneration cheesemakers and original cheeses: Franklin Peluso's Teleme and the Vella Dry Jack, but Wisconsin lives its cheese history. The locals are proud and protective of their cheesemakers, and while they readily mourn the loss of many small-town cheese plants, they still have more per capita than most other Americans.

The Widmer plant is a great example of a "factory" that is not really what most people picture when they say the word "factory." Sure, there's stainless steel and vats that hold a lot of milk, but there's also the bricks, the sagging shelves, a brine tank that looks like it was forged by hand, and the factory built around it.

And this is where some of the best cheddar in the country is made.

Many cheesemongers and cheese writers have praise for the rustic beauty of cheese. I do, too, of course. The cover of my previous book, *Cheesemonger,* is one testament to the pretty/ugly duality of cheese appearance. Parmigiano Reggiano sits regally, ID and date stamped, secure in its place in history. There are a few cheeses with extraneous molds from the trip over the Atlantic in a boat. No one seemed to notice that the Gruyère-looking cheese, that is not a

Gruyére, was extra brown because the cardboard shipping box had adhered to it at some high-moisture part of its storage, along with prettier airborne flora. Mimolette sits, unaware that soon it will be unavailable in America for a little while, so mighty (and mitey) that the Food and Drug Administration will turn it back to prevent, I guess, a large-scale outbreak of "grocer's itch."[6]

There is also a 24(ish)-pound clothbound cheddar on the same cover. It's not Bleu Mont, though it's just about the same size, and it could be. Instead it's the Cabot, aged in the Cellars at Jasper Hill in Greensboro, Vermont; more dainty than its 60-pound predecessor but still a work of handmade art: slightly ridged, brown and beige, wrapped in cheesecloth. The cheddar sits on a (not visible to the reader) milk crate, hiding behind the not-a-Gruyère as if to say, "I am so confident in my good looks that I don't even have to try to be noticed."

Cheeses like these attract the eye of the average turophile. I do not need to speak for these cheeses, though I have in the past, and so many others will in the future. No, I am here to praise the beauty of a cheese that is ubiquitous but unseen by most consumers: the 40-pound block of cheddar.

I have love for its beauty the same way I have love for a well-organized, humming factory; an old muscle car; or a well-engineered bridge. The forty is not a natural beauty; it's a beauty of formulation and human thought. Perhaps I am more a fan of social realism than I want to admit, because when I see a forty, I see food for the people.

The 40-pound block is healthy, natural food, just engineered for minimum loss and maximum storage ability. The forty can be a bone-white goat cheddar or a verging-on-red-orange annatto-bomb from Wisconsin that stains your hands no matter how much you wash that day. Good forties are evenly colored, whatever their hue, fitted tightly in their bags that are fitted tightly in their cardboard boxes. Sometimes, a little rectangle of cheese bulges where the peekaboo window in the box has been cut out.

Younger forties are tight against their plastic, but more aged forties can have more looseness. Some—and this is usually considered a defect in cheesemaking, even if the cheese still tastes great (which it often does)— come with what I like to think of as an extra "flavor pack": pooled water and whey, like a little water balloon or, actually, probably more like a little cheese colostomy bag.[7] Mongers not careful in cutting the packs open can unleash this entire puddle onto their counter, which, since a counter is usually just above crotch level, will be hilarious to everyone but the monger.

When you release the forty from its box and bag, it is a shimmering thing of beauty, slick like a wet seal and formidable like a craggy mountain. Okay, that's a bit of an exaggeration. Compared with a Parmigiano Reggiano, it's more like a moderate-size hill, but it still must be conquered.

Pretentious mongers can deny its beauty, but the forty calls out for attention. It's rare—especially when we are cutting the mild cheddar, which we do two at a time, two to three times a week—that a customer doesn't stop and stare and ask, "What are you cutting?"

I think the first thing I did on my first day working with cheese—1994 at the old Rainbow Grocery location, at 15th and Mission—was to learn how to break down a forty. Sizes of cuts vary by price, which is, obviously, higher now than twenty-some years ago, but there is a system. Our custom-built cheese cutter consisted simply of a metal frame with a cutting arm where the wire could be attached and two removable cutting boards. There was a small space where the two boards didn't quite meet, so the cheese detritus from the cuts could fall below the board to the counter.

There is cheesemonger pride involved in breaking down a forty. If you consider yourself a real cheese professional, none of the cheese ever leaves the cutter. Bam! The forty is now two twenties. Bam! Bam! The twenties are tens. Two more cuts on one of the tens, and you have a windowpane, the 10-pound piece still held together in your hands. Two to four uneven cuts on that, and you have between twelve and twenty various-size retail pieces ready to be· wrapped. Simple, easy, fast, affordable, and tasty. A cheese for The People.

Indeed, my favorite cheese image ever isn't cheese company or region based. The image isn't an immense rustic wheel or an artistic close-up of a moldy rind. No, my favorite image is block cheddar based. I saw it while watching the civil rights documentary *Eyes on the Prize*. A picture from the March on Washington shows volunteers preparing eighty thousand cheese sandwiches for the participants of that historic event. Wearing white paper hats and aprons, an interracial group of women pack a room. Assembly-line style, they are putting precut cheese on bread, wrapping sandwiches, and putting them in bags for attendees. The women are united in their tasks, preparing to feed cheddar to the people arriving in the city, many of whom traveled a long way to get there. This picture is my favorite image of cheese even though, admittedly, the folks traveling to Washington weren't there for the cheddar.

Chapter 4

Oh, Geez, What Is Cheddar Anyway?

Maybe I should have asked this question earlier. However, I think it speaks to the ubiquity of cheddar, the nature of its being the people's cheese, that I didn't really think of asking myself the question, "What is cheddar?" until I was on this cheddar journey. I'd studied the history, but I had not defined the word.

You'd think that asking the question would yield a simple answer; if not a one-sentence answer, then a specific recipe and definition. Perhaps because of the place that cheddar has in our culture and history, that just simply is not the case.

Put this way, I love both Willi Lehner's Bleu Mont Cheddar and Joe Widmer's 40-pound block. But how can they both be cheddar?

In the United States we have government-regulated terms to use for different foods. This is called the Code of Federal Regulations or CFRs. Recently there was a big kerfuffle because Unilever, a food giant that owns the brand Hellmann's, brought suit against Hampton Creek, which produces a vegan product called "Just Mayo." Since Unilever is a $67 billion company, and Bill Gates and Li Ka-shing, "Asia's richest tycoon," back Hampton Creek,[1] I don't really have a dog in the fight. I bring up this case because it would have been decided partly on whether "Mayo" is close enough to "mayonnaise" to have to follow those regulations if Unilever had not dropped the suit.[2]

A common definition, a historical definition, and a legal definition are not necessarily the same thing. But because I don't want to come off like that guy on the Internet who quotes *Webster's Dictionary* (including pronunciation symbols) to "win" every argument, let's leave the CFR definition of cheddar for later.

All cheese, even the freshest examples, is an attempt to intervene in the natural spoilage of milk. Even making a cottage cheese, a mozzarella, or a fresh chèvre extends the life of the original milk, giving humans a chance to eat something at a later date, ending the prehistoric cycle of hand-to-mouth survival.

I studied a few cheddar recipes, looking for a simple one to reprint. However, the recipes tend to be long, involved, and technical. I pictured eyes glazing over. I wrote out a "simple" version and had a hard time presenting it in fewer than twenty steps. The thing is that, without pictures, it's a very dry read for anyone who doesn't already know how to make cheddar. Besides, if I did want pictures, this book would probably retail for ten dollars more. Cheese writing for the people demands I keep the pictures out.[3]

When cheesemakers get together, as at the Gathering of the Cheddar-makers, they say things to each other like, "Cheddar-making is all about controlling acidity," and they all nod their heads knowingly. But to a non-maker or nonscientist, a statement like that can be less than illuminating. Quickly trying to remember that high school chemistry, I'm all, "Uh, acidity is the opposite of . . . what again?"

Since I am not a dairy scientist, I'll try to sum it up quickly. Please remember, though, that I am dumbing this down a little—you know, down to my level.

The parts of cheddar-making that are unique are the scald, the salt, the mill, and the cheddaring.

What does that mean? To make cheese you need milk, culture, rennet, and salt, right? Every major cheese type has a different timing or pattern for how these ingredients come together. Fermentation, a part of all cheesemaking, is the same as it is for vinegar or booze or whatever. It is turning the sugar into something else. The milk sugars, called lactose, are converted to lactic acid. One of the critical things about cheddar is not only that it develops lactic acid slowly at first, then at a steadily increasing rate, but that it is pretty much finished by the time the cheese is made. Cheddar-making is all about controlling acidity! Go ahead and nod now.

How this is done varies by cheese, of course. The combination of particular temperature (86 to 88 degrees F) and starter culture (that starts the fermentation) begins this process for cheddar. This period is called "ripening milk" by dairy scientists, though not usually by mongers. Cheese customers tend to get confused about milk ripening versus cheese ripening, so I just call it "when the cultures move into their new apartment." The cultures settle in, explore new spaces, and get the vat ready for the housewarming party when their friend rennet will arrive.

The first unique part of the cheddar process is the scald. After rennet is added, the milk begins separating into curds (solids) and whey (liquid). After this, the curd is cut into small pieces, and the tank is heated to over 100 degrees F without the whey being drained. The scald helps expel more whey from the curds and expel it more evenly. All the parts of making cheddar are what lead to its becoming a cheese that can age for a long time, and indeed, the scald in particular is what helped cheddar develop into such a durable and popular cheese. With a fresh cheese the make process keeps moisture in; with an aged cheese, the process gets it out so the cheese can age without rotting.

The rest of the cheddar-making is also dedicated to this goal of creating an ageable cheese without rotting. "Cheddaring" is the next step. In this process the whey is drained out and the curds are allowed to knit together, which, based on the chemistry in the vat, and my anthropomorphization of all things dairy, they naturally want to do at this point. Not so fast, curds! You can join up with your friends, but we are going to cut you into slabs (often called "loaves") and pile you on top of each other, and that weight and pressure will make you release more whey! And we're going to do this over and over again, making the piles higher, for a while, maybe even 90 minutes![4] Technically, the weight involved in piling the slabs not only pushes water out of the curds, but also stretches the fat and protein chains. Daniel Utano, a cheddar maker for Boosher's Handmade Cheese for many years (now with Ferndale Farmstead Cheese), says that when he was first trained he was told the cheddaring "wrings the chains out like they were sponges trying to get the moisture out."[5]

After this "cheddaring" it's time for milling. All those slabs are taken and thrown into a mill, not completely unlike the wood chipper scene in *Fargo*. This slab carnage is done so that the curds will be small enough for the salting step. Then what seems to the outsider like a lot of salt is added at this point. Salting is another crucial step that allowed cheddar to become the most popular cheese in the world because salt helps stop the fermentation process that—if left to continue—might cause a cheese to literally blow up. Salt added in this way adds flavor and affects the final texture of the cheese.

Then the cheesemakers can fill whatever form they are using with the curds, pack it tight, and press the cheese. After some time in the cheese press, it is ready to age out to desired ripeness.

So there you go: heat milk, make cultures comfy, add rennet, form curds, cut curds, scald, drain, cheddar, cheddar, cheddar, mill, salt, form, press, and age. Every step works together to create a cheese that is very tightly knit together and has expelled much of its moisture so it can transform and extend the life of that original milk for months and years. Got it?

Every dairy scientist and cheddar-maker reading this is likely shaking their heads at the parts of the process I just glossed over or skipped, and they are right to feel that way. What I didn't mention in all this, making the cheesemaker appear magical, is that all throughout the process fancy cheese gauges are used, acidity is measured, and curds are examined and measured against the concept of the texture of a chicken breast. (Measuring curd knitting against an *actual* chicken breast would violate food safety protocols.)

There are also often long waiting periods between the steps. If cheddar-making is all about controlling acidity, then controlling acidity is all about knowing when to wait and when to start the next step. As well, of course, as bending over a vat and throwing around big slabs of cheddar curd, at least for the artisan producers.

But the other way I simplified things is by relaying a classic version of the cheddar make process, not the most common one. Heat milk, make cultures comfy, add rennet, form curds, cut curds, scald, drain, cheddar, cheddar, cheddar, mill, salt, form, press, and age is the way you make cheddar. Unless you make it a different way. The cheddar make process in big factories includes a version of all those steps, more or less, but by machine and, for the most part, out of view. If I am leaving out all the measurement aspects, as I did above, then workerwise—in some large production facilities—the process consists of the following steps: press button, then watch someone take the finished cheddar off the conveyor belt a while later.

If cheese manuals and scientists use very technical and arcane language, debate among cheesemakers—while also often eventually becoming technical—usually starts out with a concept of realness based on one aspect of technology. Bandaged or rindless? Stirred curd or milled? Made by hand or by the press of a button?

To state the obvious, these arguments over definition have changed over time as technology has changed. Indeed, in many ways the story of cheddar is the story of advances in technology. True, that's the story of many foods today, but cheddar is a great example of a cheese defined on a continuum, based on the possibility of the moment.

Cheddar became so popular because technology changes have constantly been used to extend its shelf life. While "cheddar" had existed in some form for centuries, dairy scientist and historian Val Cheke dates the standardization of "Somerset Cheddar" in England to the 1850s (not coincidentally the same time period that the first cheddar factory appeared in the United States). This alone points to the fact that many definitional variations must have existed prior to this point in history.

Standardization, in this sense, is probably most accurately thought of as assembling best practices to help collectively lift all producers up. After all, if the purpose of making cheese was to extend the life of milk, there was no point in making it badly and wasting resources. In this time, before there was a common understanding of the exact nature of what caused cheese and milk to spoil, these sets of procedures pointed the cheesemaker away from what we would now probably call criminally liable practices of sanitation and food handling.

Cheke, in one of my favorite passages in any cheese book ever, writes of the problems facing the farmstead cheesemaker in aging cheese before modern refrigeration, humidity control, and stainless steel shelves:

> This process is now known to be a very complicated affair, because so many factors can affect the 'fermentations' in the cheese. In many ways the modern cheese-maker has an easier time, for his store can be thermostatically controlled in temperature and humidity, to give his standard and balanced cheese the approved atmosphere. Not so the harassed dairy-maid of old, whose cheeses demanded constant care, for some might dry into harsh and acidic crumbs, some dissolve in putrefaction in spite of therapeutic herbs, while others rolled off the shelves propelled by the gas of their own fermentation. If they stuck to the shelves in a slimy mass, the dairy-maid was to blame for lazy handling. It was her fault if they became grease spots in a hot room, or covered with mould in a wet one, and hers was the blame if flies 'blew', and maggots crawled and when mites reduced the cheese to dust.[6]

I love this passage for many reasons. The first is the image of the aging room as a dangerous gauntlet of exploding, maggoty cheeses that might propel themselves at your head at any moment. The second is because it really shows all the potential hazards of cheesemaking and underlines how amazing it is that this skill even exists.

Cheddar is defined in technical cheese terms as a "hard pressed" cheese. Not "hard-pressed," as in "you'd be hard-pressed to make that cheese because it's a pain in the ass"—though some might say that as well—but hard pressed as in during the make process the curd is weighted down so that more moisture is expelled. This, in turn, means the cheese becomes "close" in texture (eyes and fissures are defects in a cheddar, as opposed to, say, a Swiss Emmental) and can be aged until it is very firm. This is why cheddar became so ubiquitous in the United States and around the world. It stores well. It ships well. It preserves the milk longer than many other types of cheese.

However, even as cheddar became one of the most popular types of cheese in the world, it still had problems. One of the many fascinating things about Paul Kindstedt's seminal work on the history of cheese, *Cheese and Culture*, was the revelation about cheesecloth.

I'm not an academic. I like to consider myself well read, but I will fully admit that I have historical blind spots. I never connected the fact that the cheap cotton available in the United States—due, it's important to remember, to the slave economy—was a factor in a technological advancement in cheese.[7] In fact, I had always assumed that the bandage-wrapped cheddar, what I think of as the "original" form of the type, had been made that way for centuries. I mean, sure, that makes no sense if you think about it. It's just that I hadn't. It never entered my mind that wrapping the cheddar in cotton was most likely an American invention pushed by the necessity of adjusting the cheese to the climate of New England.[8] I always assumed it came that way with the immigrants from England.

Before the use of the cotton wrap, cheddars were heavily salted. However, in the heat of the average prerefrigeration American aging room in summer, these rinds would often crack and be prone to maggot infestation. American cheesemakers, in the late 18th or early 19th century, discovered that coating the outside of their cheese repeatedly with butter (made from whey) would create a coating similar to an early version of paraffin wax and a much thinner rind.[9] Not only that, it helped seal the cheese in a way that prevented moisture loss. The seal improved flavor but also was a big help to the cheesemaker financially. Moisture = weight = money. Previously, some moisture loss was encouraged because of the fear of rotting from within. Now, with less risk, moister cheeses could be created, potentially making the same practice more profitable.

Skipping ahead a hundred years or more, the inventions of the plastic-sealed 40-pound block and even the pasteurized processed cheese food make sense. If the trajectory of cheddar is the preservation of milk as food, and the constant battle is loss of sellable weight—thus profit—during the aging process, developing technologies—from salt, to bandage, to wax, to plastic—makes absolute sense from a business standpoint, if not from a flavor one.

Some technologies are farmer-centric, and some only really serve large businesses. During the years of the development of bandage wrap, cheesemaking was a small-scale project, relatively speaking. Sure, larger farms produced cheese (sometimes with the use of slaves) for export as part of the triangular slave trade,[10] but most cheese at that point was made by farm wives for personal use or local trade. After the 1850s cheese, especially cheddar, was becoming a factory-dominated food (again, let's remember these "factories" would be welcomed into artisan cheese guilds anywhere in the United States in 2015), but farmstead producers didn't die out completely for a while. As cheddar entered the 20th century, however, scale and technology continued to change.

The other interesting thing in that Val Cheke quote is the switch of pronoun. The modern cheesemaker is a male, and the prestandardization cheesemaker is a woman. This is no accident or old-fashioned use of "man" as universal. No, the standardization of the cheddar process and the rise of the cheese factory was the beginning of the end of women cheesemakers, at least until the artisan resurgence of cheese, especially goat cheese, in the 1970s. One is hard-pressed (no pun intended) to find more than a handful of women cheddar-makers in the United States today.

Since the cheese is called "cheddar," I had assumed that the "cheddaring" process was what defined cheddar cheese and that it had existed since the first wheels of cheese were created in Cheddar, England. Oddly, this does not seem to be so. I realized while doing research that "cheddaring" was part of the improvement and standardization of cheddar, popularized by Joseph Harding in England and brought to New York State in 1867 by Scottish immigrant Robert McAdam[11] or American dairyman Xerxes Willard,[12] depending on which cheese historian you want to believe; that is, about seven centuries after the first records of "cheddar cheese" exist and over a decade and a half since it unquestioningly became America's favorite cheese.

One could argue, fairly convincingly, that this is when cheddar actually became cheddar. I prefer to view it on a continuum, though. Cheddaring was another technique-based change to the cheese, helping lead it to the goal of better preservation of milk through expulsion of moisture and tighter texture of the cheese that was historically made near Cheddar, England. I suppose this is why I don't write ad copy. In all seriousness, though, cheddaring was a great technological advance in the late 19th century. It improved consistency and, by most accounts, created a more pleasurable flavor, more dependable aging, and a more popular cheese.[13] That cheddaring was a great concept was proven by its almost universal adoption by cheddar-makers of the period.

What did people do before cheddaring became the dominant form of cheddar-making? They used a method called "stirred curd"—which is pretty much exactly what it sounds like, stirring the curds longer instead of slabbing and piling them on top of each other. Stirring the curd actually took less time than cheddaring but was more labor intensive. The stirred curd method created a shorter (less elastic), curdier cheese as well, and if made with poor-quality milk one that tended toward the gassy explosive cheeses that the aforementioned dairy maid needed to watch out for when entering the aging room.

Before studying cheddar methods I had assumed that the "stirred curd" method of agitation was something designed in the late 20th century for a modern closed vat on cheese unworked by human hands. Advances in technology have helped repopularize "stirred curd" cheddar, mechanize it, and make it the dominant style in large factories in the present day. Over the course of talking to cheddar-makers who actually make cheddar by hand, I learned that many of them—who prefer to remain anonymous— view only hand-milled and cheddared cheeses as legitimate.

In fact, I would say cheddared versus stirred is the number one point of contention among cheddar-makers toward other cheddar-makers they view as "not real" cheddar-makers. But it turns out that factory technology has enabled this old method to be reinvented, the hard work of stirring now done by machines and the flaws of the process worked out with cultures that can withstand higher heat and new techniques of pressing and sealing.[14]

I figured I would be 100 percent on the side of the traditionalists, standing shoulder-to-shoulder with them to declare the stirred-curd folks betrayers of the cheddar legacy. And I mostly am. I do love the aesthetics of the slab pile and the curd mill. However, I just realized while on this cheddar journey that the pro-cheddaring people are actually the innovators, not the traditionalists. You know, in the grand historical scheme of things. And in the end the flavor is what matters to the eater.

So, finally, what is the definition of cheddar? Are you ready? Here's the CFR definition:

> (a) (3) One or more of the dairy ingredients specified in paragraph (b)(1) (Milk, nonfat milk, and/or cream) of this section may be warmed, treated with hydrogen peroxide/catalase, and is subjected to the action of a lactic acid-producing bacterial culture. One or more of the clotting enzymes specified in paragraph (b)(2) (Rennet and/or other clotting enzymes of animal, plant, or microbial origin) of this section is added to set the dairy ingredients to a semisolid mass. The mass is so cut, stirred, and heated with continued stirring, as to promote and regulate the separation of whey and curd. The whey is drained off, and the curd is matted into a cohesive mass. The mass is cut into slabs, which are so piled and handled as to promote the drainage of whey and the development of acidity. The slabs are then cut into pieces, which may be rinsed by sprinkling or pouring water over them, with free and continuous drainage; but the duration of such rinsing is so limited that only the whey on the surface of such pieces is removed. The curd is salted, stirred, further drained, and pressed into forms. One or more of the other optional ingredients specified in paragraph (b)(3) of this section may be added during the procedure.[15]

Of course the CFR also has an out:

Description. (1) Cheddar cheese is the food prepared by the procedure set forth in paragraph (a)(3) of this section, or by any other procedure which produces a finished cheese having the same physical and chemical properties. The minimum milkfat content is 50 percent by weight of the solids, and the maximum moisture content is 39 percent by weight, as determined by the methods described in 133.5. If the dairy ingredients used are not pasteurized, the cheese is cured at a temperature of not less than 35 deg. F for at least 60 days.[16]

So to sum up, the definition of how American cheddar is made is not important if the end product has the same "physical and chemical properties." There are not an infinite number of ways to achieve this, but what it does do is make the question of "what is a real cheddar" open to debate—one that is more aesthetic, political, or cultural than based in current law.

Don't you like my definition better now? Heat milk, make cultures comfy, add rennet, form curds, cut curds, scald, drain, cheddar, cheddar, cheddar, mill, salt, form, press, and age. Cheddar-making is just that simple.

Chapter 5

In Search of the First Cheese Factory

Rome, New York, is a fabled place in the history of cheddar. I knew that it had to be the next stop on my journey. Besides, fate found me only four hours away, and you already know that I will drive long distances for cheese history. My trip to see the Box-That-Once-Held-The-World's-Largest-Cheese was epic in its own failed way. I was wary of disappointment but couldn't resist the pull.

Officially known as the New York State Museum of Cheese in Rome, New York, it is actually one of two cheese museums in New York State. The Rome museum actually became a high-profile example of alleged pork-barrel politics. The cheese factory was reconstructed in the 1980s at a cost of $175,000 to the state. According to a *New York Times* article from twenty years later, the controversy of the state funding for the museum still resonated. In 2005, then-governor George Pataki used the funding of Rome's cheese museum as an example of the evils of the state budget, saying, "We've seen enough cheese museums and pro wrestling halls of fame to know what our budgets would become: free-spending free-for-alls."[1]

Whatever the source of funding, there is a good historical reason that the New York State Museum of Cheese is in Rome, New York. Cheese museum aside, Rome is honored by the state of New York as the home of the first cheese factory in the United States, the place where the cheddar revolution was born in 1851. I say, "of course," but if you asked the entire population of 320 million Americans where the first cheddar factory was built, I doubt more than a couple of thousand people would know the answer,[2] and very few others would previously even have contemplated the question. Not only that, but the claim itself is steeped in cheese controversy. I didn't want to be someone who simply repeats cheese myths without examining them first for truth or boosterism, so I decided to look more closely at what the concept of a "cheese factory" would have meant back then, and what it should mean to us today.

First off, how was cheese made before there were factories? The word "factory"—in addition to the way we use it to represent automation replacing human labor today—was sometimes used in the 1850s to simply signify the opposite of "farmstead." Just as today, farmstead cheeses of the 1800s used only the milk of the family's herd. Unlike today, though, farmstead cheese back then accounted for pretty much 100 percent of all cheese produced. For the most part these cheeses were just another attempt by farmers to make a living, and while some cheese was bartered or sold, for the most part this was cheese made by the farmer's wife to help the family survive.

There has never really been an easy time to be a farmer in America, and for most farmers of the time this utilization of resources was just one small part of an overall plan to make sure kids got fed and another year on the land was possible. Certainly some farms had professional cheesemakers and large herds. Those farms made a large part of their income selling cheese, but this was still done on premises, and those farms were in the minority of cheesemakers.

Was the Rome factory the world's first cheese factory? I had heard this said among cheese people from time to time, but even the biggest boosters of the New York State Williams factory do not make that claim. The cheese that easily refutes this idea is one of the oldest cheeses from the French Alps: Comté.

In a promotional move that made me laugh in appreciation of their middle-finger-to-the-newbies style, a few years ago the Comté Cheese Association came out with the slogan "1,000 years of artisanal cheese-making." Not a hundred: *a thousand*. In this country *ten* years of artisanal production seems practically old-timey. Furthermore, when I asked Nicki Sizemore, the Comté Cheese Association representative in New York, about when the first cheese factory came into existence, I got the following reply, "Comté fruitières, or cheesemaking facilities, go back some 800 years. The first written record of the word 'fructeries' (which became 'fruitières') appears in six texts dating from 1264 to 1280, describing cheese production in Déservillers and Levier. Farmers would pool their milk at the chalets to make the wheels of Comté (the 'fruit' of their labor). This cooperative system certainly extends back far before 1850, and the fruitières were typically located at the heart of the villages."[3] So it seems, even if her numbers are off by, oh, half a century, they probably have the Williams factory beat.

Today Comté is still made by a cooperative system of cheese production that enlists local cheese factories (the "fruitières") to collect milk from local farmers and turn it into cheese, where it is then shipped off to regional aging facilities when it is old enough to travel. Now, the fruitières system has only been around for eight hundred of Comte's thousand years—it now includes 160 fruitières, averaging eighteen farms per fruitière, producing 1,350,000 wheels (almost 11 million pounds) of cheese a year—but no American cheese factory is going to come close to that history.

Similarly, this is true of the Swiss as well, who claim factories for the industrial production of Gruyère and Emmental from the early 1800s. Similar to Comté, it is hard to imagine making cheeses ranging from 80 to 200 pounds without the pooling of milk at a central facility for cheesemaking.

So can the Rome factory be safely considered the first cheese factory in the United States?

There are other contenders. Most often boosted by the Wisconsin folks is Anne Pickett. In the early 1840s she was the cheesemaker who organized what is commonly referred to by some as either the first cheese factory or the first dairy cooperative in the United States. Hers was a relatively small operation—including the neighbors, it seemed limited to about thirty cows—and while it is a noteworthy accomplishment, what disqualifies it from being a factory is that it was a cottage industry. Literally. It was not a separate facility designed for cheesemaking, but the cottage where the Picketts lived and, in the kitchen of which, Pickett made the cheese. Pickett's cooperation with her neighbors was a big step forward for cheese in the United States, but as a model of production, her cheesemaking facility was still more farmhouse than factory.

There might be a lot more support for the recognition of the great, lost American cheese, pineapple cheese, if only it hadn't disappeared so long ago.

I had seen "pineapple cheese" mentioned numerous times over my reading of cheese history—it's often included in the "Types of American Cheese" sections of old pro-cheese brochures along with brick and Muenster. Honestly, though, I never stopped to think about it. As a child of the 1970s, I just assumed it was some kind of nasty cottage-cheese-and-pineapple thing that I associated with dieting. One day, though, while doing research for this book, I saw "pineapple cheese" and thought about my assumption. "Wait a second, that makes no sense whatsoever," I said to myself.

Pineapple cheese, it turns out, was a firm, aged cheese that was aged in forms that made it *look* like a pineapple, not taste like one.[4] It was extremely popular in some regions of the country and was the foodie bait of its time, demanding higher prices for its added labor costs, shape, and flavor. A 1935 Kraft-Phenix Cheese Corporation brochure describes it this way:

> The fancy Pineapple cheese . . . is nothing but Cheddar which has been cooked much harder than ordinary and, after pressing, is dipped into warm water for a few minutes. Then hung up to dry and ripen in a close-meshed net. It is the net that makes the diamond-shaped corrugations on the surface which, with the pineapple shape, makes it so attractive. As it ripens, linseed oil is rubbed on the surface and finally a coat of shellac, which prevents cracking and at the same time gives it a smooth, glossy exterior.[5]

Nothing says "fancy" and value-added like a coat of shellac!

Even if we wouldn't eat it today, it was popular enough that articles mention a factory built on a farm in Litchfield, Connecticut, in the 1840s. What defined this operation, as well as a few other nonfarmstead operations of the time period, was that they did not collect fresh milk; they collected curds that each different farmer brought to the factory from his own farm.

Dairy scientists and cheesemakers reading this probably cringe a little at that last sentence. It's not that people don't use the curds of others for their cheesemaking today—sometimes curds are frozen and shipped halfway across the world to be made into cheese at a later date. However, in the middle of the 1800s a curd-collection system of cheesemaking inherently had many problems—in today's parlance they would be called "critical control points," any of which could ruin a vat of cheese. The numerous individual farmstead cheesemakers had varying skill and knowledge and no access to scientific advances in testing for acidity let alone food-borne pathogens. This era was also prerefrigeration, so curd supplied for common cheese would almost inevitably have differences in age (even half an hour at this point in the process could have far-reaching effects in terms of acidity in the cheese) and would likely doom the consistency of such a cheese.

Knowing this, some might wonder if they shellacked it so that it wouldn't explode! Seriously, though, it does explain the extra "cooking" involved in the definition of this cheese—likely it was done to mitigate some of these variables. Still, I would love to try this cheese. Connecticut cheesemakers, get on it! Reclaim your roots!

When the old texts refer to the Jesse Williams factory in Rome, New York (and they almost all refer to him, even though his wife Amanda was also regarded as a talented cheesemaker. Indeed, she accompanied him when they rented out their dairy farm for an entire cheesemaking season to travel and study the cheesemaking of others[6]), they always use the phrase "associated dairying." I admit I just let that phrase roll by the first forty or fifty times I read it because it seemed self-explanatory. But then I realized that *this* was the revolutionary part of the Jesse Williams legacy; the concept makes this factory the important one to remember. A cheese factory would become known as a stand-alone building in which the local dairy farmers bring their milk to a cheesemaking expert (which by all accounts Jesse and Amanda Williams were), so that they can all work together to achieve more financial security. "Associated dairying"— whether as a cooperative (as it most often was in those early days) or as a cheese producer buying the milk of local dairies to perfect craft and increase production—was defined in opposition to *individual dairying* (or farmstead dairying), where a farm family was responsible for doing everything themselves and therefore usually limited in terms of skill, scale, and marketing ability.

While detailing a journey through old books and texts is not the most exciting thing to convey, it is one of the most exciting things to do, at least for me. It takes great effort sometimes to put yourself back into a place that doesn't exist anymore. When I realized that I might not understand the phrase "associated dairying" as well as I needed to, I turned to the pamphlet called *Associated Dairying*, written in 1879, for help. The following passage blew me away. After the author "shows" the reader around the creamery, explaining the functions of some of the tools, we get this passage in which the writer anticipates our next question:

> "But you have not told us what a creamery is. We will get our Webster and look for a definition."

> You will not find it there. It is one of the new words
> awaiting its turn to go into the next revised edition. It was
> not common enough fifteen years ago to come under the
> eye of the lexiconographer . . .[7]

Right. Duh. The word "creamery" didn't exist when all dairy products were made on a farm. "Creamery" was coined when stand-alone factories became common enough to need a word that differentiated them from farmstead dairy producers. Originally, "creamery" specifically meant a factory that collected milk to produce both butter and cheese[8] (since a factory that made just butter was a "butter factory" and one that made just cheese was a "cheese factory"). In the farmstead era of dairy, when there was no cooperation or association between dairies, there was no need for a collective word to describe the place where milks are mingled and dairy products produced. Today the word has lost its specificity, but in 1872 the phrase "farmstead creamery" would have been an oxymoron. This is one of those things that makes absolute sense when you think it through, but—when you do—you realize how the way you formulated the history in your own head had been holding you back.

The associated organization of cheesemaking—the milk of many farmers pooled to make cheese—that is so dominant in our world today had to be developed and nurtured in the late 1800s. Obviously, today the farmstead cheesemaker is the outlier, and everyone knows that, seemingly instinctively. But the Williams factory was such a revelation—and its success so all-encompassing—that by the time I got into the cheese world it had mostly obliterated the possibility of making a living selling farmstead cheese in the United States and also the memory of what had come before it.

Not only that: the cheese factory was also a source of American pride. Despite detailing the Swiss and European methods of cooperative cheese production only a few paragraphs previously, *Associated Dairying* goes on to crown Jesse Williams with the ultimate accomplishment:

> Though there were doubtless other trials made in other parts
> of the country, to Jesse Williams, of Rome, Oneida County,
> New York, is generally accorded the honor of originating the
> system of associated dairying, which bears the distinctive
> title of "American."[9]

"What is so American about it?" I wanted to ask right away. The only difference I could see is that the author viewed the Europeans (at least the ones in the Alps) who had been doing this for quite some time as "peasants" and the present-day American farmers as revolutionaries. Which, from the vantage point of 150 years later, when it is almost impossible to imagine the world of dairy before Jesse Williams, they probably were. A few pages later, Resh answers the question this way:

> Our own system differs from those of the old world because the resources and genius of our people are different. Its advantages, in the words of Professor Arnold, one of its most untiring champions, are that "the parties engaged in it become mutual instructors. First, by an examination of each other's work; the manufactories being in a manner public and open for inspection. Second, by organizations for mutual giving and reception of information relating to their art, and thus knowledge is developed by which milk is more profitably produced, goods more skillfully and cheaply manufactured and more systematically and successfully handled."[10]

When Alexis de Tocqueville traveled through the United States in the early 1800s and wrote his thoughts and observations in *Democracy in America* (1835), he wrote a sentence that has echoed until today, "The position of Americans is therefore quite exceptional." What he was referring to is that America was exceptional in the sense that it inherited all its nation building, science, and intellect from Europe but transported it to a land where there was seemingly an endless supply of land (forget the Native people for a second) and no tradition that needed to be upheld if it stood in the way of progress. He writes:

> The Americans are a very old and a very enlightened people who have fallen upon a new and unbounded country where they may extend themselves at pleasure and which they may fertilize without difficulty. This state of things is without a parallel in the history of the world. In America then every one finds facilities unknown elsewhere for making or increasing his fortune. The spirit of gain is always on the stretch and

the human mind constantly diverted from the pleasures of imagination and the labours of the intellect, is there swayed by no impulse but the pursuit of wealth. Not only are manufacturing and commercial classes to be found in the United States, as they are in all other countries but, what never occurred elsewhere, the whole community is simultaneously engaged in productive industry and commerce.[11]

The concept of American Exceptionalism lives with us to this day, even if transformed by politics and time. Through the 1930s it was used as a negative by Communists, and a positive by capitalists, to describe the United States not having the same history of class tension and aristocracy as the rest of the industrialized world. Today, as a phrase, it has lost its root in circumstance and is often used as a stand-in for blind patriotism, most notably, and often ridiculously, in the last decade to question whether a president believes *enough* in the American Exceptionalism that he promotes.[12] It has become a synonym for America-is-the-best-damn-country-in-the-history-of-the-world-don't-you-dare-criticize-it and as a moral ground for military intervention.

The way that Resh uses the concept of exceptionalism? Not too far from de Tocqueville, but with the conceit that it is the cooperation and open sharing of information (as well as some inherent genius) that, in this case, is the point of American pride. I wouldn't say this is necessarily historically accurate (I am not a historian, but as mentioned, cooperation was certainly being practiced by other cheesemakers of the time), but what is important is that they saw it that way at the time. Supporting the cheese factory became a source of community pride and American boosterism.

New York State nominally built a museum to cheese, but it is mostly a museum to the cheddar of the last half of the 19th century because that is the region's huge contribution to the world. Jesse Williams's claim to history is that his cheese factory in Rome was not only America's first cheddar factory but a model factory, one copied and improved upon over the years. Depending on how one wants to look at his factory, it could be seen as a liberating force for farm wives, reducing the amount of labor they had to perform. On the other hand, the factory professionalized women's work and then, as often happens under capitalism, gave the newly created jobs to men (for the most part). Finally, the Williams endeavor can also be viewed as the first step toward the end of handmade cheese production and the invention of push-button cheese.

Any way you see it, the result of the Williams cheese factory is that fewer farm women were engaged in cheesemaking, which many saw as drudgery. In a poem supposedly first printed in 1864, cheesemaking is considered a deal breaker for a pair of potentially betrothed:

THE DAIRYMAN'S COURTSHIP

My dear little Katy! My purse is not weighty,
    An hundred broad acres for keeping the cows,
A snug house and dairy; then say you will marry
    Me, now, Katy darling, my neat little spouse.

Dear Henry, my jewel! I think you're not cruel,
    Some leisure you're fond of, as well as the news;
Your housework and dairy I never could carry,
    The bare contemplation, sir, gives me the blues!

Now, Henry, in season, I'll give you my reasons,
    For certainly you have pondered them well;
So give your attention, while I merely mention
    Some few—but a volume the whole would not tell.

Oh! vexatious trials, and bitter denials,
    Of housewives in "cheesedom"—then what shall I do?
My baking is spoiling, my clothes must be boiling,
    And beef must be broiling and CHEESE TO MAKE TOO.

There! baby's awaiting, my limbs are all aching;
    How can I get through with this ev'ry day toil?
My house seems so dreary, and I am so weary.
    But still I must labor or dinner will spoil.

The milk in the dairy, could I only vary
    This every day routine of MAKING THE CHEESE;

Of this but relieve me, and then, Oh! believe me,
    All else is a task, I'll perform at my ease.

From all this confusion, I have one conclusion—
    A cheese factory's building just over the way;
So tackle old Billy, or Brown Mag, the filly,
    And carry the milk up there every day.

'Tis there they will take it, and into cheese make it,
    And keep, care and sell it, for, that's all they do:
Relieve me, from dippers, from rennets and skippers,
    I'll be your good housewife, so loyal and true.

My darling, I'll do it! I'll take the milk to it;
    Let them manufacture and, give them the whey,
Beside their commission for which is rendition,
    The net cash remaining to us they will pay.

This is an arrangement, preventing estrangement
    Of two loyal hearts, then, praise "JESSE" we'll sing,
Whose sure demonstration, convincing the nation.
    A cheese manufactory IS THE RIGHT THING![13]

Between this and saving the poor dairy maid from the exploding maggoty projectiles of cheese mentioned back in chapter 4, Williams comes off in dairy lore as an incredible hero to women. Undoubtedly, in a drudgery-filled environment such as a late-19th-century farm, not having to make dairy products benefited women in terms of having one fewer task to do. However, it could be asked, how many of those farm wives might have preferred a job as a cheesemaker to the compulsory work that the cheese factory did not relieve them of?[14]

One often overlooked part of history is that, while Jesse got the plaque and the credit for the first whole-milk-to-cheddar-cheese factory, his wife, Amanda Williams, was also regarded as an exceptional dairy worker.[15] They had actually been making cheese on their farm since 1830 and studying the best practices of others in the region. Jesse did a lot of the touring, seeking converts to associated dairying. History remembers his name more than his wife's. I am guilty of placing his name first, too; quoting official com-memorations makes it hard not to. We are left to wonder whether Amanda also got to travel with Jesse to spread their cheese factory gospel . . . or if she was home supervising the cheese factory, making cheddar and keeping their livelihood running.

Beyond the displacement of women as cheesemakers, another key theme exists, one also often lost to history, regarding cooperation. With the associated dairying system, the factory is a model of cooperation, an innate American rural trait. I am not arguing it was some kind of workers' democratic utopia—I have yet to find an article that discusses the work conditions of Williams-type factories. What was really revolutionary here, and what made the Williams model succeed, was the sharing of informa-tion both between cheddar-makers in England and the United States and between the farmers and cheddar-makers across the United States.

I pondered all this on my journey to Rome. I was headed to the Erie Canal Village, a re-creation of a 19th-century settlement ("on the site where, on July 4, 1817, the first shovelful of earth was turned for the construction of the original Erie Canal").[16] As with the many things I thought I knew about cheddar that turned out to be wrong, I thought I was going to the Jesse Williams factory. Instead, I was going to a factory built in the 1850s and *modeled* on the Williams factory: the Merry and Weeks factory from nearby Verona, New York, which had escaped the bulldozers and been moved to the village so that others could witness history.

The Erie Canal Village is a living history museum. It was near closing time when I arrived, but I sneaked behind a building so I could avoid the workers dressed in period costume. I don't really know why I did this . . . scarred from visiting "colonial villages" while on family vacations, I guess.

The factory was free of actors, and I was pretty much alone on my self-guided tour. An hour before closing on a day with torrential rain turns out to be an optimal time to visit a re-created village. The museum itself is just one big room that most people would probably walk through in about fifteen minutes. There were forms, boxes, and buttermakers displayed, along with mostly period pictures. The step-by-step how-to-make-cheddar display was pretty good—among the best I've seen, better than many books I have read.

Again, I wasn't there at an optimal time for tourists, but I was struck by the emptiness of the location. I was standing in a factory that was one of the first to start a food trend that would lead to cheddar's being America's best-selling cheese for 150 years, but being a New York State museum, its displays lost some of their historical steam, since cheesemaking had consolidated and New York became less important for cheese production than Wisconsin, California, or even Vermont. I wanted 1850s-dressed actor-workers to be making vats of cheese. I wanted to see an old-fashioned cheddar press pushing on twenty wheels at a time. I wanted to see an anthropomorphic Jesse Williams robot talking about making his first batch of cheddar.

As I was finishing up, taking a last couple of pictures of the cheese factory in the sunset, a costumed worker approached me. Thank goodness, she spoke in contemporary Upstate New York, not faux-period Ye Olde. She just wanted to make sure I was done before she locked up the factory for the night. She told me that she used to work at the salt museum in Liverpool, New York, before this job. "I went from an ingredient to a food!" she said.

The next stop on my trip to find the meaning of cheddar in Upstate New York was the Rome Historical Society. I dug through their Jesse Williams archives and saw that a granite memorial had been made for Williams in the 1930s. I had never heard of this before. Indeed, not only had the whole town—it seemed—come out for the dedication in 1936, the *Utica Observer-Dispatch* described the celebration to take place: "Dressed in the costumes of 1850, preceded by an ox-drawn cart of the same period, a procession of Rome citizens will make their way from the Court House, where the New York Cheese Manufacturer' Association was organized, to the site of the factory [three miles away]." After that, "two small girls, representing milk maids of the [18]50s will christen the memorial by dashing a wooden bucket of milk over the stone base of the monument." According to another source, over twenty-five hundred people attended the ceremony despite rain and cold.[17]

Could it be? Was this the monument to cheddar I was looking for? Maybe my mistake was overvaluing the huge, the spectacle. I went to see the "World's Largest Cheese" and ended up at a disappointing wooden box. Was it the punishment for my hubris, seeking out a mammoth cheese when the real story was not the bigger-than-life, but the commonplace nature of cheddar to our world? Finding out there was a granite marker only three miles away from where I sat—if it was still there—filled me with hope but also dread. What if I was too late?

I admit it, I have a history fetish. I am often disappointed by people's disin-terest in the histories of the locations where they live. I asked the workers at the society and the director if they knew about the Williams monument, but no one did. To be fair, I was getting used to the fact that monuments to cheese were more important to me than to most other people. However, the folks at the historical society were super-friendly and helpful. I would not have found the Williams factory without them, even if the next step was on my own.

Was it gone? From the description, it didn't seem that it would be an easy thing to get rid of, even if you owned the property and wanted to put in a hot tub or something. What could happen to a monument that people once traveled across the country to visit; that, I would find out later, was so important that the head of the biggest cheese company in the United States would at one point come to pay his respects?

I knew the location, more or less, from the old newspaper articles. When I hit the official blue-and-yellow state historical marker that the historical society folks directed me to as a starting point, I knew I was close. The site was dedicated in 1970, and the state signmakers were satisfied with a terse but hefty pronouncement, "Jesse Williams in 1851 inaugurated the cheese factory system thus revolutionizing dairying."

I knew that the memorial was near the town's fish hatchery, which I could see from the state marker. I drove by slowly, looking for any sign of it, knowing the roads might be different, that it might not be immediately visible, that it might even be overgrown and not viewable from the car. As I approached the intersection of Fish Hatchery Road and Williams Street, I couldn't see any sign. Old maps had shown me I should have already passed the factory at this point.

Wait, what's that? A rectangular patch of dirt in someone's yard? Had it been removed? And recently enough to leave a trace? Had I just missed my chance to see this memorial by days or weeks? I prepared myself to knock on the door of a stranger's house, asking stupid and unwanted questions about a cheese pioneer that not many people talked about anymore. To be fair, though, if the people in the house had just removed a couple-ton granite marker, they would probably remember it, if not him.

No, let me take another look. I drove back around a second time . . . and saw it.

I had to park in the "Employees Only" lot, but it didn't seem like there would be anyone around to care. I thought I might have to bushwhack to find it. I thought it might be crumbling, or hard to find in overgrown nature. But no, it was on the fish hatchery grounds, and they kept things nicely maintained. In fact, someone was driving a lawn mower in the distance. By sheer luck I seemed to have found the memorial on the regular grass-trimming day. It was as well kept up as it possibly could be. It had been built to withstand Upstate New York weather and the tests of time.

The memorial was taller than I was. There were no signs that anyone had been here recently. No flowers, no personal mementos, no Kraft Singles strewn about in remembrance or anything like them, just grass. There was no path to the memorial, which sat in the middle of a small mowed field, about 40 feet from the parking lot filled with work vehicles.

Under an image of the original factory and creek, the plaque reads:

> 1851–1936 Upon this spot in the year 1851 Jesse Williams a dairy farmer in this community set up the first cheese factory in America. This pioneer step led to the inauguration of the modern cheese factory system in this country. Previous to that time, cheese in America had been produced only on a home farm operation. Jesse Williams, for the first time in the history of American dairying, converted sweet milk from surrounding dairies into cheese at a central plant. He invented cheese making machinery, which he did not patent, but gave to posterity: aided in the creation of other factories: and trained numerous cheesemakers who carried the arts of cheesemaking throughout America. He organized the New York Cheese Manufacturing Association.

The plaque is understated compared with the historical marker that memorializes Williams's "revolution in dairying," but indeed, that is what happened. Factory growth, while slow at first, exploded to become the dominant mode of cheese production in the United States within a couple of decades after the Williams factory. The new system of dairying forever changed how cows were seen, women's role on the farm, and the entire rural landscape.

I came of age in the cheese world at a time before there was any real way to get a solid, dependable cheese education. I remember going to the local bookstore and buying multiple copies of Steve Jenkins's *Cheese Primer* when it came out—one for everyone in our cheese department—because every other book I could find was so outdated. The Internet didn't exist in any functional way for civilians at that point.[18] The information we got was by word of mouth, and the quality of mouths varied.

So it makes sense—with all the other information we needed to uncover—that our working history of cheese was rudimentary. I was starting to realize that the foundations I had were really just place markers, waiting for better information to cement everything together. Even so, I read a particular fact a few times before it really sank in, one at the crux of this journey.

Even now, sourced from many places, I feel unsure about typing this. It makes no sense in the cobbled history of American-made cheese that my peers and I "knew" to be true. There's traditional English Cheddar, then the Americans bastardized it, Taylorized it, cheapened it, processed it, used it to dumb down a food culture. Then, nearly a hundred years later, a few brave souls rediscovered the awesomeness of the old format and copied the few folks in England still holding on to the original recipe to bring it back to the States as part of a food movement that celebrates history, traditional foods, and small producers.

So the most unexpected fact I came across while researching the history of cheddar was the fact that, very soon after the factory system was started, much of the cheddar being made in the United States was being exported to England. This was during a relatively short time period, but still it blew my mind. After all, I started mongering at a time when the amount of cheese the UK was importing from the United States was pretty much zero. How did the export of American cheddar happen so quickly after the factory system began? Why did the UK need to buy cheddar at all? What did America do to screw it up?

I felt guilty about asking that last question. I mean, why did I assume it was *our* fault? Maybe there was just a temporary glitch in English production due to a cow disease or natural disaster. Maybe American cheddar was just a food fad and ran its course. Maybe England could have been so threatened by the quality of our cheddar that they banned importation because of the national shame and the effect it was having on national morale . . . farmers abandoning their herds, makers burning their factories, mongers crying so inconsolably that they could not cut a pound to order.

No, my assumption was right. The Americans screwed it up.

For the last few years, at the cheese counter, I kept thinking about this fact of exportation that had been previously unknown to me. How did a country that was—very early in its factory cheesemaking days—exporting a third of its cheese, almost one hundred million pounds,[19] wind up as a country exporting almost none, and importing large quantities? Not only that, in the 1990s when I started working in cheese, this was a country in which people seeking out "good" cheese wouldn't even buy American varieties. As snobbish as that was, it still shows what a lot of people thought of American cheese at the time. How did we get here?

The height of American exports of cheese, mostly cheddar, to the UK was in 1881, with almost 150 million pounds of cheese shipped. However, by 1900 it had dropped to almost nothing.[20] The factory system of associated dairying led to a lot more volume of cheese, and even increased quality overall compared with the more amateur, when-time-allowed home farmstead method. However, the biggest problem of the exported cheese was that it became associated with low quality, a reputation that American-made cheese has been suffering from in the rest of the world ever since, at least until the last decade or so.

The main villains that caused this decline in quality? Butter skimmers and milk fillers.

Throughout history it wasn't uncommon for some cheesemakers to think about skimming the cream off their milk before making cheese. In Switzerland skimming milk for cheese is practically the national pastime, yet their cheeses are considered among the best in the world. However, when one is making a traditional style of cheese that originated in another country, then trying to sell it back to that same country, people might notice the absence of the satisfying fat they are expecting. Indeed, skimming the butterfat from milk—to increase profit—had killed the reputation of Essex and Suffolk cheeses within England;[21] how could the United States cheesemakers expect to fare any better?

The really egregious violence against good cheddar, though, was done by "filled cheese."

Back in the nineties—the 1990s, not the 1890s, believe it or not—someone once tried to sell me "filled milk cheese." It was an exchange that started badly and never got better.

"Your girl Sylvia said I should come in about 11:00 a.m., but I'm running late," said the person on the phone, to whom I had never spoken before. The voice was like the outside of a moldy clothbound cheddar, abrasive and fuzzy. I'd never met this rep. At that point I had a weekly 11:00 a.m. appointment with a local cheese company, so I doubt anyone told her to come in at that time. And I also don't have any "girls," let alone one named Sylvia.

She didn't show up.

She called the next day and said, "So I know I said I'd be in today, but I'm running late. . . ." We renegotiated a time.

When she arrived she had some guy in tow who was either her boss or the marketing person for the cheese company. She never introduced him beyond a first name. She was from a fancy-ass specialty distributor but not one I deal with on a regular basis because they were based in Southern California. I was expecting her to pitch me on a fancy line of something moldy and French, or maybe an air-ship Italian program, but she surprised me. She pulled what looked like a small orange ham out of her bag and went into her spiel. After the third or fourth mention of "filled milk cheese," I stopped her.

"What is filled milk cheese?" I asked. "I've never heard of that."

"We simply replace the butterfat with vegetable oil." She smiled.

My coworker looked up from the cheese she was wrapping and looked down quickly, trying not to laugh. The sales rep went on talking about how great this product was because it had no cholesterol or lactose and only a third of the fat and blah blah blah. I know I was slow to get it, but finally I realized she was coming to the natural food co-op and thinking that we would, of course, be looking for diet cheese instead of a real cheese.

Then she pulled out the brochure, and I saw the cheese company logo. The product was a punch line, not a name: "Earth's Answer."

"What is the question again?" I asked, but she didn't acknowledge my jibe. She kept it moving. When she got to the part about replacing the butterfat with soybean oil, I had my chance to stop the madness. As a natural food store we don't generally carry soybean products unless they are organic. The rep realized the game was up and started gathering her things. "Well, let me leave these samples. Maybe your girls will like them."

"I don't have any girls," I said loudly to their backs.

After they left I noticed the names on the products. I thought the samples were mozzarella, cheddar, and Swiss. Nope. "Mozz," "Ched," and "Swis."[22] I gathered them up and put them in our store's "free box."

I refused to buy it, thought it was a dishonest and bad product, but I had no idea of its history or the fact that it was viewed, historically, as the product that killed the reputation of the American cheese business overseas for over a century. Boy, I wish I could have that conversation again. Not that the company trying to sell it to me in the late 1990s exists anymore. . . .[23]

While I had never heard of filled cheese when I started cheese buying, one hundred years earlier it was a very hot topic. In 1895 Henry E. Alvord, chief of the Dairy Division of the U.S. Department of Agriculture, wrote the following, which then was quoted at a hearing before the House Committee on Agriculture in 1921:

> "Filled cheese," which is regarded as having so injuriously affected the cheese interests of this country within very recent years, and especially our foreign trade is by no means a new article. . . . Very soon after oleomargarine began to disturb the makers, merchants, and consumers of butter in America, oleo oil came into use in the manufacture of cheese.
>
> As already stated this oleo cheese, lard cheese, or filled cheese comes into market under every name except its own. Its true character and designation are recognized only while in the hands of the manufacturers agents and when it moves from the principal distributing points the various brands upon it give ample evidence of the intent to deceive and defraud. Reputable merchants and exporters generally refuse to handle the article.[24]

Indeed, when asked to assess what had done the damage to the U.S. export of cheese, Alvord wrote, ". . . the exportation of so much low grade cheese or skims and of adulterated goods or filled cheese in defiance of the requirements of the British markets and the consequent degradation of a well earned reputation."[25]

These American-made cheddars were not replaced by English ones. Indeed, a growing population in England meant that import of cheddar was necessary, and the vacuum was filled by cheese from other English-speaking countries. In a whimsical piece about cheddar written in 1938, a famed English food writer laments visitors to the shops of Cheddar leaving with

Canadian cheeses. "I have to confess regretfully that Cheddar cheese of commerce seldom comes from Cheddar . . . although it is held to be foolish to carry coals to Newcastle, cheeses are carried to Cheddar!"[26] One history of the time tells about the astounding turning point when England refused 30 million pounds of U.S. cheese in the same year that they accepted an equal amount from Canada. After that, U.S. imports went into a decline. Dishonest London mongers didn't help; selling the good American cheddars that did arrive as "English" and the bad English ones as "American."[27]

In a very short time cheddar-making in the United States went from influencing the world to showing the world that our cheese couldn't be trusted.

It's easy to think, when visiting Willi Lehner's cave or looking at the beautiful wheels of clothbound cheddar in the aging rooms at the Cellars of Jasper Hill, that maybe 1851 is the moment when everything went wrong.

Forget for a moment that history doesn't really work like that. If not Jesse Williams, someone else would have brought the factory system of associated dairying into being. Joseph Harding in England, Robert McAdam in Scotland, Xerxes Willard in New York, Hiram Smith in Wisconsin, or any of hundreds of farmers whose names are lost to history. The information was being gathered in the mid-1800s, best practices being recorded, technology being developed, science starting to understand dairy and cheese. It was a period of time devoted to such matters; the Industrial Revolution was not just about steel and cars.

I have been trying to think of a food (not a crop) that wasn't changed by making it in a factory. Bread, beer, wine, pickles . . . anything you can think of has a corporate mass-produced analogue. I tried to think of regional foods, or rather foods we think of as regional because, perhaps, they never industrialized. My Texan wife tried to help me out, but even such things as praline products, if not nationally big sellers, have their factory versions.

And while the 1851 cheddar factory wasn't much of a factory by today's standards—pre-Taylorism, the work was not cut into tiny efficient bits, and mechanization was still limited—clearly it was thought of that way in the press of the times and the historical accounts. The most important thing about it is that it was the first factory that was trying to develop and perfect a factory method of production, rather than just creating a bigger space to make cheese. The one thing it really separated, the first part of this process, was dairy farming and cheesemaking.

But what if it hadn't happened? What if cheese had remained as a farm project?

Well, no matter how much we think about the Bleu Mont Cheddar and the Cabot Clothbound as traditional products with preindustrial roots, those cheeses are made in cheese plants much more mechanized than the ones that existed back in 1851. The Cabot especially—even if care is taken to source the milk of one farm and perfect a bigger, more complex flavor than any other Cabot cheese—is not even slab-cheddared. Although, if we remember our history, 1851 cheddar producers had not yet widely accepted that step in the process.

So no, the Williams factory was not the wrong step, but a step with inevitable consequences. Cheddar, well built for both travel and factory production, was bound to boom.

Chapter 6

Vermont Is Not Wisconsin

When I think of important cheesemaking states outside my home state of California, Vermont and Wisconsin are the first two that immediately come to mind. Indeed, Vermont is first in the nation in percentage of dairy in "farm cash receipts," which means that their dairy farms contribute a larger portion of state income than dairy does in any other state.[1] A theme for this journey to the heart of cheddar seems to be that I should lower my expectation level for cheese excitement among the general populace, but I always figured Vermont was exempt from that self-imposed rule. Upon my arrival I assumed I would feel the same kind of cheese excitement and boosterism that Wisconsin, "America's Dairyland," offers up at the slightest provocation.

That's not the way Vermont works, it turns out. In Wisconsin, I would always tell cabdrivers that I was a cheese buyer visiting cheesemakers and farms. Then, without fail, they would tell me about their favorite cheeses, where to get the best curds, and what cheese factories had tragically gone out of business. Continuing, they would also let me know that whoever I thought I was coming from California, and no matter how many years I had spent professionally buying cheese, anything I had to say would be suspect because I was not from Wisconsin and never would be.

In Vermont the conversation went like this:

Cabdriver: "What are you doing while you are in Vermont?"

Me (smiling, waiting to get an excited response in return): "I'm a cheese buyer, visiting Vermont cheesemakers."

Cabdriver: "Did you hear what Rush Limbaugh said about illegal immigrants?"

I am not making the claim—far from it—that all Vermonters are ditto-heads. I am just saying that cheese is a dominant form of communication in Wisconsin, more valued than political affiliation, tourist information, or even weather. Confusingly, Vermont not only is home to many great cheesemakers, but is also the home of one of the most distinctive styles of cheddar made anywhere in the country. What could I learn about cheddar in a state where the locals didn't seem to know how good they had it?

Maybe it was just coincidence, but my journey to Vermont started on a number of unfriendly notes. My Limbaugh-loving cabbie was helping me flee at 1:00 a.m. from a bed-and-breakfast in Burlington that I had booked online and that turned out just to be some dude's house in a dark residential neighborhood. It was dirty, cat filled, and sticky and had no locks on the doors. When I arrived—too late to pick up my rental car because the company was closed for the night—the "proprietor" was asleep. I knew because I could hear his snoring throughout the house. Except for a prominently displayed license, there was no sign that this was actually a "bed-and-breakfast" and not a wrong address. Well, there was one . . . a handwritten note saying, "Fruits & Juices & Jam & Eggs Hash brown patties in freezer door. Sorry I only make breakfast for Sunday brunch."

Post-cabbie, when I went to get my rental car the next morning, the guy behind the counter took one look at me and asked, "Don't you think you need a bigger car?"

"Are you calling me fat?" I wanted to ask but didn't. In retrospect, he may have been trying to warn me that most of Vermont is gravel road.

Vermont has a lot of cheddar tradition and is still a major producer, so to more fully understand cheddar's place in our culture, I organized a tour of some of the state's most famous and important makers. What, I wondered, would I find here that would help me understand cheddar's place in the American mind?

My first stop was Cabot Creamery, the most well-known and biggest cheese company in Vermont. Interestingly, the two slightly upscale block cheddar makers, Cabot and Tillamook in Oregon—probably the two best-known cheeses nationally, outside of Kraft—are both agricultural cooperatives. Both have long histories and still exist from the time when cooperatives were the obvious way to organize a dairy-based project.

Being a co-op worker myself, I always want to find solidarity when visiting farmer co-ops. Every sector of cooperatives (worker, consumer, student, housing, and agriculture) seems to be a little wary of each of the others, however. When a consumer cooperative grocers' association formed, for example, I heard through the grapevine that some of their members felt that the workplace democracy of our worker cooperative would undermine their more traditional management structures and unorganized workers. When student co-op members inquire about "interning" with our co-op, there is definitely a feeling among some workers at our store that they won't want to mop floors; they'll just want to tell us what to do—even though we've been in business longer than they've been alive. Ag co-ops are sometimes seen as unconcerned with the issues of both worker and consumer natural foods stores, and among small farmers they are sometimes talked about as bullies.

The week before I visited Vermont, I was doing a cheese talk at the Natural Foods Co-op in Sacramento, California. The cheeses were some of my favorites: Teleme, one of two California originals that I always keep in the case; Miette by Baetje Farms in Missouri, a company I had judged to make one of the top goat cheeses in the country—even though I had never heard of them—when I judged cheese at the American Dairy Goat Association competition; and Green Hill, made by Sweet Grass Dairy in Georgia, a cheese I almost always use in classes I teach to demonstrate the color and the richness of grassfed Jersey milk.

We had a fun class for about an hour, tasting and talking, gossiping and gabbing, until finally a man in the back of the class had a question. "What's wrong with cheddar? Is it just not 'hip' to talk about it anymore?"

I told him, no, in fact I was working on a book about cheddar, and he probably just made it in as a voice-of-the-average-American anecdote. After the class we talked, and he told me that he was from Heuvelton, New York. Even though my talk was in 2014, the man was still bitter about Cabot's parent co-op Agri-Mark closing down the McCadam Cheese packaging plant in 2003 after they acquired McCadam from a Finnish co-op (which had previously purchased it from multinational food giant Dean Foods, which had purchased it in 1972).

McCadam[2] was founded in 1876 in Heuvelton, and even though they moved most of the cheese production to Chateaugay, New York, during the Great Depression, the man told me that closing the packaging plant had ripped the heart out of that small Adirondack town. As he talked about it, I felt his hometown anguish, the loss of what once was.

One of the selling points that cooperatives have is that they are rooted in the community. At our store we can guarantee that our profits aren't shipped to another state or overseas. Our workers live in the community. We have investment in the place we do business. Consumer co-ops, owned by the shoppers, can pretty much guarantee the same thing. Agricultural co-ops can grow much larger than the other two main co-op sectors, though. While offering guarantees for the farmers, the Heuvelton packaging factory was not a stakeholder, so it could become expendable.

I am not privy to the financial information that went into the decision to close the plant and am not offering this example in condemnation, only as a way to illustrate that nothing about cheddar-making is easy, and there are no financial guarantees, even in the places—most of which are now considered geographically undesirable—where cheddar was born in the United States.

At Cabot I met up with Craig Gile, who had been working as a cheddar grader for Cabot for the previous few years. Together we entered the biggest warehouse I have ever seen in America that was dedicated almost entirely to just one cheese. The scale was something to behold. Forty-pound cheddar blocks upon forty-pound cheddar blocks piled forty-eight blocks per pallet. These pallets were stacked upon more pallets and piled four pallets high. In another section, wooden crates holding 640-pound cubes sat on more identical wooden crates, stacked up to six high.

If the average American eats 33.5 pounds of cheese a year and lives to seventy-nine years of age—ignoring the fact that babies and toddlers wouldn't eat that quantity—that amounts to 2,646.5 pounds over the course of one's life; that is, just over one pallet's worth of cheddar. The Cabot factory, my friends, holds a lot of cheese.

All of it is run by one woman, who came riding through the factory on her pallet jack, trying to figure out who was intruding on her space. Craig and I tasted cheddar after cheddar, him showing me how their grading process works and how they decide which "green" cheese will become what finished product.

We tasted relatively freshly made cheddar and ones aged five years. We poked at the 640-pounders through their little rectangular glory holes. We tasted the ones made with different flavor (alpine-style) cultures, and one made in a 40-pound block with basically the same recipe as the Clothbound Cheddar that is aged at the Cellars of Jasper Hill (though unlike the Jasper-aged one it is made from pooled milk, not a single selected farm's milk).

We spanned the gamut of block cheddar flavors! Grassy, sweet like milk, sweet like caramel; some rich, some acid, some a little bitter; some that gave that Northeast sulfide bite; some undeveloped but showing character; some undeveloped, and I had to take Gile's word that they would become distinct once they were allowed to mature.

In such a large operation, the cheddar grader plays a crucial role. Cabot does not sell its cheddar by age, but by flavor profile. Thus a very bitey cheese at eighteen months might become a "Seriously Sharp" cheddar, but another at the same age may only be graded as a "sharp." The Seriously Sharp used to be known as "Hunter's" cheddar, which amuses me because when I think of hunting I think of gun oil for a clean, safe shotgun and lighter fluid for hand warming. I do not taste petroleum in the "Seriously," but another Vermont producer, Shelburne Farms, markets their slightly-out-of-control and unpredictable blocks of cheddar under the name "Tractor Cheddar" and once bragged of one of its many flavor components being reminiscent of "diesel."

The thing that really unites Vermonters in their cheddar-making is that they are not afraid to showcase what denizens of other states, and cheesemongers, too, might consider off-flavors. Vermonters are proud of their sulfury and bitter-sharp cheeses, and even the way the plastic around their 40-pound blocks sometimes blows up like a cheese balloon.

Well, that might be going too far. They don't really like it when their blocks balloon from gas expansion—they are hard to sell and generally, when popped, exude an egginess that can overwhelm a cheese cutting room—but you can see in their eyes a little pride in the ruggedness of their product, and I think they appreciate making a cheddar that says to a customer, "I dare you to try this."

Terroir is a concept often used for food in high-end circles. It means, roughly, "sense of place," and is meant to reference why certain foods or wines can only taste a certain way if they are made in a certain region. While this term does have real meaning in many cases, I have mocked the term *terroir* before for its pretentiousness when used inaccurately. Another cheese professional, I wish I could remember whom so I could credit him or her, once referred to the concept of *terroir* for pasteurized cheeses as ridiculous since the heating kills any native microflora in the milk and flavor has to be added through secondary cultures introduced during the cheesemaking process. "The only *terroir* in a pasteurized cheese is the *terroir* of Danisco," he said at a workshop at a national cheese conference, referring to the Swiss cheese culture company.

That might be a little further than even I would go, though really, probably not. However, in Vermont, there is something to the notion of *terroir*. All the Cabot cheeses are pasteurized, but they still make them in the New England style—the style developed when all cheeses were made from raw milk—to have bite.

After many Vermont block cheddars are aged over two years, they become a polarizing force. I think of the flavor in all caps: THE VERMONT BITE. It's the kind of cheese that some people call "inedible" but others call the only cheddar that tastes like cheddar should. If I sample these super-aged Vermont cheeses out to ten customers in a row, one might say, "Finally, a cheddar with real flavor. I'm going to make an apple pie just to serve with this!" Most customers will appreciate it. And then one customer out of the ten, not used to strong flavors, might ask, "Did you dig this sample out of a bag of farts?"

Grafton Village Cheese Company, a much smaller cheese company than Cabot and one that still makes unpasteurized cheese, is famous for their biting Vermont cheddars. If *terroir* means "sense of place," then Vermont cheddar gives you that more than any other cheddar, and Grafton more than any other Vermont block cheddar-maker. Dane Huebner, the cheese-maker at Grafton, believes that cheese, and especially cheddars, from the region have their "own taste of place with slight sulfur flavors like hydrogen sulfide and dimethyl disulfide, which has a garlicky/truffle aroma."[3]

Huebner is a microbiologist by education, hence the big words, and he has won awards as a cheesemaker in three states for three different companies. He knows cheese.

The aged, block versions of Grafton cheddar can be a great divider at our store, between the folks who like the sweeter, cleaner cheddar style made in every other part of the country and those who prefer the traditional Vermont style. We commonly use words such as bitter, sulfur, sharp, and bitey to describe this cheese, and if you like that kind of flavor, those words will not be seen as negatives. There are two Grafton factories in Vermont, and I visited the one in the Village of Grafton, a town rehabilitated by the Windham Foundation, "dedicated to promoting Vermont's rural communities." Grafton is also listed as a must-see by travel writers, making *USA Today's* "10 Most Beautiful Places in America" list in 2009, among other honors.

Grafton the town seemed nice enough to me as I drove through, but you know I was really just there for the cheese. Grafton the cheese company was originally founded in 1892 as a cooperative but currently operates under the nonprofit structure of the Windham Foundation, like the rest of the town. Still, in the cheese room, it felt like a cheese room anywhere else in the country.

The most common Grafton cheese is a raw-milk block cheddar. It's milled curd, made in 40-pound blocks, and from the outside looks like an unassuming box of cheese. Grafton has been making different types of cheese in recent years as well, including some sheep and blended milk ones, and they also make two clothbound cheddars,[4] one with their own milk and one with the milk of fellow nonprofit-owned Spring Brook Farms' prized Jersey cows. The Spring Brook milk cheese is sold under the name "Queen of Quality," and the clothbound recently won Best USA Cheese trophy at the 2014 International Cheese Awards and has won numerous honors at the American Cheese Society (first in category 2014, second in category 2013).

While the 40-pound Grafton block has the flavors we've come to expect from Vermont cheddar, the Queen of Quality, with the milk from a 100 percent Jersey herd, underlines the distinction between block cheddar and farmhouse style. Block cheddars can be sharper and bitier, but the depth of the farmhouse style is unsurpassed. The Jersey milk makes the Queen richer as well.

Back in the homeland of cheddar, Jersey milk—much higher in butterfat content than the milk of other cows—was not thought to be good for making cheddar; it was just too rich for the style.[5] Indeed, even the folks considered by many to be the best cheddar-makers in the world—the Montgomery Family of Somerset, England—won't use Jersey milk for cheddar. The Montgomerys kept making traditional cheddar through World War II when it almost went extinct; they are one of the few who get to label their Montgomery's Cheddar as "West Country Farmhouse Cheddar"; and they are recognized by Slow Food, a movement set up to defend and promote traditional methods of food production. All the very best American clothbound cheeses are compared against their cheddar, which is made only with Friesian milk. The Montgomerys have a herd of heritage Jerseys, but they use their milk to make an incredible (and incredibly rare in the United States) cheese called Ogleshield that is nothing like cheddar.

In America through the 20th century there was prejudice against using the milk of Jerseys for cheddar for another reason: volume. Jerseys produce high-fat milk, but a lot less of it than Holsteins, especially after the selective breeding of the last 150 years. Jerseys are making a big comeback, but in American dairy, especially for fluid milk, Holsteins are still king.

As I write this, I have more than half a ton of Jersey milk cheddar coming my way, so while I defer to the Montgomerys on all matters cheddar, I have to say that I can appreciate a Jersey milk version, too. It's also one of the types of cheese I like to buy because it was just sitting around a warehouse with nowhere to go. That award-winning Spring Brook "Queen of Quality" clothbound? It came about because Spring Brook was unable to make cheese for a while back in 2011. Spring Brook needed to do something with their milk. Instead of letting it go bad; pouring it down the drain; or, I don't know, filling swimming pools with it for fancy, therapeutic milk baths, they sent it to Grafton. Some of this milk became the Queen of Quality clothbound, but the rest? Made into 40-pound blocks with no obvious place to call home.

Since they had to age, there was no immediate need to find a buyer. However, eventually, when they were ready to go, Grafton realized they had a lot of cheese that no one knew about and that, even if they made a vat today, would not be available again for another three years or so.

I love cheese like that. I think of it as "event" cheese, like the cheddars made at the Gathering of the Cheddarmakers that never got out to California. Some of the best milk in the country—Spring Brook's Tarentaise Reserve won Best of Show at the American Cheese Society Conference in 2014—combined with one of the oldest and most distinctive cheddar-makers in the country at Grafton is almost definitely going to make a memorable cheese. The Queen of Quality block doesn't have the depth of the Queen of Quality clothbound, of course, but it has the extra butterfat you'd expect from the Jersey milk, the bite you'd expect from a Grafton cheddar, and a sweetness I didn't expect at all. These blocks will be cheese that customers will be asking about for years after we run out. It's at times like these that I feel I am teaching folks an important lesson about the ephemeral nature of amazing food.

Ephemeral . . . like the buffalo milk cheesemakers who pop up occasionally in the United States, only to disappear again not too long—relatively speaking—after starting in business. In fact, the next stop on my cheddar tour of Vermont was a company using the facility originally built for a company making buffalo yogurt.

When I parked in front of Vermont Farmstead Cheese Company,[6] Bob Marley was blasting from the cow barn. As a co-op worker, I felt right at home. Behind the counter at Rainbow, we make up cheese songs all the time for different cheeses. There is an Italian cheese called Quadrello di Bufala, which is basically a Taleggio made with water buffalo milk. Because Marley is a staple of any old-school natural food store's playlist, the song for this cheese came easily, sung to the tune of "Buffalo Soldiers": *"Buffalo Taleggio, dreadlock bison. Refrigerate on arrival. Refrigerate for survival."*[7]

I was humming this tune while I walked in the door.

When I entered, cheesemaker and vice president of creamery operations Rick Woods was making Lillé—a Coulommiers-style soft-ripened cheese that is one of the best soft-ripened cheeses in the country—not cheddar. Lillé is a great mushroomy-rich cheese that is almost unknown on the West Coast right now, so I was excited to see them work on it. The make process is a two-person job, turning over the cheese in its draining racks. The flipping didn't take long, though. Vermont Farmstead is not a large operation.

Vermont Farmstead got its start because the water buffalo dairy failed. Vermont Farmstead is on the site where Woodstock Water Buffalo Company used to be. Woodstock (later, under other owners, known as "Spoondance Creamery," "Vermont Water Buffalo Company," and "Bufala di Vermont") was one of many attempts to produce buffalo milk cheese in the United States, almost all of which so far have ended in acrimony, mystery, or failure. Woodstock was trying to make mozzarella, ricotta, and yogurt when they started, and they had a tantalizing business plan. Why import the freshest, most perishable product from Italy when you—theoretically—could make it a few hours away from America's largest urban area?

Unfortunately, it turns out there are many reasons, including lack of good herd genetics, lack of experienced buffalo milk cheesemakers, lack of knowledgeable veterinary care, and lack of specialized cheesemaking equipment. Critical mass of production in a given region solved these problems for cheddar in New York, then Wisconsin, 150 years ago. With cheddar the sharing of best practices, needed tools, science, and information lifted everyone up. Water buffalo cheeses have not yet been able to achieve that in this country. Woodstock gave it a better run than most but, in the end, went out of business as well.

Vermont Farmstead is the only community-owned farmstead dairy/cheesemaker in the country as far as I can tell. Neighbors banded together to buy the farm and keep it a farm, formed a new cheese company, and hired Woods, who it turns out started in cheese at Grafton Village Cheese

Company just about the same time as I did at Rainbow. He, however, learned a useful-to-society skill: cheesemaking.

The Vermont Farmstead Governor's Cheddar is named after Vermont governor Peter Shumlin, who visited the farm, and Woods made him make a whole vat of cheddar instead of just a one-off photo op. "Not so fast, Gov! We have a whole vat of cheese to make!" That's not an actual quote, by the way, that's just how I picture it in my head: the governor harping, cheddaring, and milling. Governor Shumlin was successful in his inaugural cheddar make because that batch actually won third place at the American Cheese Society in 2012 for cheddar aged over one year. Since the first place was Canadian and second place was made with goat milk, Woods says proudly, "We made the best cow milk cheddar in the country."

While I wished I could have visited another ten or twenty Vermont cheesemakers, I was working my journey of cheddar around my actual work schedule. I would love the reader to think that I can spend my cheese-buying time flitting around from farm to farm, plant to plant, just tasting and chatting, occasionally buying batches of cheese to ship back home, like William Randolph Hearst buying statues or something. No, not for a buyer who actually spends most of his week working counter shifts or receiving cheese. Not for a buyer who works for a cooperative that has only one store.

Before I left Vermont, though, I knew I had to visit Jasper Hill. They are celebrities of the new cheese movement, the focus of articles and sections of sociology books, and not only do they help produce great cheddar, more clothbound cheddar is aged, graded, and sold from their "cellars" than anywhere else in the country.

The last time I was at Jasper Hill Farm, I had been traveling with my friend from Sonoma, Sheana Davis, who is a shop owner, cheesemaker, and chef. We were traveling from Maine to Massachusetts, and we wanted to check out what the Kehler brothers were up to, since we had met them at some cheese event and loved their enthusiasm and what we had tried of their cheese. Also, their totally isolated location was directly in our path. I remember hearing co-owner Andy Kehler tell me about the plans they had to build a series of aging rooms for cheese. It was a huge project to help save dairy farming in Vermont. They were going to start construction in the coming weeks when the weather improved. We were there during "mud season," which I hadn't, until then, known was a season.

"Yeah, yeah," I thought. "We'll see if this thing goes anywhere. . . ."

Because, you know, at cheese events you hear a lot of talk. Cheese that never gets made, farms that never farm, the Next Project to Save Family Farms that never gets off the ground. . . . I'm not jaded: I often meet with these folks, share information freely, and hope they can put together their grandiose plans; it's just that I usually never hear of them again.

We had visited Jasper Hill in 2006. In 2014 when I went back it was hard to believe I was in the same place. I mean, it had the same gravel roads, the same small herd of cows. The barn was the same, though now covered in a mural of cows grazing on the moon, which may be the Kehlers' next plan. Judging from the transformation made since my last trip, I wouldn't dismiss the idea of Jasper Hill moon cheese outright.

When I visited before, it was just Jasper Hill Farm. Now it was Jasper Hill Farm and the Cellars at Jasper Hill. Seven different aging rooms have been decked out to fit the needs of the cheeses that are aged there. No longer farmstead—even if some cheeses are only produced with their own milk—they buy the milk from neighboring farms as well and have increased their production. No longer just the family and one or two others, there are forty-six employees, including a number who left urban cheese selling to come to Jasper and become part of something big. Big in the sense of important, of course. Like the migration of all those folks who moved to San Francisco in the sixties, Greensboro, Vermont, is one of the places where cheese is happening right now. It's the place to *be*.

They partner with Cabot in producing the clothbound cheddar, but just one wing of one of Cabot's warehouse dwarfs the quantity of Jasper's production and store of aged cheeses. Jasper is still pretty impressive, though, especially the cheddar rooms. Cheddars are aged with their batches and piled at least twelve high to the ceiling on aging shelves. Cheese is graded, notes are kept, and peak timing is decided on by taste, not age. Vince Razionale, who somehow manages to include "Purchasing, Inventory Management, Sales, Customer Service, [and] Tasting" in his job responsibilities, gave me a tour.

Cabot makes these cheddars, but unlike the rest of Cabot's production, the milk only comes from one particular farm, picked for the quality of their milk. The cheese is made in a much smaller batch than the usual Cabot production run, formed into wheels, and aged in the Cabot warehouse until it can be safely transported to Jasper Hill. At Jasper the cheese is wrapped in cloth, larded, aged, tasted, evaluated, cleaned, relarded if needed, and finally sold when it reaches the correct flavor profile. Some cheddars that don't make the grade (literally) are disposed of in different ways but not under the name "Cabot Clothbound aged in the Cellars at Jasper Hill." While I was there I also got to taste the version made from pooled milk for a private label. It wasn't bad, but the lack of depth and flavor development was notable. It was a decent cheese, but you didn't need to be a cheese professional to taste the difference.

Razionale and I tasted a lot of cheddar. Some had big fruitiness, some were sharper, some were more acid, some more buttery. An opportunity to try so many cheeses at once is a great way to develop one's palate. It's similar to monger training at our store. Education is great, reading books is great, talking to customers is great . . . but tasting is what really teaches you about cheese.

The difference in flavor characteristics between wheels is one of the special things about clothbound cheddars, something you do not get in 40-pound blocks. Sure, there are differences between blocks—that's why Craig Gile and I tasted so many at the Cabot warehouse—but it is nowhere near the same diversity of possibilities. With clothbounds, flavors could possibly be tracked to different things—what the pasture was like, time of year, was the aging room slightly different during a crucial moment, who made the cheese—and those differences are amplified by the more porous aging method. Larded cheesecloth simply allows more air exchange than does sealed plastic. The grading that goes on at Jasper Hill is not a free-for-all of acceptance. Quite the opposite, in fact: attempts are made to develop and bring out the best flavors and learn why certain batches may taste different. This is what good cheddar-making has always been about, standardizing practice to get the most out of one's cheese.

Oh, and you know what I said about not being William Randolph Hearst? Well, I ended up tasting a batch of cheddar from the shelves that was so good, I had to buy a couple of hundred pounds for the store right away. I had shipping confirmed through my distributor before I even got my hairnet off.

Between visits to cheddar plants, I drove to my sterile-funky business hotel for the night. In my suitcase was a foodie's wet dream: a pound of Queen of Quality, a pound of Cabot Clothbound, and a can of Heady Topper, a

Vermont IPA brewed by The Alchemist Brewery in Waterbury and rated best in the world in 2013 by *BeerAdvocate*. It was in such demand that the brewery had to close its retail shop because it was attracting such large crowds. Luckily I was inconspicuous in my tiny rental car, and either there is a dearth of violent foodies in central New York State or I just managed to avoid them. At a hipster food event in San Francisco, I would have been in fear for my life with this bounty.

I staged a taste-off in my hotel room. First I put on "Battle" by Gang Starr to set the mood. Then I cracked open the beer. Heady Topper . . . holy crap. This is not a beer book, and I claim no real beer knowledge beyond the fact I've been drinking it since I was thirteen, but I could tell this was something amazing. It's a double IPA with none of the hoppy bitterness you can get in other IPAs. Fruity, citrusy, woodsy maybe? At 8 percent alcohol it tasted boozy but in a just-enough kind of way. Supposedly it's in such short supply that it's hard to get this beer even in the town of Brattleboro, in southeast Vermont.

In the Bay Area we have a similarly popular, small-production brew made by the Russian River Brewing Company called "Pliny the Elder." It sells out within hours of arrival at our store every week. I think almost every store in the Bay limits amount of purchases because there could be a profitable resale market, and our entire week's supply would disappear within minutes if we weren't vigilant. You might laugh at that, but when our store gave out 20 percent off coupons, people were trying to sell them online. And yes, "Pliny" is named after the same Roman food critic that wrote about Cantal, the precursor of cheddar. It's a small world for the foodie who's looking for historical inspiration.

But the cheddars. . . . Oh, man. How many people get to have two of the greatest cheeses in the world given to them straight from the cheese companies? Not only that, one was given to me by the actual cheesemaker, the other by the person in charge of the aging. I am a lucky guy.

I kept tasting notes even as the Heady Topper started going to my head. I hadn't really eaten much of anything besides cheese samples for two days at that point. I started with the Queen of Quality because I hadn't had a chance to eat very much of it in my lifetime, and I couldn't wait to try it again, the first time since it had taken international honors. The paste was a dark yellow from the beta-carotene in the grasses and the Jersey milk, visibly darker than the Cabot Clothbound. I thank those Jerseys for making it richer than most farmhouse cheddars. The Queen was buttery, salty, grassy, mushroomy, dank, and cellary. The number one distinction of a good farmhouse cheddar to me is depth. This cheese was deep but also completely accessible and without pretension: more Flannery O'Connor than William Faulkner.

I couldn't remember which batch of the Cabot Clothbound I had gotten; we had tasted so many in the Cellars at Jasper Hill. Whatever batch it was, it was awesome. Rounder than the Queen of Quality, more earthy and animal, crystalline, yet fudgy in texture at the same time. The Jasper Hill aged cheddars, in their multitudes of taste, almost anticipate your desires. When you start wondering, for example, "Where's the sweetness?" the sweet hits you before you can finish the thought. I couldn't tell at first if it is milky sweet or caramel-y sweet . . . and in the end I just have to say there are bits of both. Somehow stripped down and complex at the same time, there are a lot of tastes to name. Before you put that piece in your mouth, you didn't know it, but every step in the journey seems essential and obvious when you finish. More like a James Baldwin essay than one by Thomas Wolfe.

Both cheeses are less pretentious than my comparing them to great American writers. My point in this comparison is a simple one, though. The quality of cheese made in this country is one of those factors that we can use to compare our present time historically to other eras of creation. I get that cheese is more ephemeral than other forms of art, but the level of talent in cheesemaking these days is comparable—though not identical—to other eras in American history. Novelists of the Southern Gothic, the Harlem Renaissance, essayists during the Civil Rights era, punk bands in disparate urban-based scenes in 1977, 1979, 1981, and 1984, and so on. For a variety of reasons, talent was encouraged and coalesced in different ways in different locations at specific points in history. There are two periods of time when the United States made clothbound cheddar as well as anyone in the world: the late 1850s . . . and right now.

Here's something to think about, though: the time periods when America was making its greatest clothbound cheddar bookend the century and a half when cheddar was America's most popular cheese. In the early 21st century, block mozzarella took cheddar's crown away, and if you want a shorthand reason as to why, go look at the variety of frozen pizzas on your grocer's shelves.

Vermont still claims a greater concentration of great cheddar-makers than anywhere else. Great cheese is one of the reasons that Vermont is special. But this is no accident. People, concerned with the land, the farmers, and the state's economy, had to figure out some alternative models to preserve cheesemaking, and especially cheddar production, in a state where you always seem to have to go over a mountain to get to the next town and where more roads are gravel than paved. Think of a Vermont cheddar producer: Cabot, the biggest producer, the company whose partnership with Jasper Hill has helped them succeed? Agricultural cooperative. Grafton, the most distinctly Vermont-tasting cheddar? Run by a nonprofit. Shelburne Farms, the company that helped bring clothbound cheese back to the United States? Also run by a nonprofit. Vermont Farmstead Cheese Company, a newer company that took over the land where a failed water buffalo yogurt operation used to be? As far as I can tell, it's the only community-owned cheesemaker in the United States.[8]

That these cheddar-makers were able to survive, or start up, after the consolidation of the cheese business and go on to prosper shows us that some people really do care about the taste of their cheddars. That they all have succeeded with some sort of alternative business model shows us that textbook capitalism and myths of bootstrapping might have spelled the end for Vermont cheddar if folks hadn't worked out some creative and cooperative solutions. With all that, you'd think the cabdrivers would have a little more pride in Vermont cheese, eh?

Chapter 7

Eat My Wookey Hole

Though this journey is about American cheddar, I do love English cheddar as well. We sell it, of course, so even if it won't occupy much time on this voyage I want to acknowledge that the English farmhouse cheddars are still the inspiration for many a cheesemonger and cheese eater. Though other countries have influenced English cheddar-makers as well, the original recipes, style, and flavor of clothbound cheddar from southwest England have always been the lofty goal that other cheesemakers aspire to reach.

I usually meet the English cheddar folks at my desk at the co-op, rather than, say, with all of us wearing our fox-hunting gear and drinking ale before we have a vertical tasting of cheddars from farmstead West Country dairies. I am not a very tidy person. My desk is cluttered and stuffed. I usually have a milk crate under my desk that has my recent sale flyers, cheese spec sheets, and important papers. It sits on top of the milk crate that's filled with older sale flyers, company spec sheets, and important papers. Like an excavation, I can find things if I can approximate the date.

However, my desk is also the place where I bring vendors to meet and taste cheese. My usual sales reps are used to it. I'm used to it. My coworkers begrudge it, and it is a consistent negative on my work evaluations. I always remember to be a little self-conscious when I bring someone new up to my desk, and one day I had two new people with me: an English cheddar man and his American rep. I tried to quickly make an empty spot on the desk by piling up some invoices on the corner.

The visitors had a traditional cheddar for me to taste. When I first started in cheese, traditional cheddars were a rarity, but now there are many available. We now have our choice between top-of-the-line English ones such as the Neal's Yard–distributed Montgomery's Cheddar, and Keen's Cheddar, Quicke's Cheddar, and some great American ones (none of which existed twenty years ago) such as Cabot Clothbound, Fiscalini 18 Month Bandage Wrapped, Bleu Mont, and Flagship Reserve.

So this was going to be a hard sell on his part. While there are many great cheddars, retailers still need to limit themselves to what they can actually sell in a reasonable amount of time. We carry more now, but at that time I was pretty much stuck with one English, one local, and one other American. And even that was pushing it if I was just going by actual customer interest instead of my own.

The cheese itself was very good, if not as complex as the higher-end, more mature, English cheeses. The price point was incredibly good, coming in lower than pretty much anything I already had of that style. I asked him to tell me a little about the cheese.

He said it was cave aged, matured for over six months. This cheese used "traditional methods," I was told, but this sample, being too young, did not have the name-protected West Country Farmhouse Cheddar designation.

"What is the name of the cheese? " I asked.

"Wookey Hole," he replied.

I am sure he explained something about the process, the age of the caves (which turn out to be quite a tourist attraction, it seems), the volume of output, the care and handling of the wheels . . .

"Wookiee[1] Hole?" I said.

I have written previously about how when people come up to the cheese counter and make a variation of the "cut the cheese" joke, my fellow mongers and I pretend to not understand. It's my defense mechanism born of years of people making the same joke but always thinking they are the first one. So I am not sure if the cheese person was giving me my own medicine by looking at me blankly after I said this or if there was a cultural barrier.

"Yes, Wookey Hole," was the response.

"Uh," I said. "That sounds kind of . . . *dirty*, doesn't it?"

He and his local rep looked at me like *I* was crazy. He patiently explained that Wookey Hole is a town and that it's aged in the Wookey Hole Caves. Further, a wookey hole is a place that, back in the day, was an animal trap. Villagers supposedly would push game through the forest from all directions, converging on a pit they had dug for this express purpose. When they met at the wookey hole, they'd have a feast of fallen wildlife. He did acknowledge that the visual image of a pit full of wounded bloody animals was probably not a good selling point for cheese.

But I guess when it comes down to it, I have the humor level of a sixth grader because the whole time he was talking I couldn't get X-rated *Star Wars* images out of my head.

I took a breath and decided to be professional and not mention this again. However, just then, my coworker came up, saw the promo material, and said, "Oh, my God, Wookey Hole?!?!" Other workers overheard this, and soon there was nothing but Wookey Hole jokes for the rest of the day.

"Hey, Gordon! Eat my Wookey Hole!"

"My Wookey Hole is salty and pungent!"

"I'm going to the *Star Wars* cantina to get me some Wookey Hole!"

On the face of it, this would seem to encapsulate some differences between the old world and new world of cheese: Americans showing little respect for tradition, mocking without bothering to understand, and basically being brats. However, while not defending our mockery, and certainly without denouncing it, I will say that this interaction actually tells us more about the evolution of cheddar than it seems at first glance.

The six-month-aged Wookey Hole Cave-Aged Cheddar I tasted is a good, larger-production clothbound cheddar, but not considered traditional enough to achieve the name-controlled designation. Indeed, if there is anything I was learning on this journey, it is that nothing is really "perfectly" traditional. Changes and compromises happen over the course of time. Some are improvements, and some may cause regret, but food production has never been a static art. The maker of Wookey Hole also makes a cheddar that does age long enough to qualify as a Protected Designation of Origin (PDO), name-controlled, West Country Farmhouse Cheddar.

I am not picking on the Wookey Hole. I like it. I have sold it. It's very good, if younger than many other English clothbound cheddars. The milk is from Dorset, which is one of the counties included in the PDO. But the concept of "traditional" can sometimes be a moving target. In fact, there are now more American producers of "traditionally made" cheddar than there are English ones, even if we lack the name control.

The great English clothbound Cheddars are truly what all cheddars with aspirations of immortality should be measured against. They are also some of the best cheeses in the world. But the thing is, not every cheese sets out to be the best cheese in the world. The history of cheddar, in particular, seems to be the story of the tensions between compromise and pricing, between flavor and efficiency. A cheese such as the young, non-PDO Wookey Hole I tried at my desk has a great niche. It is a clothbound cheddar, with the flavor attributes of that style of cheesemaking, and one that is affordable for a larger segment of the population.

But what about the PDO cheddars? While I defer to them as the envy of many cheesemakers, can it be said that they are truly traditional? While the original cheddar-makers were likely of a certain region, it is unlikely that they had codified rules rather than oral and practical traditions for the first few hundred years of cheesemaking. When the world wars hit, the cheesemakers adapted, even temporarily abandoned, their styles. Mary Quicke's amazing cheddar, made on a 450-year-old farm in Devon in beautiful, full-size, bandage-wrapped wheels, did not qualify for the name-control designation for many years because during the cheesemaking process they scald at 1 degree more than is allowed by the regulations.[2]

Some have criticized the West Country Farmhouse Cheddar PDO for being less traditional than it could be, however. For example, the requirements to qualify for name control status are specific for many traditional aspects including region, age, and many steps of the cheddar-making process, but the PDO allows for nonfarmstead milk, nonartisan starter culture, pasteurized milk, and even block, not clothbound wheel, production.[3]

A PDO is really a marketing device in service of maintaining a regional tradition. In that capacity I am all for it. It's vaguely sad to me, though, that PDO came too late to save the simple word "Cheddar," making the official designation the seven-syllable mouthful. The morality in my head tells me that the newcomers—the blocks, the waxed, the underaged—should be the cheeses with more qualifiers in their names. Bland sixty-day-aged orange blocks made from factory-farmed milk in an industrial park outside of Whatever-Town are also considered "cheddar," and to differentiate themselves, contenders for the best cheese on earth, made in their original region, need to be called "West Country Farmhouse Cheddar." It is a mild outrage, to be sure, but still an outrage.

And it's not as though we really honor or understand PDOs in this country anyway. We have no domestic cheeses that are name protected. Cheesemakers and mongers, mostly out of the necessity of comprehension, are loath to start calling, say, a local feta-style cheese "Redwood Hill white brined cheese" just to make some Greek Feta makers happy. There is some truth to the idea that mocking the name "Wookey Hole" shows an American predisposition to go for an easy joke over pushing to understand historical context. But there is also truth to the idea that adherence to tradition over the needs of the people, or, more crassly, the demands of the market, will not really work either. Especially when the cow has been out of the barn for quite some time.

Speaking of crassly meeting the demands of the market, though, I did bring in the Wookey Hole cheddar. A block away from the store, there was a short-lived annual street fair. Held on Harrison Street, it was called the "Hair"rison Street Fair, and it was set up for "bears, cubs, otters, chasers, and their friends." While primarily about male carnal appetites, drinking, and building community, I figured that a weekend where big hairy men would be descending on our neighborhood from all over the world was the perfect time. I bought about 300 pounds of Wookey Hole, my coworker made a huge display of Chewbacca action shots from *Star Wars*, and we piled the cheese high.

It sold almost as fast as we could cut it. It turns out that the bears just could not get themselves enough Wookey Hole! They probably did not get the history of the cheddar or of the region or of the villagers rampaging through the forest leading wild animals to their deaths in a wookey hole (our sign did try to explain these things, but I'm afraid Chewie[4] got more attention), but they made their own meaning, at least for one weekend.

Still, it's an amazing thing to be able to taste the world from my cramped, messy desk in San Francisco. I'm mostly leaving out the English cheddars from this book except to put the American cheddars in context, but just so the Brits don't cut me off or anything, I do have a little bit to say about them.

It surprised me to find out the level of communication between cheesemakers in England and the United States, both historically and more recently. Cheddar was developing concurrently in the 1850s with visits between representatives of both continents spurring ever-improving lists of best practices. The sharing of information enabled both English and American cheddar-makers to increase their quality tremendously. One can look at importation and see that the best cheesemongers of London were bringing in cheese from New York State. One could say that the best American-made cheddar might not be a duplicate of the best English cheddar—in those prepasteurization and cheesemaker-grown culture days, there was less homogenization of flavor, and the French concept of *terroir* could be used for most cheese with a straight face—but there was certainly a lot of very good U.S.-made cheese.

Not only that, though: the communication between U.S. and UK dairymen was also developed because the cheese merchants of the day were attempting to play them against each other, telling the English that they needed to push their cheese to market quickly and cheaply because of coming American imports, and telling the American cheesemakers that there were vast reserves of English cheddar.[5]

I cannot really do the history of English cheddar justice in this book, but a few things are important to know. English farmhouse cheddar came close to extinction twice in the 20th century. During World War II, for obvious reasons, and in the sixties when—being sold against cheaper block cheddar—it was having a hard time surviving in the market. Parallel to the food movements in the United States attempting to restore and preserve local and traditional foods, what saved traditional raw milk farmhouse cheddar in England was a rediscovery of flavor.

From the perspective of this Californian cheesemonger, Neal's Yard Dairy also helped preserve these great cheeses, as well as other traditionally English cheeses they refer to as "territorials." Neal's Yard didn't put English cheese on the map, but through yearly visits, tastings, and a constant crafting of the importance of these cheeses to world cheese culture in general (and any individual cheese case in particular), they kept historic cheeses from being wiped off that map. They've not only helped cheesemakers from the United Kingdom but helped nurture American cheesemakers and get across to an American audience what English cheese authority Patrick Rance describes as the most important attribute of an English farmhouse cheddar: that the best ones "have always varied, from farm to farm, from season to season, and cheesemaker to cheesemaker."[6]

There are only three producers left who qualify for the Artisan Somerset Cheddar designation of the Slow Food Presidium, which is more stringent than the West Country name control: Montgomery, Keen's, and Westcombe. Of those, Montgomery is the most famous in the United States and has become the cheddar all producers in the United States compare themselves to, even if they are trying for a different flavor profile, adjusting to the characteristics of their different milk or the taste of their local market.

Additionally, in every conversation I had with American producers about their relearning the techniques that had been lost in the United

States, they credit English cheese folks—usually Jamie Montgomery of Montgomery's Cheddar, or Randolph Hodgson of Neal's Yard Dairy—with patiently helping them along the way. Clothbound cheddar has exploded in the United States, even since I started conceiving of this journey. About twice as many companies are commercially producing one now as there were even five years ago. We have the communication of cheese people across an ocean to thank for that resurgence, proving that information can be shared and best practices considered without making every cheese taste the same.

English cheesemakers also felt the threat that eliminated clothbound cheddar from the U.S. market for a period of time. If one romantically wants to think of all things over the ocean as more traditional and pure or that somehow the English take more pride in their history of cheese than we do, the antidote is surely turning to Patrick Rance's opinion of most cheddar being produced in England in the eighties:

> Even our most generous gift to humanity, Cheddar is really known to comparatively few people. Most meet it in name alone. What they eat is some hard-pressed rectangular substitute, often foreign, usually emasculated in character and chilled into irredeemable immaturity.[7]

The choice of "emasculated" here is ironic, even as I can cheer the rest of the quote. The cheddar factory, historically speaking, displaced women from being the cheddar-makers, after all. It's more like the factories *defeminated* the cheese. However, we know what Rance means, even if his language is inaccurate for once. He goes on to refer to it as "Mousetrap fodder";[8] then, still not finished with his grievance a few pages later, claims that, despite his experience as a cheesemonger that the public wants better cheese, factory cheesemakers "have shut their ears and emitted almost nothing but plastic coated extruded curd. This they call Cheddar."[9]

Heck, with that level of vitriol, possibly the greatest English-language cheese writer of all time sounds like a food blogger talking about American cheddar, though clearly more informed and a lot more eloquent.

Speaking of eloquent, Michael Raffael, in his book about West Country cheesemakers, describes the wonder of the Montgomery's Cheddar the following way:

Like the stalactites in the Cheddar Gorge caves, Montgomery's cheese represents the culmination of the slow drip from centuries' experience . . . something on another plane from the industrial dairy that sets itself a standard and takes pride in maintaining it.

This isn't some Luddite refusal to accept change, nor is it founded on some whimsical notion of what may be authentically rustic. It's the recognition that accepting uncertainty, making it work in his favour, is the only way of ensuring that cheddars leaving his store will all have character and that the outstanding ones will be among the finest cheese of any kind being made in the world.[10]

With these goals it is no wonder the clothbound cheddar-makers would feel a kinship, even if some were eight thousand miles away from one another.

Chapter 8

Curds and Raines

The reason that a search for the meaning of cheddar had to involve an actual journey is that it is one of the most region-specific cheeses we have in this country. Regions that are cheddar powerhouses continue to think of one style—their style—as true cheddar no matter how far removed from the Cheddar Gorge, the farmstead, or the Williams factory it may be.

That's why I was shocked when I was invited to judge cheese curds at the American Cheese Society annual cheese competition in Sacramento, California, in 2014.

Cheese curds are something that most non-Wisconsinites don't really understand, even the ones, like me, who make their living working with dairy products. Sure, I knew that to make cheddar a cheesemaker coagulates milk into curds (the milk solids) and whey (the liquid runoff), then makes cheese with the curds. But driving through rural Wisconsin you can't help but notice the FRESH CURDS signs along the road. You also can't help noticing that these places with the FRESH CURDS signs are packed. Everyone eats curds there.

On a business level, since good curds are sold only—at most—a day or two after they are made, they are a quick return on one's milk investment. They're a cow's milk, cash flow answer to the goat cheesemaker's fresh chèvre: the offering that sells fast and helps keep the doors of the business open. This cash flow issue really comes into play when you are going to age some of that cheddar for a year or two. All that cheese sitting on shelves waiting to be ready to sell is money you have already spent. It might be on its way to being an awesome, sharp, snappy cheese as well, but during hard times it must be difficult for a cheesemaker not to look at the aging shelves and see piles of cash that they could use right about now. . . .

Daniel Utano, the cheesemaker who made the Beecher's Flagsheep that took Best of Show honors at the American Cheese Society in 2012, puts it this way:

> Cheese curds can be great for a business model because it
> brings cash flow in while cheddar is aging out. . . . At the
> same time, it's a very time-consuming thing to do. You go
> through the entire cheddar-making process, which if by
> hand, is a long, tiring process. You've cut your curd, cooked
> it, drained your whey out, cheddared your curd, milled your
> curd. All you have left to do after that is press your curd
> and then age it out. It always seemed like a ton of work
> to just get these squeaky bites. Even the best cheese curds
> aren't booming with flavor and most likely you'll get less
> money from curds than aged cheddar. You have greater risk
> with aged cheddar, but greater reward. But ultimately it is
> a great means of making back money right away, getting
> your name out there, and ultimately moving your business
> forward while you age your cheddar out.[1]

Curd eaters are also quite picky about the freshness of their curds. When I used to buy "fresh curds" from a local California cheesemaker for our store, Wisconsin transplants living in the area just shook their heads in frustration. Not only were they sold in airtight plastic; they had a six-month shelf life.

Beyond that, though, there is a bigger crime against tradition. Those California curds don't squeak. The squeak is how you can tell if your cheese curd is truly fresh. Many would say that the cheese "curds" we sold back then were actually not really curds at all, but just mild cheddar cheese balls. Tasty in their own right maybe, but only sold as "curds" in a place that doesn't know any better.

In Wisconsin people eat curds like Pringles. Except they are loved and devoured there in ways that Pringles, if potato chips were sentient, could only dream of. I simply can't think of a legal equivalent of anything that we consume so enthusiastically in California. I actually buy frozen curds from Wisconsin now, an irony on a "fresh and local" level, but something that makes the people who want curds—mostly those Wisconsin transplants and chefs who make poutine—much happier.

I would argue that even though they are just a step in the process of cheddar-making, fresh curds are one of the most regional cheeses in the country. If I were in charge of making a Designation of Origin name control for American cheeses, this would be my order:

1. California dry jack
2. Vermont raw milk cheddar
3. Wisconsin cheese curds

While my California-ness should disqualify me from writing about cheddar curds, an examination of cheddar without a few words on curd, well . . . that just wouldn't be right. In their uncooked state, they can be everything you want in a fresh cheese and more: squeaky, fresh, subtle, salty, milky, sometimes even a touch citrusy. Of course, while the Wisconsinites gobble them up out of the bag like potato chips, they also cook with them. The last time I was in Wisconsin I ordered fried cheese curds with every meal. Every place we went had them. I think the only place in my hometown to get fried cheese curds was at A&W, and only there because they are part of the national menu. I never saw anyone order them.

The Wisconsin cultural excitement for curds is really a brake on "progress" in its own way. That curd mania really only exists in one state is because Wisconsin is the one state where—despite many losses—there still are small-town cheese factories dotting the landscape. Every town may not have one anymore, but there is likely a plant no more than a couple of towns away. Every local seems to know where they can get fresh curds and on what day. Those FRESH CURDS signs put up by cheesemakers when they finish a batch are only partly signs promoting commerce; they are also signs proclaiming, "buy local," "this is a decentralized economy," and "support our cultural heritage" . . . except without any of the pretense, expense, and judgmental sentiment with which the latter phrases would be used in an urban environment.

Wisconsin cheesemakers at the ACS competition, of course, noticed that no Wisconsinites were judging curd, and they were worried. How could anyone else truly understand the understated power of curd? I was worried, too, and asked for help. My cheese friend and second-generation cheesemonger at Larry's Market in Milwaukee, Patty Peterson, had judged the inaugural curd competition the previous year and gave me this curd advice: "They've gotta have a good squeak, flavor—there really is a difference between them—some are sweet and milky, others are drier and sharper. As for shape—I preferred the hand-cut—not as uniform and usually bigger than the factory-milled, which are very consistently sized."

Great effort was taken to taste the cheese as soon as possible for the judging at the American Cheese Society. That's the actual reason there were two Californians judging: We had to be there a day before everyone else to get at them fresh. When I sat to judge curd, I really hoped we would pick—blindly of course—a Wisconsin cheese somewhere in our top three. It was only the second year of curd being in the competition. I had a feeling that if no Wisconsin curd was picked, it might be the last.

I couldn't let that affect my scores, but luckily, even if I had wanted to, there really is no way to have a curd judging of thirty-some entries that isn't blind. I defy the most Sconnie of the Wisconsinites to say they can recognize the origin of that many curds. The judging went fairly quickly. My partner is well known as one of the fastest judges around, and honestly, there is often less to write about fresh cheeses in the maker comment part of the judging form.

Curds, obviously, are not the only regional aspect to cheddar. As a judge at the American Cheese Society, I mentioned before that the aesthetic judge is paired with a technical judge. Both of us use technical terms—for the most part—to evaluate the cheese in front of us. Before talking about regionality, it's probably wise to look at these words.

The terms vary a little based on what aspects of cheddar the dairy scientists are trying to study, but one paper uses the following: "cooked, whey, milkfat, sulfur, free fatty acids, brothy, nutty, catty, sour, bitter, salty, sweet, umami."[2] Another food scientist, Michael Tunick, research chemist with the USDA, writes the following:

> Experts have developed a specific lexicon of words to describe possible flavors in cheddar; these include bell pepper, brothy, catty, cooked, cowy, fecal, fruity, milkfat, moldy, nutty, floral, scorched, sulfur, waxy, and yeasty. Ideally, the texture is firm and slightly crumbly; possible body and texture defects include corky (dry and hard), crumbly (falls apart), curdy (rubbery), gassy (eyes or holes), mealy (grainy), open (spaces in the interior), pasty (sticky), short (flaky), and weak (soft).[3]

A lot of work has gone into the science of taste in recent years. In France, the Comté Association—early adopters and creators of the village cheese factory—have created a flavor wheel for their cheese that has eighty-three descriptors. All of these groupings have their own use. You can use them to grade the properties you are looking to study.

As it probably should be, judging can be a sterile experience. At an American Cheese Society conference one year, I went to a workshop by MaryAnne Drake, a professor of sensory analysis and flavor chemistry at North Carolina State University and one of the leaders in the study of cheese tasting. I am used to tasting cheese in smelly, loud, small environments—like my desk at work. The workshop was clearly just an approximation of what would be done in a multiday training for tasters, but when we arrived there was no open cheese. It was already cubed and lidded in airtight plastic cups.

One by one we went through the cheeses, opening them up, breathing them in, touching them, tasting them. Each cheddar was an example of the difference in flavor profile from the same type of cheese. It was a very scientific way, dumbed down for a large conference room, of course, to learn what tastes were and how we can find and describe them—certainly better than my training of how to taste that basically consisted of . . . nothing. Well, nothing but eating. Brothy? Nutty? Cooked? We found those. Thankfully she was being kind, and we didn't identify any "fecal."

One of my favorite things about ACS judging is that—besides the non-commercial purity of it that I mentioned before—we work in teams. The technical judge—a dairy scientist, grader, or otherwise acclaimed expert—is the bad cop. With them the cheese starts with fifty points and they grade down for defects using the attributes above to look for flaws. Me, I am the aesthetic judge—the good cop—the one who starts from zero[4] and finds only positives. The beauty of this system is that it incorporates science (the technical judge) with flavor (the aesthetic judge).

The funny, and sometimes contentious, thing is that sometimes the technical judge will grade down for the exact same attribute that the aesthetic judge awards points for. Their negative-one-point "too sweet" is my plus one (or two, or three . . .) for exceptional sweetness. This balance, different from the U.S. and World competitions, which are purely technical, is to highlight the fact that often a non-textbook-perfect cheese is something that a lot of people will want to eat. Additionally, how a technical judge or a grader will react to flavors and textures is somewhat regional. The English cheddars I talked about in the last chapter, for example, all have a higher acidity and more crumbly texture—by design—than American ones and would likely get graded down for those attributes if judged by someone who grades cheese in Wisconsin or California. When international cheese people discuss "American cheddar," the acidity difference is often what they are referring to.

It's not just the acidity level that affects cheese flavor, of course. In cheddar-making, according to Neville McNaughton (owner of CheezSorce and a cheese consultant who has had a hand in the development of many of the country's best cheddars), the crucial aspect—"the platform you build your cheese on"[5]—is the cultures chosen combined with the make process. He writes:

> Industrial cultures are linear, harsh and hard to control. In their selection for speed of acid production, which leads to low cost, they have lost an important element of their makeup and that is aminopeptidase activity, a complex enzyme system that produces the fine flavors and suppresses bitterness. The faster of the two primary Cheddar cultures is *Lactococcus lactis* subspecies *lactis*. This has become the primary culture in industrial cheddar cheese. Compare that to cheese I made 30 years ago where *Lactococcus lactis* subspecies *cremoris* was the dominant culture and *lactis* was used sparingly as part of the blend. Those cheeses from 30 years ago were mild at 90 days, medium at 180 days and mature at 12 months. They were smooth, a little fruity, slight sulphur with a full and rounded profile and would age for two years with no sign of bitterness. Compare to many U.S. cheeses and being a bit low on salt will run bitter in six months stored at 40 F.[6]

And about that sweetness I was just awarding extra points for in the judging? This has definitely been a point of contention among cheddar eaters over the last decade. Cheddar purists might not like it, but the American palate loves a sweet and crunchy cheddar. To achieve this, you do something that was a lot harder twenty years ago and impossible back in the farm-cheddar days: You design a culture cocktail.

What cheesemakers can do in this day and age is a bit of both science and aesthetics: Add a combination of cultures to the milk at just the right stage of the make process and—if everything else is done correctly—a unique cheddar will appear. Here you get the science of a complex chemical interaction resulting in the flavor of an amazing cheese.

The culture cocktail accounts for the newer-style, extremely popular block cheddars on the grocery store shelves like Dubliner, Coastal, Skellig, Oscar Wilde, and Flagship (to name just a few) that have an unexpected, almost sugary-sweet crunch. Because what cheesemakers and mongers have found is that now that customers don't think those little white amino acid crystals in cheeses are mold, they really like their taste and want to buy them.

My favorite of this genre is the Prairie Breeze, made by Milton Creamery in Iowa. The milk is from the cows of Amish farmers, and the cheese is made by a Mennonite family, who also oversees the amazing Flory's Truckle, a clothbound cheddar made not far away in Missouri. The Prairie Breeze is a great balance of sweet, sharp, and salty, and it crunches. I'm not the only one who thinks it is the best of the new wave of blocks. *Cooks Illustrated* magazine actually voted it in as a tie for best cheddar in the country.[7] Because we were the only store on the West Coast that carried it at that time, people were driving up from Los Angeles to buy it.

McNaughton, who helped develop Flory's Truckle and Prairie Breeze, discusses the popularity of the new, sweeter cheddars this way:

> [I]t is growing and quite quickly. I think that you have to hold this up against the background of declining industrial grade cheese, characterized by acid, sometimes sour and commonly bitter. The new cheeses are full, rounded and non-confrontational, a warm satisfaction. There is nothing more gratifying than watching faces when they taste good cheese, defined as: a warmly returned smile, closed mouth savoring expression of joy, and then the excited response when they ask, "Oh my god, what is the name of that cheese?"[8]

As mentioned previously, different regions sometimes still hold fast to styles they are accustomed to, but with the increasing awareness of cheesemakers of the options they now have to design cheddars, they are not bound to create cheeses similar to what is already being sold in their area. As for the crystallization so often requested by consumers ("I want the cheese with the crunchies in it"), once the province of very aged cheese like Parmigiano Reggiano, old Gouda, one-year-aged Gruyère, and mature cheddar, McNaughton points out that by concentrating on *Lactobacillus*, a cheesemaker can achieve "good crystal formation before a year of age."[9]

Very traditional cheesemakers don't go in for the newfangled culture cocktails. The Montgomery's Cheddar, for example, still uses "pint starters." What that means is that they develop their own cultures for their cheese themselves instead of buying it from a chemical company. Yogurty and thicker than you'd think, to be used for the Montgomery's Cheddar the cultures must be grown (a pint at a time) in local, unpasteurized milk from naturally occurring bacteria.

The flavors in a clothbound cheddar are not the same as the ones from the type of cheddar we more commonly eat today. The traditional flavor is usually bigger and more complex, with grassy, earthy, fruity, and even caramel notes. There are similarities as well—for example, you can taste sharpness in the traditional cheddar, but it is not the dominant flavor. In tasting clothbound cheddars, especially before the recent boom in makers, I made the assumption that I was tasting something that would be similar to what I would have tasted if I could go back in time and buy a hunk of cheddar from the Williams factory of 1851. I assumed an almost direct line of flavor from the preindustrial farmhouse cheddars to today's versions. However, much like when I had the should-have-been-obvious revelation that pineapple cheese did not contain actual pineapples, I suddenly realized that a lot has changed in a century and a half.

When confronted with an obscure cheese question, I do what I always do. I ask a dairy scientist. The opinion of Paul Kindstedt? That over the last 150 years cultures, not process, have made the biggest difference in flavor.

> What of course was different [from roughly 1851] is that Williams et al. were not using starter cultures but simply relying on the raw milk microflora at a time when refrigeration and chemical sanitizers, both of which are used routinely and mandated by law today, did not yet exist. The resulting microflora that fermented the milk that made the cheese in 1851 was thus far more complex and varied far more from day-to-day, and especially across season (for better or for worse) than anything that we would encounter today. I would argue that the effect of clothbound packaging versus laminant barrier film packaging is likely smaller (by far) than the effect of 1851 milk microflora versus modern milk microflora on the character of 1851 Cheddar cheese versus 2015 Cheddar cheese.[10]

A cheese like Montgomery's, because it is still made with local pint starters, would still likely be the closest cheddar to what was eaten before cheddar factories changed the cheese world. But it also seems obvious that even with those homemade cultures, the result is a lot more predictable in the present than it was in the past. When I visited Jasper Hill Farm I tasted dozens of batches of clothbound cheddars, finding some differences in all of them. I can only imagine how huge that variation would have been, for better or worse, in the days of no refrigeration, no real dairy science, and microflora running wild.

And indeed, the flavors we are seeing these days are not created from nowhere. They are the result of identifying the strains (or combinations of cultures) that create desirable flavors and then controlling the process to have those cultures dominate. Kindstedt refers to the cultures of the present era as "souped-up," and McNaughton says, "Historically there were a varied range of organisms appearing in and evolving in our cheese as a result of the production environments."[11] That wild microflora mentioned above! "Some of what we recognize today as new age could actually be the past on steroids."[12]

Still, the way that most people want to describe cheddar, of course, is on the sharpness scale. Mild? Medium? Sharp? Extra sharp? At our store we actually arrange our block cheddar on display in terms of sharpness, left to right. However, we do not go by what the labels say. Most people don't know this, but the labels are meaningless.

When I first started in cheese, people—makers, vendors, distributors, and especially customers—tried to explain what "sharp" meant, as if there was actually a legal definition. There is not. The label will generally relate to the age at which the cheese is sold, but this varies by company, so a "sharp" from one maker could be a "medium" for someone else. Sharpness level, the holy phrase of cheddar buying and selling, is thought by most customers to be a taste grade, but to most producers—Cabot, as mentioned in the Vermont chapter, being an exception—it is simply an inventory designation.

Drake's workshop looked at the differences in cheddar-making across the United States and—while more intricate than I will be able to represent with my high school science—pointed to the fact that, yes, consumers often look for different flavors in cheddar in different regions. Those differences may exist, but they are primarily different, flavor-wise, due to the way that a producer makes or ages the cheese, not just because of what region the milk is from. Furthermore, customers might be buying "sharp" cheddar for flavor preferences that they associate with "sharp," but this has more to do with the taste of a specific brand.

Hence the most common complaint we receive in our department. "Dear Cheese Department, your Brand X[13] cheese labeled 'sharp' is not sharp. Please make sure your products are labeled correctly."

Another major area of cheddar preference that is more perception than reality is color. First off, I wish people would stop using the term "yellow" altogether for cheddar. Calling that Department of Corrections jumpsuit-orange cheese "yellow" is just confusing. I admit that calling most non-orange cheddars "white" is also not quite accurate since a lot are yellowish, certainly more yellow than the orange cheese often called "yellow," but at least it is clear what side of the spectrum they are on.

There is no regional tell bigger than looking for an orange cheddar, except for perhaps asking for curds. I am not judging. I love a nice orange cheddar myself, but if you are looking for it you usually either are from the Midwest or live near the Tillamook plant in Oregon.

One of the few things I actually knew about cheese when I started working with it professionally was that the orange cheddar had added color. I even knew it was (usually) a natural color derived from annatto beans. I know that because I shopped in real, old-fashioned hippie co-ops. But I must admit to a form of blindness that I have succumbed to for the last twenty years. This is embarrassing, hold on. . . . I hadn't realized that many large production cheddars add annatto even when they are "white" cheddars.

I was especially embarrassed because I am a label reader by nature and a cynical label reader by profession. I have fought with European companies because I have taught myself ingredient-French and ingredient-Italian and double-check the non-English labels against the made-for-export ones and sometimes find differences. For whatever reason, however—maybe a cheese rep told me this, maybe I just made it up—whenever I would see "annatto" listed on a non-orange cheddar I would ignore it (and this is the embarrassing bit), assuming that the company simply was using the same label for both its colored and white cheddars.

In this day of FDA crackdowns and increasing labeling laws, I hadn't realized that my assumption had become so quaint until, while visiting a cheese factory, my tour guide mentioned that they add a little annatto to each batch to stabilize the color throughout the year. Of course that is something a big company would do! Standardization of color is right in line with the trajectory on which cheddar has taken our food system.

As for why it's used, well, it's steeped in cheese history and yet another example of fat-shorting that has always plagued the cheese business. Paul Kindstedt, of course, has the historical answer, and on a National Public Radio show said, "The cheesemakers were initially trying to trick people to mask the white color"[14] of their fat-skimmed cheese. That's not the case anymore; you can buy your orange cheddar with, usually, full-fat pride.

Have you seen the recent wave of Kraft commercials? Kraft is attempting to re-enter the higher-end cheddar market these days. They have even taken some ribbons at the American Cheese Society competitions. In recent years their commercials have featured "cheese judges" in a cheese competition wearing yellow lab coats.

This is amusing for a couple reasons. The first is the color. At the Gathering of Cheddarmakers that I attended in Wisconsin, a group photo was taken. It is unintentionally color-coded. Every single cheesemaker—with, of course, the exception of the indomitable Willi Lehner—is wearing all white, while the five or six non-cheesemakers are all wearing colors. At the real judging competition, the aesthetic judges rush to a pile of rented white lab coats—well at least us big folks do—to find one that fits, while the technical judges arrive with their own white coats, usually with their name embroidered or patched on the front.

The second reason those commercials are funny is that the advertising firm trying to get the Kraft account approached me, wanting advice. Yes, me. The buyer for a San Francisco worker cooperative that started as part of a group of collectives—retail, wholesale, trucking, and producers—trying to upend the food system. I am not sure they knew that when they contacted me. No, they saw that I was doing a class at The Cheese School of San Francisco on cheese judging and sampling out some winning cheeses.

The advertisers wanted to film the class. I said no. They asked The Cheese School if they could film it. The Cheese School said no. Or maybe the advertsisers asked the other way around, I'm not sure. Finally, the agency representative asked if they could take me to lunch to pick my brain, to find out about how judging worked, and what they needed to know for their proposal.[15]

I said no again. I am not above getting a free meal in exchange for a little discussion, but this was practically the definition of the old saying "there's no such thing as a free lunch."

At least that's what I thought until I realized that the very origin of that phrase "no free lunch" was tied to cheddar. I'd never really thought about the phrase, to tell you the truth, figuring it was just a very old and fairly self-explanatory saying. The phrase has a particularly American bent to it, I suppose, with an inherent moralism, not far removed from the Puritans. We need to work for what we get. No one owes you anything. Work or starve. Labor is virtuous in our society.

Cheese history is steeped in virtuous labor, after all. The Benedictine monks, for example, not only gave us the concept that "to labor is to pray,"[16] but set the landscape for amazing families of cheeses, making possible Brie, Crottin, and Livarot. In fact, they created so many cheeses, and those became such a big part of monastery life, that it was internally critiqued and mocked by 20th-century Trappist monk and writer Thomas Merton as being a misplaced priority with the memorable phrase, "Holy Jesus, buy our cheeses."

However, the reaction to laborers who were often considered non-virtuous—ones who dared organize for fair wages, unions, and sometimes revolution, or ones who just liked to drink—put a crimp in the economic production of New York's cheddar-makers in the 1890s.

In the late 1800s, the center of cheddar-making was already shifting west as the population did. The lucrative export market to England was also on its way to being completely lost due to the filled milk scandal and competition from Canada. But back then there also actually were free lunches, not simply the concept of "free lunches" as a political metaphor. As with any history, blaming the woes of New York cheesemakers solely on prohibitionists is too simple, but let's go on a trip back to the 1890s for some revisionist history anyway.

Saloons commonly offered free lunches to customers for the price of a drink in major cities of the day, especially in New York City. Cheddar cheese was a main component of this "free lunch." Let's recall that the 1890s were a time of huge economic depression and labor uprising. Many people were out of work and those who did work usually worked six-day weeks. In 1893 hundreds of banks collapsed and unions held successful strikes against the railroads. Unrest—and unemployment—continued with nationwide strikes in 1894. Laws were passed across the nation by politicians fearful of an organized working class. Centers of working-class life—and therefore also "agitation"—were obvious targets, whether this was the overt rationalization or not. Where could poor workingmen be found at the time? In bars eating free lunches that were helping stave off starvation.

The force of the Temperance Movement got the Raines Law passed in New York in 1896. While this law, if thought about at all today, is remembered for its ban on Sunday drinking, Progressive Theodore Roosevelt fighting Tammany Hall to enforce it, and the infamous "Raines Hotels" where saloons added squalid rooms to qualify as lodging places to be exempt, this law also outlawed the "free lunch" and was a huge blow to cheesemakers and dairy farmers.

This was done to get men out of the saloons. A burgeoning, Progressive "home science" (later "home economics") movement was also taking form. In fact, one writer urged, "By using every possible means to educate the wives and daughters of working men to be more intelligent homemakers, we can do more towards the solution of the labor problem than all the anarchists, the communists, the socialists or even the labor organizations . . . have ever been able to do."[17]

How did this affect cheese? Secretary of the New York State Dairymen's Association, B. D. Gilbert said at the time:

> It is estimated that the saloons of Greater New York used from eight million to twelve million pounds of cheese per year; and if those of the rest of the State be added to this it would bring the total consumption by means of free lunch up to at least fifteen million pounds, or about one-sixth of the total production of the State last year. This law is one of the severest blows yet inflicted on the cheese industry.[18]

The phrase "there's no such thing as a free lunch" has been used to promote everything from anti-corruption movements to libertarian economics. The debate can rage on—if anyone is still interested—about whether these "free lunches" or urban saloons were a place of degradation and anti-Christian tumult or—as urban reformer William Stead wrote in 1894—these profit-motivated promotions "fed more hungry people in Chicago than all the other agencies, religious, charitable, and municipal, put together."[19]

What is interesting to me in searching for the meaning of American-ness in cheddar is how different the use of "free lunch" is today. I mean, I am not the most capitalistic person in the world, but it is interesting that a marketing device with unintended social good, set up to aid the accumulation of wealth by saloonkeepers, was opposed and regulated against during a time of near economic collapse. Unemployment, for instance, had improved from its low point in 1894 but was still three times higher than at the start of the decade. A measure that reduced cheese consumption—overnight—by as large a percentage as claimed by Gilbert must not have contributed to helping the economy.

In today's usage of "free lunch," the implied scold is that the cost of the lunch is paid by someone else. If one is on the Mitt Romney–ish side of history, it is paid for by the "job creators" to the freeloading 47 percent. On the other hand, there is also a warning to the eater of the free lunch, a synonym with "if things look too good to be true, they probably are"—but there's an added jab in there. Are you a sucker for trying to get a good deal? Are you the one who is "born every minute"?

Back in the 1890s, if one believed—and a lot of people did—that free lunches were simply a practice set up by booze interests to trick people into a life of alcoholism, I suppose the idea that the lunch wasn't really free made sense. But if we view these urban working-class folks as people with intelligence staving off starvation while sharing a commons, building community in their neighborhoods while at the same time supporting relatively small-scale dairy farmers and cheesemakers, then the "free lunch"—that people of the time were urged to forsake in the name of morality—has a totally different look. A "free lunch" in New York State at the end of the 19th century may have been, in essence, a nongovernmental agricultural price support preventing rural poverty and feeding the hungry.

In fact, as Stead notes elsewhere in his book, in Chicago a number of saloonkeepers wanted to eliminate the free lunch in order to increase their profits but were afraid to act, in absence of legislation, because they were afraid of losing business.

Indeed, the "free lunch" *is* always paid by someone. But it wasn't the "moochers" who made up the concept; it was the people trying to make a profit off them. That the free lunch eaters collectively wielded such power that at least some of the businesses were afraid to act without government action shows that there was a community of working-class drinkers simply looking out for their own interests, trying to get the best deal and simply survive—not a bunch of people trying to get something for nothing.

Well, anyway, that's one way to look at it. But who knew that a phrase you hear every day has such cheddary roots?

Back to 2014 and back to the roots of cheddar: the curd. When the ACS awards ceremony started I was worried. Who did we pick? Utano's company at the time, Beecher's, took first place for their plain curds, and the cheesemaker who developed the Beecher's cheddar recipes, Brad Sinko (now at Face Rock Creamery in Oregon), took first in the flavored category. As it turned out, though, we awarded three of the six ribbons to Wisconsin curd entries: two to Cedar Grove Cheese, run by master cheesemaker Bob Wills.

Hopefully, blindly awarding half the ribbons to Wisconsin cheeses means that I will be allowed into Wisconsin again in the future. Whew!

Chapter 9

Velveeta:
A Crowning Achievement
of American Science

"You're an anti-family store!"

The outraged customer had moved up close to the counter to yell this. She was letting us know she would never be back.

I am actually surprised we don't hear this more often. "Rainbow Grocery," "San Francisco," "Cooperative" . . . none of those are signifiers of anything good, at least to the kind of person who would accuse you of running an "anti-family" anything. Maybe it's just that the people who would use that phrase as an insult already self-select out of our store.

What did we do to deserve this ire? My coworker, a woman raising two small children at that time, told this customer that we didn't carry Kraft Singles.

The reasons we don't carry Kraft Singles, or its brother food product Velveeta, are numerous. We're an up-from-hippie store trying to carry food without preservatives or extra ingredients, trying to carry food with good nutritional value and flavor, and trying to buy from smaller producers. At the time we were called out on our "anti-family" nature, Kraft was owned by Philip Morris (or "Altria," their post-cigarette renaming), and while I cannot claim—in this era of corporate acquisition of formerly independent natural foods brands—that we do not carry any huge corporate brands, we certainly do not seek them out. If only I knew that, years later, an advertising company trying to make commercials for Kraft would want my help, I guess I could have proven we weren't anti-family.

Where did Kraft come from? Well, back in the days of my great-grandparents, from modest beginnings it seems. The story (from Kraft) goes that in 1903, a young J. L. Kraft, son of Canadian dairy farmers, spent all his money on a horse and wagon to buy cheese at a central location and resell it to the cheese stores of Chicago. If Kraft had continued with only his local distribution, it is likely we wouldn't—in 2015—know the name Kraft. However, in 1914 Kraft and his brothers started producing cheese, and by 1916 they had patents for their variety of processed cheese.

Why would anyone even want to process cheese? This is a question born of the excess of our current times to be sure, but there are two main reasons: food safety and the continuation of the cheesemaker's centuries-old goal, to age protein for as long as possible with as little waste as possible.

Clearly the history of cheddar shows us a lot about the invaluable uses of technology. Scientific advances changed cheddar from a risky and regional cheese into the most popular and dependably edible cheese in the world. But did technology go too far? And what is too far? I skimmed through a quick version of the history of cheddar in chapter 2, but to understand Velveeta we need to dive a little deeper. Let's look back to the beginning of the 20th century. The United States had screwed up its export business to Europe, probably forever, but the conversion from farmhouse to factory cheese was in full swing.

Advances in science during this time period were incredible to the folks living then. The popular development of things like commercially available incandescent lightbulbs and refrigeration were practical applications of science that improved people's living conditions. Why wouldn't science improve food production?

And where science would really improve food production was clearly going to be in the factories where food was increasingly being produced. In 2015, we can view a farmstead cheese as a thing of artisanal beauty, its variability manifesting qualities of nature and earth, its unexpected flavors being a selling point. But in the early 1900s, some of these aspects foodies admire today were seen by many people as indications of imperfection, lack of quality, and often danger . . . in short, things to be fixed by scientific methods applied to food production.

Indeed, in that era of fascination with food technology, often the further away something got from traditional food, the more highly it was regarded by food inventors. From their point of view, they were trying for cheese that would last longer without spoilage, would be healthy (even if vitamins would start to be added as nutrition was lost in the process), and could feed people more cheaply. Additionally, these more processed versions were often marketed as a safe alternative to traditionally made cheese, which, being a living food, contained all sorts of enzymes and microbes. Some food technologists saw artisan, or even factory-made, nonprocessed food as imperfect. Flavor varied; the food could go bad (which wasted resources and lowered profit margins); and even nutritional quality could be different at different times of the year. Why would anyone want that?

And it's not like eaters of the time didn't have reason to feel this way, too. It's easy to look back a century later and see evil in intent and deed—paving stones being laid for the corporate takeover of the food supply—but some health concerns were very real. The Williams factory and the Harding methods, it should be remembered, actually relied on consulting the best, most recent science possible. And a lot of science was happening in the early 1900s, as well as a lot of discussion and political action around food safety.

In the early 1900s, milk safety was a big issue. Fresh milk was relatively new to the cities in those years. In the 1850s, "Swill Milk" from cows fed on the leftovers from distilleries had been linked to the deaths of thousands of children in New York City. This epidemic meant that milk was not widely consumed in urban areas until improvements in refrigeration occurred in the 1880s and 1890s.

Interestingly, in today's cheese world, cows fed distillers' grains can be a selling point. The makers of Isle of Mull Cheddar from Scotland, considered one of the world's best cheddars, credit the distinct flavor of their cheese to the fact that their cows are fed spent grain husks from the nearby whiskey distillery. By highlighting flavors that may—in other situations—be described as defects, Chris and Jeff Reade have built a loyal following for their cheese, which, in addition to the sharp earthiness one would expect from a clothbound cheddar, can be described as yeasty, bitey, and boozy. While the island where their dairy is located does not have grass for much of the year and this is a great solution to their feed problem, one of the reasons they can do this is because of the development that changed the course of dairy history in the United States: germ theory.

When milk started to be sold more regularly in urban areas again in the late 1800s, there were more problems with devastating illnesses. First, large typhoid epidemics in the 1880s and 1890s hit the population, especially children, very hard. While milk was a common source, it was assumed that "greedy farmers and milk peddlers" were diluting it with dirty water,[1] which was causing the problems. It was not until 1900 that milk itself was revealed to be a great host for certain harmful microorganisms.

Then tuberculosis hit next. *Hoard's Dairyman*, the voice of progressive dairy farming, was on this issue from the beginning, warning dairy farmers that they needed to get with the science or go out of business. The link between tuberculosis and milk was so clear in the public's mind that it was referred to as the "white plague."[2] If you've ever wondered why pasteurization of fluid milk is almost completely mandatory today, this is the historical reason. Groups pushing for "pure food" waged political campaigns. Numerous and very public "milk stations" that gave free pasteurized milk to the poor and orphanages opened, and the resulting declines in death rates were highly publicized. By 1914 New York City required pasteurization, and by 1917 most other U.S. cities did as well.

In an argument that mirrors the debate today around raw milk, the proponents of mandatory pasteurization—for the most part—won the day against people who argued for a proposed system of certification of safety from teat to table. Pasteurization was cheaper and easier, from the governmental point of view at least.

Pasteurization, along with the outbreak of World War I, radically changed the dairy industry. From farmers and small bottlers providing milk directly to consumers, suddenly one needed more capital to sell milk, which was once the easiest source of profit from a dairy farm. After all, milk is not aged. Unlike cheese or butter, money to pay bills could be made right away with fluid milk. Massive consolidation followed mandatory pasteurization, leaving two main companies in charge of national distribution and large companies and cooperatives in control of production in most dairy states.[3] In terms of cheese production, this, too, began to centralize, and national brands like Kraft and Borden emerged. However, these big national brands spent most of the 20th century contracting with local cheddar-makers to make the most popular cheese in the country under their large corporate labels.

Besides the development of the ability to apply germ theory to cheese, another development in American culture came out in the first decades of the 1900s that also has altered the cheese landscape for generations: the popularization of the discovery of vitamins in food.

Think of how disconcerting it must have been to a culture that once only worried about having enough food to eat! The way people thought of food, at least in middle-class communities, changed forever: not only could the food you acquired be dangerous from something contaminating your food from the outside, but that the food itself—even if filling and tasty—might be harming you over the long run by not giving you what your body needs to be healthy.

We are all familiar in this day and age with the advice to not eat certain foods—or *to* eat certain other foods—and then being told that recent studies show just the opposite. I still lovingly recall one commercial I saw as a child. Eggs were locked behind bars in a high-security prison, one to a cage. Suddenly the clang we all know from TV, movies, or personal experience rang out. In a precursor to the Innocence Project that frees people wrongly accused of murder, the eggs were being let out of jail. New studies showed they weren't guilty and you could eat them more often.[4] This was a mind-blowing experience watching television as a child, even if the revised nutritional guidelines were only for, if memory serves, an increase of one egg per week.

Margarine was considered healthy and an improvement nutritionally (and texturally) over butter in my household and is another good example of the back-and-forth of the public's understanding of scientific studies. The concept of good fats and bad fats is still being fought out, and I have faith the good fats will win. But the idea of vitamins—as a societal concept—is much bigger than any one food battle. It was a revolutionary change of paradigm for every food produced or grown.

"What food is good?" became a question, so rather than simply acquiring enough food, one of the most basic functions of humans became problematized. It is no wonder that food historians who study this time period discuss it in terms of psychological issues. *Fear of Food* is the title of Harvey Levenstein's book about food in 20th-century America. "Anxiety and Aspiration" is Charlotte Biltekoff's chapter on the development of vitamins in her book *Eating Right in America*.[5] As a cheesemonger in a natural foods store, I can attest that this anxiety exists to this day.

When Jesse Williams built the Rome factory and John Harding developed his best practices—enlisting the best science of the day—perhaps what came next in the United States was inevitable. Those first factory cheeses must have been revelations of flavor and quality.

But efficiency, safety, and corporate dominance eventually became the end result.

Tuberculosis and typhoid fever, combined with the shift in population from rural to urban areas, shifted priorities in all food. Germ theory came first, and then came nutrition science. Flavor became, if not exactly suspect, then certainly a nonpragmatic value. Science, efficiency, and American know-how could fix all these problems. Factory food—safe and designed with nutrition in mind—was America's contribution to the world.

At least that's what the companies who promoted it would have you believe. Processed food as the culmination of progress is communicated in different terms and words these days, but the 1935 Kraft-Phenix pamphlet, "The Romance of Cheese," lays out the thought process better than I can. A multipage tale of cheese starting in 2000 BCE (including a beautiful rendering of the apocryphal traveler who was storing milk in an animal stomach and . . . oops! Cheese!)[6] wanders through the time of the ancient Greeks, Romans, and the biblical period, detailing original Camemberts and Emmentals, Limburgers and Guyères, Goudas and cheddars. Finally, climactically, all of dairy history leads us to: Velveeta.

The same Velveeta that the hipster public voted for at the mac and cheese contest that started this journey.

It's easy to laugh and dismiss this as just a commercial marketing ploy, and on some level it was, but this reasoning had traction. From the earliest days of cheddar production there were two main concerns: rot and moisture loss. Both lead to losing money. What better cheese than one that never loses moisture, never goes bad, and—given the changing paradigm of food itself—is nutritionally balanced by scientists? One can mourn the loss of traditional cheesemaking methods but still see why the appeal was successful.

Invented in the early part of the 20th century in Switzerland and experimented on in a few other countries, processed cheese would come to dominate what people think of when they think of American cheese. Processed cheese would later even take that name. While in the 1800s, cheese being shipped to England made in the innovative American factories was sold as "American Cheese," today it is hard to find a natural, unprocessed variety. At first the recipe for processed cheese was more intricate than a reader in the 21st century would think. Companies worked on their blend of aged and young cheddars (and emulsifiers) to create flavor profiles that people would buy. Gradually, however, distinctive taste began to go away as a goal of the process. After two world wars and the advent of the "American Century," flavor—that nonpragmatic bugaboo of scientifically perfect cheese—was becoming less important.

The methods of Joseph Harding and the other pioneers of cheddar were ahead of their time in many ways. In an increasingly industrializing country, taking the individual parts of cheddar-making, creating what we would call now "best practices," and then standardizing them created—overall—higher-quality cheeses and more efficient cheesemaking. The 1850s was an era in which everything improved for cheddar, even for the remaining farmstead producers. However, looking back it is easy to see how every advancement in cheddar led to processed cheese and, later, to assembly-line production and the subsequent lessening of the importance of flavor. Recipes were altered and standardized, salt was added to curd, atmospheres controlled, contact (human and other mammal) minimized, efficiency improved, and bandage wraps applied . . . then paraffin. Every step of the way this was done to create more cheese from milk when it was sold to the final eater.

From a profit point it makes total sense. That milk (and whatever else is in there to emulsify it) is converted to cheese at just about the largest possible ratio in the history of the world. Every drop of moisture lost is another penny lost forever. It's like filled milk cheese or the watering down of butter, but actually legal.

I must say here that it has also created a food trend that I, as someone married to a Texan from Lubbock, must acknowledge. Though it originates from a Mexican dish called *queso flameado*—which uses traditional Mexican-style cheeses like *asadero* or Oaxaca—*chili con queso*, or just queso dip as it's commonly referred to now in Texas, at least by non–Mexican Americans, pretty much has to be made with processed cheese. To be sure, there are fancy restaurant versions, and home foodies who will make a roux and mix in cheeses from the global economy, but it just won't taste right. Heck it might even be better, but few Texans looking for that comfort food will find it satisfying. Processed cheese has been with us a long time, longer than almost anyone living on the planet today. It's no wonder that food made with it can be considered "traditional" in some ways, too . . . again, like the People's Choice mac and cheese.

From a food safety standpoint processed cheese certainly was safer than anything that had come before, at least on the level of food-borne pathogens. Nothing can really go wrong with a Velveeta, and come the Bad Times or Zombie Apocalypse, you will be happy to find it when you are looting your dead neighbors' pantry for food.

Beyond profit and safety, processed cheese was also seen by many as—simply—progress. Let us read the words of the company most associated with processed cheese:

> Another American development, unique in its importance, has been the perfection of an American Cheddar cheese food especially suited for children, but none the less delicious and nourishing for the seven ages of man. The history of this distinctive American-produced cheese food, although comparatively brief in the light of ages of time and cheese production, is a convincing demonstration of the enterprise and scientific spirit of modern cheese manufacture in this country.[7]

In other words, "Hey Europe, thanks for the primitive, unscientific cheese. We'll take it from here" (American cheese industry to Europe, 1935).[8] Indeed, processed cheese began to make big inroads into the cheddar cheese market in the first half of the 20th century.

In searching for the meaning of cheddar in America, I honestly did not think I would find such stark references invoking America in the service of cheese production. But there it is: eating factory-made, processed food that has been vetted by "experts" is not only good for you but shows your faith in America. Good Americans eat "American process cheese food."[9]

Thus only an anti-family store would refuse to carry Kraft Singles.

If one wonders what's next for food technology, the tech workers of Silicon Valley have given us something hard to argue against if one believes in a purely scientific, progressive future. I have a hard time believing it is not a joke, especially since it is sold under the name "Soylent" (based on the 1973 movie *Soylent Green* where Charlton Heston is horrified to find out that the new trendy superfood is actually made out of people), but I have had Internet friends extolling its virtues. Sold with the slogan "What if you never had to worry about food again?" it is a powdery blend "developed from a need for a simpler food source. Creator Robert Rhinehart and team developed Soylent after recognizing the disproportionate amount of time and money they spent creating nutritionally complete meals. Soylent is a food product (classified as a food, not a supplement, by the FDA) designed for use as a staple meal by all adults. Each serving of Soylent provides maximum nutrition with minimum effort."[10]

It promotes what Val Cheke criticized more than half a century ago. At a time when the term "fast food" had just been coined, Cheke wrote about the speed-up of life and working conditions that led to the change in eating:

To those who enjoy the rich, mellow flavor of raw mature cheese, the processed-cheese appears very jaded indeed. For gone are the cheesy flavours, hot and strong, subtle, biting and tasty. In their place is the smooth, mild, spreadable product with a flavour little resembling the initial cheese. . . . Nevertheless its popularity spread far and wide, for it was a development suited to the increasing speed of life, when lack of labour began to tell, and the leisurely preparation and slow appreciative chewing had perforce to be replaced with the quick swallowing of a 'prepared' meal.[11]

Soylent, following the tradition of food in the United States since the understanding of the vitamin, is more nutritionally balanced, efficient, and cheaper than any meals you likely make on your own. Clearly this is the new pinnacle of food, surpassing the processed cheese slice. Soylent doesn't push itself with American themes—the Cold War is over, after all—but it certainly follows the long tradition we have of scientifically developed and marketed foods.

Shut down the family farms and inefficient producers of food who waste time and resources with the development of flavor and their insistence on a diverse agricultural economy. A better, safer, more efficient and affordable life is here.

Chapter 10

Boosting the Cheese Centennial

"How's the old horse-thief?"
"All right, I guess. How're you, you poor shrimp?"
"I'm first-rate, you second-hand hunk o' cheese."[1]

When I visited the site of the Williams factory, my purpose was to find the monument to cheddar built there in 1936. When I got there I learned that there had been another big event at the same location: the "Cheese Centennial" in 1951.

This was a big deal, at least to Upstate New York and to cheddar professionals. The Williams monument was rededicated and the local newspaper dedicated a whole "Cheese Centennial Section" to the planned events. Cheese "dignitaries" from all over the country came and were treated to a reenactment of Williams's life by the Rome Theater Guild. John H. Kraft traveled from Illinois to make a speech thanking God that such a man started the factory system and praised Williams's "service to man."

Some of it was pure boosterism for the town and its hero. Numerous articles proclaimed of the wondrous life of Jesse Williams—his wife Amanda was falling more and more out of the picture at this point, especially since her name didn't make the granite memorial—and attempted to shore up his legacy by stating that the Rome factory indeed was the first in the nation. It almost goes without saying that a community celebration in the 1950s would have to crown a young local woman. And indeed one was elected, not only to serve as "Miss Rome Centennial," but to travel to Washington and hand-deliver New York State sharp cheddar to President Truman, the elected New York senators, and whoever else they could drag into the Senate restaurant for a photo op.[2]

Many of the local businesses got in on the action, buying ads in the *Rome Daily Sentinel*:

> "Jesse Williams Had An Idea. IN MANY COUNTRIES THAT IDEA WOULD HAVE DIED AT BIRTH. HERE IN AMERICA THAT IDEA FOUNDED A GREAT INDUSTRY" (B. Levitt and Sons Hardware and Plumbing)
>
> "THE SOLE AIM of CHIROPRACTIC is to relieve suffering Humanity and enable it to enjoy health to the fullest extent. America's Cheese Centennial" (Federation of Chiropractors of New York International Chiropractic Association)
>
> "May The Next 100 Years Be As Progressive As The Last. OUR CONGRATULATIONS TO THE CHEESE INDUSTRY" (The Edward Barnard (luggage) Co.)[3]

The chiropractors don't really seem to be getting into the spirit of things, but everyone else is seizing the moment. The ads are beautiful Babbittry: the celebration of can-do spirit and the boosterism of local business. No one seized upon the centennial more than Kraft, however. Not only did the president of the company come and give a special speech, but they also dedicated much of an issue of their in-house publication, "The Kraftsman," to memorializing Williams.

Kraft really went all out, though, in their ad for the Cheese Centennial. They were not content with simply honoring Jesse Williams as the first dude to start a cheese factory. You'd think that might have been enough of a stretch because it left Amanda Williams, Anne Patchett, Lewis Norton (of pineapple cheese fame), and many examples from other countries out of the picture. No, Kraft doubled down on Williams, making him a model of what 1950s business leaders wanted America to represent:

> Let Freedom Ring always . . . as it rang for Jesse Williams and his great idea.
>
> MUCH WILL BE WRITTEN AND SAID this year about the material success of Jesse Williams, as Rome celebrates the hundredth anniversary of the event which made him famous. You will

read how, in 1851, Jesse built the first commercial cheese factory . . . and started a vast new industry.

You will read how his Great Idea brought fame and fortune to Rome and the Mohawk Valley. BUT THE SPIRITUAL VALUES in Jesse Williams' life work, and the climate of freedom which made his success possible, are likely to be overlooked, even though they are the true source of his distinction.

EVERY AMERICAN CAN LEARN from Jesse Williams. He was many things—dairy farmer, cheesemaker, mechanical wizard, teacher. And, more than that, he was a creative personality. He built instead of tearing down. He shared his knowledge and his skill for the good of his Rome neighbors and, ultimately, of the whole dairy industry. He worked— and watched his work bear fruit, for himself and for others.

ABOVE ALL, JESSE WILLIAMS' LIFE and work prove the worth of these principles that have helped make America great:

The right of an individual to turn an Idea into an Enterprise.
The right to grow and prosper in the best possible way— by pleasing one's customers.
The right to reward for improvement in the quality of one's product or service.
The right to search on and on for new and better methods of manufacture.

TODAY, THERE ARE PARTS of the world where a career like Jesse Williams' would be stopped dead because these principles are denied or their application limited. That's why it's a good idea to reaffirm them from time to time.[4]

The phrases used throughout this tribute were dog-whistle anti-Communism that was typical of the time: "climate of freedom," "spiritual values," "built instead of tearing down," the "parts of the world" where "Enterprise" would be "stopped dead." Kraft's retelling of the Williams factory story was more about positioning a story of cheese production as super-patriotic

American capitalism, about an ideological soldier in the fight against the Russians, Chinese, and North Koreans. Kraft, as the nation's leading brand, was implicitly fighting Communism by carrying Williams's legacy forward.[5]

Williams's old friend Xerxes Willard had a slightly different view than Kraft. Willard was every bit the evangelist for the associated system of dairying that Williams was and headed the American Dairymen's Association for many years. Willard had actually opposed the memorial to Williams because he felt that it did not embody his true spirit and believed that an educational scholarship for dairy farmers should be set up instead. Upon Williams's death, Willard wrote:

> One most remarkable feature connected with the inventions of Mr. Williams, is that he took out no patents and claimed no royalty on any of his cheese-making devices and improvements. He could have laid a heavy embargo upon the cheese factories of America by taking out patents, thus accumulating an immense fortune for himself, but he preferred to give his inventions to the public, and leave to the world such acknowledgment as it saw fit to offer him.[6] Indeed, letters came to Williams, in his lifetime, from farmers wanting to start factories in their hometowns across the country. Having only heard mentions of what had happened in Rome, New York—or perhaps having only read the moving poetry about him but desiring to find a wife someday—people wrote to him and addressed the letters simply, "Father of Cheese Factories, Rome, Oneida County, N.Y."[7]

What is especially ironic here is that Kraft had come to dominate the cheese world, especially the processed part of the cheese world, in the decades before this centennial by filing suit at any perceived infringement on their patents[8] or merging with other patent holders to such an extent that a "monopoly of monopolies" was warned about as early as 1912.[9]

America traditionally likes taking credit for factories and Fordism more than other countries, though, so the one thing we can definitely say about Rome, New York, in 1851 is that it was the beginning of the American love affair with cheddar, happening at the time of the beginning of the

American love affair with industrialization—the kind of industrialization of food that would eventually lead to the normalization, and then expectation, that traditional dishes such as macaroni and cheese would be made with a processed cheese product like Velveeta, instead of a traditionally made cheddar cheese.

A less Kraftian vision of what cheddar could become and mean to the community is the Tillamook County Creamery Association. A vacation snowstorm led me to visit the Tillamook factory without a scheduled appointment. It was an unusual snow. I have been going to the beach my whole life as a Californian, but I had never seen snow stick on the sand before. It was beautiful. I felt like I was trapped inside a snow globe, or in an odd sandstorm that didn't hurt. Even my wife who's from Lubbock, Texas, much tougher than me, and usually doesn't stray from her belief that "it's not weather unless your eyes are bleeding"—admitted it was an unusual and noteworthy phenomenon.

It wasn't really unseasonable, though. We aren't rich. Our beach vacations are always taken off-season.

For a West Coaster, Tillamook cheddar is a familiar cheese. California's historic lack of good block cheddar-makers means that Tillamook is often considered the go-to cheddar when one is stepping up from the cheapest one can buy. At the store we carried only assorted pre-packaged blocks until an Oregon native joined the co-op. From then on we always had at least a couple of Tillamook cheddar 40-pounders in stock. She was right—our department was not complete without it. When things would get too pretentious—in meetings, behind the counter, in future planning sessions—she would yell, "Tilly is great for that!" You know a food has reached the people when it has a nickname, especially when that nickname sounds like it could be your favorite aunt.

For my own protection, I limit myself to one cheese-related event per vacation. I need to choose wisely. I wanted to go visit Briar Rose Creamery—a goat cheese operation run by ex-Californians who make amazing cheese. Sarah Marcus, the cheesemaker, actually went to high school near me and got me hooked on her goat milk truffles when her cheese plant was only a dream. Their Freya's Wheel is a soft Ticklemore-style cheese, and their Lorelei is one of the few well-made washed-rind goat cheeses in the country. They were certainly worth a trip during our vacation.

Unfortunately, there was a mountain between us. And steep windy roads. And inches of snow on those unplowed roads. And black ice on the roads that were plowed. Then I realized how close I was to Tillamook and how easy it would be to take the next step to find the meaning of cheddar.

Snow was melting and the blizzard had become pouring rain when I drove the 20 miles from our vacation rental to the factory. I kept switching CDs along the way. There is nothing that makes me feel more American—for good or ill—than listening to loud music while I drive fast and alone in my car . . . but nothing seemed to fit. All the music I had with me was specific to other regions. X, Big Boys, Mountain Goats ("All Hail West Texas")—they all felt like the equivalent of pairing a California fresh chèvre with a piece of apple pie at a diner in New England. It might be great elsewhere, but at the specific time and place it just felt wrong. Finally, I settled on Hank Williams. It did the job, even if it didn't really scream "Coastal Oregon."

Approaching Tillamook, it was the first place in miles where the smell was more manure than coastal spray. The town was just like you'd expect an off-season coastal town to look: some businesses were open, many were closed, and the theater marquee stated, No Movie This Week. Still, the slightly beaten-up, wind-burned, fog-dampened feel soon gave way to the big, clean, freshly painted Tillamook cheese factory that sits just outside of town.

It was such a wet, miserable day that I thought I might be the only one there, but the Tillamook factory is built for visitors. A lot of visitors. It may have the best-organized flow and viewing area of any large cheese plant I have visited, ending, of course, in the corralling of visitors through the tasting area to an expansive gift shop, ice cream parlor, and café. I knew I was being herded like a dairy cow, but I didn't really care. That's how good it was.

The viewing area above the factory floor was spectacular. I have a pet theory, which I assumed was just in my head, that anyone of my generation, at least those who don't work in factories, can't help but hear the *Laverne and Shirley* theme play in our heads as we view a large assembly line. I figured that theory was something to think, not say, until I returned from this trip and showed people the photos I took. More than half immediately started singing "schlemiel, schlimazel, hasenpfeffer incorporated" out loud!

Perhaps to drive the seventies sitcom out of the collective heads of visitors, Tillamook had a machine where you could send a video of yourself at the factory—for only $1—that kept yelling at us, "You've got Cheesemail!" That was enticing to me, as professional cheese-obsessive who often actually does get cheese in the mail, but it didn't seem to make anyone present reach for his or her wallet.

I am used to having buyer privilege. It was unusual for me to visit a factory and not be on the factory floor. In fact, I am not sure I had done just a viewing tour since I started working at a grocery store. Mingling with the nonprofessional cheese fans was fun. Seeing mechanized cheddar production for the first time, most were pretty amazed how their cheese is made. They debated what happens to the trim from the 40-pound blocks when the exact weight pieces got cut out, they argued over whether cheese was Colby[10] or cheddar (indeed, hard to tell from the viewing area upstairs!). They marveled at the machinery. Almost everyone loves machinery. All that intricate precision, timing, and realization of vision makes you feel good about being human.

Tillamook is a pretty amazing story. The co-op started in 1909 as a way for farmers in Tillamook to survive, as most agricultural cooperatives do wherever they start. Tillamook was a particularly hard place to make a living as a dairy farmer because, according to one Tillamook promotional video, the roads there didn't come until the thirties, forties, and fifties.[11] No, cheese was shipped—in an actual ship—from the Oregon coast to Portland to be sold at market. Milk would spoil on the journey, so the only choice available to dairy farmers was to band together and make cheese. The weather and soil in the region made other kinds of farming impractical.

After a long passage about stumps, rocks, and too much rain, Tillamook's general manager (at that time) Harold Schild—born and raised in the Tillamook Valley—said, "Grass is really the only thing that will grow here consistently, so you build a shelter and your cows could eat grass and make milk."[12] True, the source of this quote is the cooperative-approved *Tillamook Way*, but that book shows an honesty not usually found in company-produced literature, starting with the revelation that the first cheesemaker in the valley managed to con the U.S. government and steal the land from the Native tribes. Later *The Tillamook Way* details intra-cooperative battles and reveals environmental issues the cheese factories had to deal with as they grew.

Dairy farming and cheesemaking, especially when they get large scale, clearly can cause environmental damage. How refreshing to read the histories of Tillamook that not only acknowledge this, but discuss resistance among its member-owners to environmental legislation and to fixing issues around water contamination and stream temperature. Ultimately it is the story of Tillamook producers educating themselves and overcoming their fellow farmers who didn't see the importance of change and improvement. It's almost impossible to imagine any other company of this size that is not a cooperative airing this kind of complex and contentious history in public.

Because Tillamook *is* big. When nondairy people read the word "cooperative" they tend to underestimate the size. One hundred and ten farmer-owners own the company, which produces 167,000 pounds of cheese a day. If the average U.S. lifespan is seventy-nine years and the per capita cheese consumption rate is 33.5 pounds per year—the same game we played at the Cabot warehouse—Tillamook makes sixty-three American lifetimes of cheese consumption per day. Indeed, of name-brand cheese produced in the United States, Kraft is still number one, but the Tillamook and Cabot cooperatives are the next in line.[13]

I could talk about the block cheddars, the technology, and the hardworking union cheese packers all day, but what was really my lasting memory of the Tillamook cheese plant was the community atmosphere. Like I said, we were there off-season. Not only that, even though the blizzard had ended, it was still rainy and cold. But the Tillamook visitor center was packed.

Sure the upstairs viewing areas had some other work and machine fetishists like me, but the action was down below in the gift shop. There was an ice cream section, a restaurant, tons of cheese samples, gourmet foods, T-shirts and books, and, of course, lots of cheese to buy. Here we found the trim from those aforementioned blocks being sold at a super-discount price—and being scooped up by happy cheese eaters. This is incredibly anecdotal, but the whole place just seemed happy.

While Tillamook had no single commemoration to focus it, my visit made me think of Rome, New York, in 1951 celebrating the "Cheese Centennial." The Tillamook factory was practically an everyday regional celebration of dairy all on its own. Sure, there was no Cheese Queen walking the room preparing to go to Washington, D.C., to bring Tilly to the president, but there was pride in the room. The local high school's team name is the "Cheesemakers" after all. And, fittingly, the high school was founded in the year of the Cheese Centennial, 1951. The cheese pride of Tillamook is more similar to the community cheese pride of parts of Wisconsin than anywhere else I have ever visited in the United States.

It was also interesting to visit a factory where I am a small buyer. Our store sells about 5,000 pounds of Tillamook cheese a year. Most cheese-makers I deal with would be taking me out to dinner and putting me up in a hotel if I bought that much weight, but here I was anonymous. I bought some fresh curds and a rubber, squeaky toy cow named "Tillie from Tilla-mook" and was on my way.

Chapter 11

The Cheddarpocalypse

The week before Thanksgiving—the busiest week of the year for grocery stores—is the worst possible time for an unknown cheesemaker to send a cheesemonger a sample. It's like going to the leather bar in Dockers and a T-shirt on a Saturday night and expecting to get action. Cheesemongers during Thanksgiving week have in mind one very specific task—sell all the damn cheese they bought for the holiday in a very short time—and are not interested in anything not directly related to that task. The last thing any of us wants in that moment is more cheese or any distraction.

No phone calls. No appointments. Nothing extra to think about. Even exceptional samples sent in November can end up as notes on my to-do list that keep getting pushed down to the bottom as customers and crises get dealt with first. Sometimes they even stay there so long that I get too embarrassed to call and just cross them out.

Yet cheesemakers and distributors send cheese samples at this time of year anyway. Don't tell my parents this, but I often bring these free samples over to their house for the holidays. For the record—just so you don't think I'm an awful son—I actually purchase and bring over family favorites as well, but it's a good time to try out cheese on unsuspecting eaters, especially when I can't even find a few minutes during those workdays to give a fair tasting to an unknown cheese.

A few years ago, I unexpectedly received a sample from someone I thought would know better. Brad Dubé—who grew up selling cheese at his family's grocery store and whom I have worked with almost my whole cheese life—had probably told me the story of this cheese, but I had no time to listen. In fact, I ridiculed him. "You sent me a sample on the Tuesday before Thanksgiving? Is this your first day as a sales rep?" I asked.

"Just try it," he said patiently. He'd become immune to my mocking over the years.

I packed the cheese sample over to my parents' house without even looking at it, so I didn't know what to expect from the Dunbarton as I unwrapped it in the kitchen. I knew that it was from a cheddar-maker in Wisconsin, so I kind of assumed it would be a big orange wedge that would have the usual Wisconsin taste—more creamy-sharp than bitter, something everyone would like. It was a big sample, so I knew I could count on it to take up a quarter of our pre-dinner cheese plate.

I panicked a little when I unwrapped it. It was covered with mold. It was so moldy for a white cheddar that I looked to see if there were maggots as well. I once brought a cheese covered in maggots over for a family holiday, but I disposed of it so calmly and quickly that—until now—they never even knew. Was this a repeat of that disaster? How was I going to serve this cheese plate when the biggest piece of cheese I brought was bad? That'd teach me to serve freebies!

And certainly I wouldn't buy a cheese from this company if they couldn't even send a sample in good condition.

In desperation, I looked at the cheese again. Then I said a silent apology for the customers I had mocked when they returned cheese when it wasn't really bad, just unfamiliar. Because on second look I noticed that the blue veining was intentional and uniform, not invasive. Plus, this was a hard, natural-rind cheddar made traditionally with cheesecloth, larded, and aged well. It looked like a "happy accident" cheese I had tried in my first years of cheese buying.

I mentioned the Montgomery's Cheddar earlier on this cheddar voyage. That's fitting because—even to American cheese workers and cheese eaters—they are unsurpassed in importance. After all, the Montgomerys have been making cheddar for generations and were one of the few families not to give it up during World War II when cheesemakers were pushed—by the U.S. government and necessity—to sacrifice flavor and tradition for better yield and a more dependable product. But I didn't know this the first time I tried their cheese.

One of the first times I sold a Montgomery's Cheddar—after I got over my shock at its size and weight (a dense 60- to 70-pound barrel of intense earthy, fruity cheese goodness)—I was shocked by the bluing. It wasn't uncommon, especially twenty years ago, that when traditional cheddars got slightly bruised or cracked, ambient mold from their aging rooms could get into the cheese. This was in the mid-nineties and I had never paid more for cheddar than I had paid for that Monty's. "It costs twenty bucks a pound and it's got this crap in it?" I said out loud. I cursed it loudly even though I was behind the cheese counter. But then, at the urging of the person who sold me the cheese, Kate Arding, I tried it.

And I loved it. I called coworkers over to give them tastes. I cut a bunch and put it out on the shelves. Furthermore, I soon found that certain customers looked for the moldy pieces because they liked it that way even more than the unblemished version. Blue mold—even if accidental—will definitely punch up a cheddar.

Other customers, of course, brought it up to the counter—either showing off or trying to help us out—saying, "This cheese has mold in it!" The show-offs refused to take a sample when we offered it. The helpers often became seekers of the blue after they tried it, looking for the moldy bits on their next shopping trips. I started circling the mold spots in wrapped pieces with a Sharpie to highlight them, both for the people who wanted the blue bits and so no one could return it saying it had gone bad.

I am not shy about tasting cheese, even if I think it may hurt me. Risking a mouthful of bad cheese is an occupational hazard. In my parents' kitchen, with the Montgomery's Cheddar in mind, I cut off a piece of the Dunbarton and put it into my mouth with a silent prayer that this wouldn't be the cheese that did me in.

The Dunbarton Blue was amazing. It tasted like a well-balanced version of the blue-veined bits of the Monty's. The Dunbarton, an intentionally molded, traditional cheddar, was one of those cheeses that as soon as you tasted it, you wondered why people hadn't been making it for years. Everything about it seemed so right and so obvious. The cheese was sharp, fruity sweet, and earthy. The blue was unmistakable, but didn't overpower the other flavors. The cheese was moist but would crumble at the veins if you wanted to serve it that way.

It's a rare thing to taste a new cheese and feel like it is a masterpiece, but that was the experience I had there in my parents' kitchen. Indeed I put the Dunbarton Blue on the cheese plate wondering if it would just be me—with my new-taste-seeking, professional curiosity, and nostalgic memory of my first real cheddar—who would be impressed.

It wasn't just me.

Usually a blue is the last thing on the cheese plate to get eaten. Blue lovers get mad at me when I say this, but it is generally true. Eaters go for the fat and sharp first, in terms of not only bites taken, but how much cheese they stuff in their mouths at one time. I've had many a party where the Brie rind looks like a discarded snakeskin, the hard outside of the Ossau-Iraty looks like a carcass, but the hunk of blue is still half there looking like a wedge of cheese, polite bites taken out instead of greedy gashes.

But the Dunbarton? Devoured in minutes. This cheese was a winner. Despite having a cooler full of pre-ordered cheese already en route for the food holidays, I ordered the Dunbarton the next day. It was too good to wait.

Dunbarton Blue was a cheese that almost never existed. Fresh out of college and ready to take over the family business, Chris Roelli looked forward to the challenge of making cheddar like his father and grandfather had. His dad and grandfather knew about Chris's aspirations. That's why they shut down their factory.

Are the prospects of making a living selling America's most iconic cheese so bad that a family with three generations in the cheese business would lock their doors rather than see the next generation come back to work in the family business? In the case of the Roelli family of Shullsburg, Wisconsin, yes.

The Roellis have been in the cheese business since before Chris Roelli's great-grandfather emigrated from Luzerne, Switzerland. The line of cheesemakers may even go back further than that—no one in the family really knows—but the Roellis have been making cheese in Wisconsin for almost one hundred years. Yet Chris's grandfather Walter was making so little by the early 1990s that he felt ending the tradition was preferable to saddling the next generation with the albatross the business had become.

In retrospect, Chris could see the reasoning: "We were a bloody fish swimming with sharks. It was just a matter of time until we were someone's lunch."[1]

How did a multigenerational cheddar-maker get to that point? The ability to understand germs and nutrition in the beginning part of the last century weren't the only changes in society leading toward the cooking, emulsifying, and extruding of cheese and the consolidation of the cheese business. The devotion to using the newest science that had fueled Williams, Harding, the Wisconsin Idea, and the Progressive Era were also being incorporated more fully into aspects of human behavior and organization by the end of World War II.

Deborah Fitzgerald, professor of the history of technology at Massachusetts Institute of Technology, in her study of the period shows that, from the 1920s onward, many business leaders considered agriculture a "sick industry" and that the best hope was to model their operations in a more "modern" way. She writes:

> Timeliness of operations, large-scale production sites, mechanization, standardization of product, specialization, speed of throughput, routinization of the workforce, and a belief that success was based first and foremost upon a notion of "efficiency"—all these principles were drawn directly from the factories and businesses only recently declared successful. Henry Ford's production facilities, for instance, stood as a dramatic example of the efficacy of rational management techniques, which many felt should now be applied to farming. As an International Harvester promotion exhorted, "Every Farm a Factory."[2]

Looking at the advertisements for cheese that have appeared in magazines and newspapers through the last couple of centuries, one thing is obvious: the push to progress. Through these ads, you can see the argument that every development from science was a net positive and that going from an always-a-little-different, lard-rubbed, raw milk, 60-pound cheddar that tasted of local flora and fauna to an always-the-same hunk of Velveeta was an ultimate accomplishment of humankind. In magazines during World War II, Goodyear Rubber was already trying to persuade industrial manufacturers and family food buyers to change their habits to use the Pliofilm that had been developed for, and tested in, war uses. Even though the war was still raging, it was clear that if their substance could protect bomber engines, it could certainly protect cheddar,[3] even if, as yet, there was none to be spared from the war effort. Ironically, a 1948 *New York Times* mention of this revolutionary new substance said, "There's been an innovation in the packaging of natural cheddar cheese that eventually may make the familiar round wheels of store cheese as obsolete as their former accompaniment, the cracker barrel."[4] Kraft's still-sold, nonwaxed supermarket natural cheese is, of course, called Cracker Barrel, ironically created in 1954. Evoking the old-timey while being a departure from tradition is a hallmark of every-farm-a-factory marketing.

In my assumptions about cheddar before I started this journey, I had assumed that the clothbound cheddar led to the waxed wheel, which led to the 40-pound block, which led to processed cheese. But no, while it seems like experiments had been done with making rectangular cheddar as early as the 1890s,[5] it wasn't until the post-WWII technology of plastic polymers that the "forty" became the ubiquitous variety of natural (unprocessed)[6] cheddar. Even then, sizes varied depending on cheese plant.

Most cheddar-makers in the postwar period were selling to the large companies such as Kraft, Borden, and Armour to survive. Those big national brands had regional producers, sometimes a lot of them, contracted to make their cheese to meet demand. They would have requirements, of course, about sizes and quality of the cheesemaking, but at this point cheese was still regionally made, even if it was nationally distributed.

The postwar period is also when the dairy farms started getting bigger, even if today's mega-dairies hadn't even yet been imagined. Still, the concept of "farm as factory"—something that had been around since the Progressive Era as a way for family farms to prize efficiency in order to make a better living—began taking on a whole new scale.

The problem with the model of the "farm as factory" is that it put all the farming practices on the table as negotiable in the name of efficiency, science, and progress. In the dairy farmer and cheese world, at first this model resulted in a professionalization of the cheesemaker. There were farmstead producers making great cheese in the 1800s—indeed Jesse and Amanda Williams were two of those people before they built their factory—but the specialization inherent in the factory meant that *cheesemaker* became a vocation: a cheesemaker was now someone who spent his or her life making cheese for pay, but who was not tied to one particular location.

Which meant, of course, that along with developments of infrastructure—first rail, then roads, and then refrigerated trucks—location became expendable, too.

Consolidation is the theme of both dairy farms and cheese plants for the last fifty years of the 20th century. The statistics are so stark, they deserve their own line each:

- Today there are only about 10 percent of the number of dairy farms that existed in 1950.

- In 1960, there were more than 1,400 cheese plants producing an average 1 million pounds of cheese per year. In 2003, there were an estimated 399 cheese plants producing an average 21.5 million pounds per year.
- U.S. per capita cheese consumption has more than tripled since 1960.[7]

In other words, people are eating a lot more cheese, made in fewer locations, from the milk of increasingly larger-size herds. This can be, rather bloodlessly, described the following way: "Cheese manufacture, except for artisan cheeses, is now a centralizing industry in which the raw materials travel to the technology in large factories."[8] Such is what happens when you strive to make "every farm a factory"—farms get larger, "family" roles get professionalized, and scale gets larger and larger.

In the 1850s, the desire to codify practices and take cheddar-making off the farm—beyond profit—was also a desire to improve the flavor and consistency of the cheddar being made. In the dairy speeches of the time, such motivation was a never-forgotten foundation. While we may, retrospectively, wonder how much of that framing was sales pitch, it is clear that technical innovation, shared information, and the better understanding of the science behind cheese made the end results a lot easier to predict.

Most Americans today would not know the name Frederick W. Taylor, but his work was so important to industrialization—as well as the consolidation that happened in the cheddar world—that his name itself represents the developments in factory production of the early 1900s. "Taylorism" is also known as "scientific management." Basically, Taylor's theory was that it was possible to study every aspect of production, determine the best possible way every step should occur, and then build a rigid system based on those processes.[9]

You can see where this theory comes from. After all, folks like Harding were doing this kind of thing in their own way, determining best practices, drawing out "ideal" factory layouts and sharing them. Combined with the devotion to science of that era, which was making huge leaps in developing an understanding of the physical world—including germ theory and nutrition—theorizing that work could be combined with science was sure to create a popular movement among venture capitalists of the day. Indeed, Taylorism is what built the factory system of Henry Ford.

Taylor had envisioned his "time and motion" studies to be liberating to workers in the blind spot that philosophers of that time had. He thought increased wealth would be shared with workers; that workers could work less in an efficient system. Everyone would work in a job that would be suited to his or her abilities and be adequately compensated! However, this system leads to ends that we now wouldn't even question. Workers, treated like machines, get bored and frustrated. Workers, treated like spare parts, are easily replaced instead of rewarded with leisure. Workers with no input on their job are not happy workers. The repetitive motion of doing the same small task over and over leads to workplace injury.

While pure Taylorism had only a few decades of devotional appreciation, its influence is still felt today.[10] Both Taylorism and Fordism required mass production and mass consumption, as well as the centralizing of factories and distribution chains. Both systems are almost the exact opposite practices of the first farmstead cheesemakers. What is interesting here, in terms of cheddar and America, is how the move to factory production—which at first increased desirable characteristics of cheese and, in many ways, was an improvement on a quality and flavor level, as well as an efficiency one—eventually became mostly about efficiency and cost. The link was the public perception of science.

That Taylorism is called "scientific management" is not incidental. Branding a theory of tight management control—which, let's be clear, has not much to do with science done in labs—made the ideas seem inevitable, especially in an era fascinated with the idea of the scientific improvement of everyday life.

While the Wisconsin Idea, Progressivism, and the farmers and cheesemakers who would take dairy from the farmstead to an industry invoked science, rightly, as a main focus in the improvement of their animals and, mostly, in the improvements to food safety, they also had political power. This political power showed that, as is true today, not all science is pure. While processed cheese consumption continued to rise, and many cheesemakers sold their cheddar blocks to Kraft and the few others who made processed cheese for a time, Wisconsin actually blocked the sale of another scientific "achievement": margarine.

Margarine was invented only a couple of decades after the Williams factory was built and cheddar-making started to become a factory-based process. It actually pre-dates the development of processed cheese.

Wisconsin banned the dyed version of margarine in 1895 and had an over-all ban on it from 1925 to 1967. Even today, margarine cannot be served unless specifically asked for in Wisconsin restaurants.

Dairy farmers, who already had considerable clout in the 1890s in Wisconsin, saw margarine as a fraud perpetrated on the public, who would be confused while looking for butter. Also, Wisconsin's reputation for butter was just being repaired: during the time of the Civil War, butter was regarded as so poor in quality it was usually called "Wisconsin Wheel Grease."[11] Remember also that "filled milk" cheeses—cheeses that, like margarine, replaced expensive butterfat with cheap oil—had been at least partially responsible for ruining the export trade of cheddar to England.[12] The dairy business was too important to the state to let something similar happen again.

However, this development shows that devotion to science can take a backseat to protecting one's industry when push comes to shove. Especially when the margarine-ban years coincided almost perfectly with the commercial introduction of processed cheese. Let me state for the record that I am not pro-margarine. I do, however, have a taste for it. I grew up with it and didn't really taste much real butter until I was an adult. You know, much like the way I grew up with Kraft Singles and Velveeta. Only years later would I realize the alternatives and change my relationship with processed cheese and embrace the real thing.

In fact, I am having a hard time constructing a logical, scientific argument for why margarine would be banned yet processed cheese allowed to prosper. True, a dairy farmer raised the cows that gave the milk that made the cheddar that was sold and processed. But a farmer also grew the vegetables that were turned into the oils of margarine. Could it be that not all use of science is equal, even to those who proclaim it ideologically as their highest goal? The scientific advances that have been made in the United States are truly things to be proud of—advances in vaccines, food safety, that whole going-to-the-moon thing—but it's important to remember that those with access to power in any given era will try to use science to their own end.

Taylorism's biggest success story of the time is the Ford assembly line. Not only was it efficient, it upped the wealth for everyone. It reduced prices, like the reduced price of protein raved about by Progressive Era dairy farmers for everyone, and a Model T was in the reach of many workers.

But there's another example of "scientific management" that I think provides a more complete picture of Taylorism when paired with the "success" of Ford: the Triangle Shirtwaist Company. A shirtwaist is a woman's blouse,[13] one of the first that crossed class lines, much like the Model T and cheap cheddar. It was at the same time a symbol of women's liberation: away from more restrictive clothing, to being able to work. And, later, a symbol of women's oppression: working at a factory in terrible working conditions where you are doomed to die in a fire. Because that is what happened at the Triangle Shirtwaist Company in New York City. When a fire broke out, 146 piece-work laborers, most of them young immigrant women, died from fire or from jumping to their deaths from the tenth floor where no fire ladders would reach.

Usually the Triangle Shirtwaist Factory fire is remembered as a tragedy, and the aftermath—the social movement that gained power immediately after—was a demonstration of the power of unions, a feminist example to discuss immigrant women in the workplace, or the start of legal reforms in industrializing workplaces. However, in addition to all of those, there is another way to remember the fire. The tragedy also illuminated the downside of a "scientifically managed workplace," one where, in the name of efficiency and organization, the women who worked there could not leave, even for bathroom breaks, and the exits were locked.

Why bring all this up when talking about cheddar? Because, locked into a system of anonymously creating cheddar cheese for large companies who were increasingly trying to maximize efficiency and profit, small-scale, family-owned cheesemakers were heading toward tragedy in the way that is obvious to us now, looking back through history.

This consolidation of flavor and method created a kind of "broadcaster voice" of cheddar: a highly standardized product that attempted to disown its regional accents. Though this also helped to brand some cheddars that did have more distinctive traits with their states, it was no accident. As Janus writes:

> By the early twentieth century the large and powerful national marketers catering to the nation's newly developed mass market demanded the end of poorly made cheese. *Consistency* was, and remains, the word on the lips of every cheesemaker in the state. Long shelf life, consistent quality, and mild flavors made Wisconsin cheese a huge success in national and international markets. Farmers

were enriched and grew prosperous as cheese was drained of its sometimes-eccentric "personality." This was the great achievement of the Age of Cheddar.[14]

Sid Cook, master cheesemaker and owner of Carr Valley Cheese Company, a multigenerational business, can speak to the history of cheesemakers and Wisconsin dairy in a way that few people can. A conversation with him can encompass the very beginnings of Wisconsin becoming "America's Dairyland," including how fresh springs were used to cool raw milk and enabled so many cheese plants to be built in the state, and how dairy farmers didn't want to haul their milk very far in the old days so cheese factories got built about "every six miles." Cheesemaking, not just in Wisconsin but everywhere, was once a very regional calling. The reason that every town or village that has a dairy history once had a cheesemaker is because until the 1900s, there wasn't the technology and infrastructure to do anything else. If not used on the farm itself, milk was collected from local dairies in milk cans. Once milk becomes cheese it is a more durable food, but until the advent of refrigerated trucking there was only so far away one could transport milk before it went bad.

There came a point—at different times in different regions—where the big national brands decided to start building, or buying from people who built, big cheese factories, continuing the logic of efficiency and standardization. This practice would take care of the problems these national corporations had with the cheese from different factories tasting a little different, as well as increasing profit and controlling other expenses. Again, the urge to standardize pushed another transformation of the cheddar system.

Then came the era I like to call the "Cheddarpocalypse," even though none of the cheesemakers still active from that era really warmed to the name when I tried it out on them. There came a day when somewhere between fifty and eighty small cheddar factories in the Midwest were told—with thirty days' notice—that their cheese would no longer be purchased. Cook explains it this way:

> If they could buy all the cheese from one place, they wouldn't have to worry about all the different flavors. They could have less graders, less warehouses, not have to deal with so many factories and they could have the same cheese all the time.

> . . . A good share [of the cheese factories that built Bor-
> den's business] went out of business; some went to other
> companies, some of them started making other cheeses. The
> only one that I can think of, well . . . I can't think of any of
> them that survived making 40-pound blocks.[15]

It's not that folks stopped making cheddar, at least the ones who survived. It's that cheddar alone just wouldn't do it anymore, not when faced
with wholesalers wanting to pay less and less for block cheddar, if they
wanted it at all from a smaller producer.

Cheesemakers, if they wanted to survive, had to get creative. Tony and Julie
Hook, for example, broadened the lines of cheese they made. Though they
are best known these days by consumers for their once-in-a-while releases of
super-aged cheddar—ten, fifteen, and now twenty years aged (retailing for
over $200 a pound)—their first bit of success was with an American original
similar to cheddar, called Colby cheese. Most Colby these days is more factory
cheddar than traditional Colby and is dyed orange so that it can be combined with Monterey Jack to make "Co-Jack" cheese. Julie's cheese, a more
traditional version, took Best of Show at the World Cheese Championships
and, according to Tony, "This gave us the ability to start marketing our own
cheese ourselves and is what kept us in the game even though we were still
pretty small." To this day no other woman has made a cheese that won the
World Cheese Championships, though women have won the U.S. Cheese
Championships and the American Cheese Society competition.

The Cheddarpocalypse can be seen in the context of the family farm collapse in the late 1970s and early 1980s that hit all aspects of rural America.
Family farms took a huge hit in America when large, corporate food
manufacturers—with the money to invest in the new technology—began
to consolidate themselves through agriculture. Indeed, the eighties and
nineties were particularly hard on Wisconsin cheese businesses when the
oft-repeated Earl Butz mantra "get big or get out" reached its final stages.
The concept of super-efficient, large-scale agriculture certainly didn't start
with Nixon's secretary of agriculture Butz, but the options at that point
had dwindled to few. According to Roelli, 60 percent of Wisconsin cheesemakers were lost during those years. Many of those who survived did so by
getting larger themselves or by taking on corporate partners. The concept

of "get big or get out" not only got out many folks who resisted growth, but also—in the farm debt crisis that spawned Farm Aid—forced out many others, as well, who actually tried to get big, seeing it as their only chance.

In fact, according to Roelli, many of the small country cheese plants that once were staples of local farm communities and economies were being bought by larger interests just for their milk contracts with dairy farms. The small plants were no use for cheese production because that was being centralized and sent to larger, more efficient factories. The big cheesemakers needed milk, not locals.

The consolidation of the cheese industry continues to the present day. The trend of the last century has been more milk, fewer farms. In the name of science, technology, and profit, first the cheddar business was changed from farmstead to factory. Cheesemaking was professionalized, and men replaced the women who had made cheese for generations. Then the cloth-bound wheels were replaced with rindless cheddars and processed cheeses, devaluing location and flavor for maximum weight retention. Finally, mega-dairies and mega-plants replaced family farms and town cheesemakers because, after all, an eigh-thousand-cow dairy is more efficient than a smaller one, and a plant making a million pounds of cheese a day is easier on logistics than a bunch of small plants spread throughout the region.

Times change. In the early 20th century, viewing the farm as a factory was an obvious metaphor designed to show farmers that they needed to see the farm as an integrated system in order for it to work. In the era when "factory" did not evoke the image of ecological destruction, this made a lot more sense, and if one can step back into those old shoes, it still does. All my experiences with farmers over the years show me that their work is all about maximizing the resources they have in order to make a living off the land. However, with living off the land being an end goal, preservation of that land is usually kept in mind, at least by farmers who are planning to pass their land down to their children.

If "the farm as factory" was a metaphor at first, the "factory farm" would become a descriptive reality decades later. The earth a factory sits on has no intrinsic value. In fact, that land is easily left if political conditions or cheaper labor and tax breaks make moving that factory outta here more profitable. If the goal of the Progressive wedding of scientific management to farming was to lower the price of protein—a benefit to all—that goal has been achieved. But was the Progressives's goal also to create a system where the "yeoman farmer" cannot survive on the land or really compete against bigger, more efficient operations?

Chris Roelli's father and grandfather, not wanting to condemn Chris to a futile pursuit, made a clearly rational decision to stop producing cheese, one that many other cheesemakers had already made. There was no way to compete with the Krafts and Hilmars of the world, so instead of saddling his son with a business that was sure to fail, Chris's father locked the doors to concentrate on the milk-hauling aspect of the dairy world.

It's not hard to see the economic problem that small cheesemakers were faced with. Cheesemakers—unless they are farmstead producers—buy the milk they need to make cheese, but the cheese they make with it needs to age. So, while the milk bill needs to get paid (or if they are farmstead, the feed bills, the vet bills, etc.), the cheese sits around, costing money in utilities for refrigeration until it is mature enough to be sold. Many cheese-makers need to make young cheeses in order to get a quick return on their investment and pay off the bills that are owed. However, making a young, mild cheddar—a cheese that could be sold relatively quickly—became a volume game with these bigger, more efficient factories involved.

When people speak of cheddar as a commodity, that is not a figure of speech. It is bought and sold at the Chicago Mercantile Exchange, recently renamed The CME Group. This trading, as well as various complex federal and state regulations, sets the price of block cheddar. Indeed cheddar is the one cheese that I get price quotes on every single week from my commodity suppliers.

All purchases made at the CME must be taken into possession within two working days. Since the purchases are made in "carload" quantities of 40,000 to 44,000 pounds, that's no joke. It also, clearly, is not for the little folks.

Since cheddar is traded as a commodity, producers became tied into the pricing system. If you are making only a penny or two per pound and producing only 1,000 pounds of cheese a day, you are going to have a hard time feeding your family anything but cheese on that $10 or $20 a day. If, however, you are on the other end of the spectrum and producing 1 million pounds of cheese a day, you'll probably be doing quite well.

But Chris Roelli had other ideas. Never losing the itch to make cheese even during the years his family was out of the cheesemaking business, he had a bit of luck. He managed to convince a local company that was making portable, pre-fab cheese plants (basically a tiny cheese factory in a mobile home!) into letting him use one as a demonstration model to get into the cheddar business.

Secretly, though, Chris was scheming. He had to keep it a secret because his idea was a cheddar blue cheese. He started experimenting but didn't tell anyone because the last thing you are supposed to do in a cheese plant is introduce mold. As Roelli says, "According to the Old Guard, you don't even *mention* blue cheese in a cheddar plant or the free mold will turn everything blue." Not wanting to conjure up images of hundreds of pounds of unusable cheese curds, he kept his mouth shut.

Slowly Chris Roelli developed, through trial and error, one of the most original cheeses made in this country in the last century. After a year of secret tinkering, he knew he had to commit to finding a place to age his cheese without endangering the newly reformed family cheese business. Luckily, after some reluctance, Master Cheesemaker Willi Lehner agreed to age Chris's wheels in the dugout aging room/cave Lehner had built for his own cheddars.

As luck would have it, the same woman who sold me my first piece of Montgomery's Cheddar entered the picture. Now a well-respected cheese consultant (and cofounder of *Culture Magazine*), Kate Arding visited to help Roelli with another cheese. That attempted cheese was a disaster, but that meant there was a lot of time to stand around and talk. Roelli told Arding about his cheese experiments.

"I looked in the aging room and saw a lot of fuzzy lumps," Arding remembers.[16] "Some were awful, but some were the Dunbartons. We wiped off the mold, took a plug and I thought, 'This is really something.'"

Arding, whose cheese résumé is among the most impressive of anyone living in the United States, is originally from England and had gotten her start at Neal's Yard Dairy, one of the companies many cheese lovers credit with helping to save traditional cheddar in England. She put Roelli in touch with a local cheesemonger, who bought it all.

Arding knows her cheese, and when word spread about the Dunbarton in the cheese community, people wanted to try it. Unfortunately, there were no more wheels in process, and the Dunbarton takes four months to age. Not only that, but it is notoriously hard to replicate a cheese with as many variables as Dunbarton. Chris Roelli was at the point where he had to stop keeping his mystery cheese a secret. "Suddenly I realized I was on the interstate, so I needed to either speed up or pull over."[17]

While Roelli gives Arding a lot of credit for encouraging him to move forward with the Dunbarton, Arding will take none of it. "I think Chris was just thinking of it as a cheddar gone-wrong, whereas I tasted it and thought of it as a blue with great potential. [The bottom line is] he's the cheesemaker."

Luckily for people who love cheese, Walter Roelli, after fifteen years away from cheesemaking, had come to miss it. Even though the elder Roelli had originally tried to keep his grandson out of the cheese business, together they decided to build a cheese plant for the new product. Of course, all they needed after that were customers to buy this cheese that almost no one had ever heard of.

While I was happy to be one of the first West Coast cheesemongers to carry the Dunbarton Blue, that the Roellis had to search so far afield for customers is the sad story of the cheese economy these days. Quite often, for small cheesemakers to earn what they need to make a living they need to export their cheese to an urban area where food is trendy enough and there is enough disposable income that people are not purchasing solely on a subsistence basis. For the Roelli Cheese Company, located in the poorest county in Wisconsin, this is certainly the case.

The Roellis use only milk from one farm for the Dunbarton Blue and pay a premium for its high quality. At large factories, the technology of today allows the process—from the pumping of milk to the packaging of the cheese—to be controlled by computers and button-pushers, never coming into contact with humans. But at the Roellis' plant, they make cheese in the traditional way: "Like it or not, my two hands touch every wheel."

Dunbarton Blue is uncommon in taste but absolutely typical in the way it underscores the dramatic difference between traditionally made and factory-made cheese. On the one hand you have a family business in the same area for a hundred years buying high-quality milk that they use to make small batches of cheese that is then aged until deemed high enough in quality for sale. On the other hand, a large company buys milk as cheaply as possible and creates a huge volume of cheese using a pre-programmed, mechanical process that does not allow for individual input. The cheese is then sealed and sold as quickly as possible.

The cheese produced by machines and button-pushers is seen as the norm, of course, and to most folks spending anything more per pound is seen as an extravagant indulgence. In a factory food economy, many people simply do not have the choice to support the people more like themselves—regular folks trying to make a living—because it would cost them money they don't have. In a de-industrialized and de-agriculturalized nation, this irony is widening.

Though the Roellis do sell the Dunbarton Blue at their shop along with their curds and a few other basic cheeses, Chris says, "We have to take our product where people can afford and appreciate it. Most people just eat what they are used to or what's in front of them. You're not eating a frozen pizza because it tastes good. [Handmade] cheese is just the opposite." It's different, you have to seek it out, and it's more expensive.

Rural folks selling their quality food to relatively wealthy people in urban areas is not really a new concept, of course. For the last hundred years or so, the population of the cities needed to eat, and rural life—at least since the Industrial Revolution really got going—has always been closer to the bone. What is newer is the consolidation of food production, which has made factory food so cheap that quality food is now seen as elitist. Some farmers always marketed (or were marketed) to the upper class promising superior quality at a premium price. But now, without a value-added product like handmade cheese, making a living off the land at all as a small operator is in question.

Still, Chris Roelli has found a way to make a small-scale cheddar-style cheese in this day and age and not go broke. That in itself is a remarkable feat.

Chapter 12

Cheddar-Making or Myth-Making?

The American Mind was raised upon a sentimental attachment to rural living and upon a series of notions about rural life that I have chosen to designate as the agrarian myth. The agrarian myth represents a kind of homage that Americans have paid to the fancied innocence of their origins.[1]

A farmer or cheesemaker telling their story can be fascinating, inspiring, and empathy provoking. Indeed, at pretty much every cheese event I go to, makers are urged to talk about themselves, their family, and their farm or food. In many ways, the strategies of what I would lump together as the "New Food Movements"—farmers markets in urban areas, niche market grocery stores (and niche sections in grocery stores), Slow Food, community supported agriculture, land trusts, and so on—have been successful, mostly, in the ways they provide a podium for farmers and small-scale producers to speak to potential customers.

I've always found something a little distasteful in this: the urging of "telling your story." Don't get me wrong, it's the urging not the actual telling that seems *off* to me; just a bit of gristle that sticks in my teeth. When Chris Roelli came into our store to sample out his cheese to our customers, I finally realized why.

The food producers would never say it—at least to me; I don't pass as "rural" in any way—but it seems kind of demeaning when urban people, who have never farmed anything beyond a small marijuana plant,[2] question farming decisions based on an academic and sometimes arrogant view of agriculture. The standards that some folks set up for farmers can be unattainable, setting them up—in the critics' minds—to fail.

Dogmatists have a hard time with Dunbarton Blue. That is one of the things I love about it. Roelli makes the cheese with raw milk when it comes from the summer-pastured cows but pasteurizes it when the milk comes from animals confined to the barn during the harsh Wisconsin winters. This variation seems reasonable. I mean, I'm neither dairy scientist nor dairy farmer, but if a cheesemaker thinks rotating seasonally between raw and pasteurized milk is the best and safest way for him to proceed, I'm not going to tell him otherwise.

Of course, that doesn't mean that other empowered, urban shoppers won't. I feel protective of cheesemakers who come to the Bay Area, sometimes, because it's such culture shock. Don't get me wrong—I'm not leaving the city anytime soon, and I love our cheese customers—but the willingness that city folks have to tell farmers what to do is not a good look. When confronted with the Dunbarton Blue sometimes-raw, sometimes-pasteurized dilemma, both the raw-fearing and raw-seeking shoppers tried to get Roelli to choose a side. Roelli, the poor guy, started talking about somatic cell counts and haylage and things like that, and one person eating free samples, whom I doubt had heard those words before, bullied right by him. "You should pasture the cows all the time," she blurted.

In Wisconsin.

Now, I'm a true Californian, but I think most people would agree that the winters in Wisconsin are kind of cold. And the cows might not like it when they can't find forage through two feet of snow.

Talking down these experts-without-experience when you "tell your story" is a part of what you have to do to sell small-scale, handmade cheese these days, along with the more common and more reasonable educating of urban people about farming that you would expect. The crisis of low milk and cheddar prices—combined with the new food movements' promotion of farming heroes—has created new handmade cheeses in numbers undreamed of even fifteen years ago. But one would have to be a little Pollyanna-ish to herald that development as an unmitigated good.

Most of the trends to come out of the food movements are consumer focused, not farmer based. By this I don't mean that farmers didn't found some of these movements or that farmers don't benefit; it's that much of the way these trends work in practice is as a market-based strategy to develop a niche where small farmers can survive. There is nothing wrong with that.

Continuing to chew this gristle, I wonder if it isn't enough that these folks have to work the land and feed us without us—both mongers and consumers—making them sing for their supper as well. Richard Hofstader wrote about the "agrarian myth" over half a century ago, and a version of this myth still prevails in much of the world of retail cheese-selling. An important distinction Hofstader made when he wrote his seminal work was between the self-sufficient farmer (the nostalgic myth) and the commercial farmer (the reality). The concept of "American Exceptionalism" morphed over time from no-country-ever-formed-this-way-in-history to if-you-say-anything-bad-about-America-you-should-be-deported. Similarly "the agrarian myth" seems to have transformed. Now, though, the "self-sufficient farmer" is not the vessel for our nostalgia. No, today the nostalgia and myth-making are reserved for an idealized view of the possibility of small family farms making a living off the land.

I am not immune to this mythologizing myself. I used to bristle a little at the new cheesemakers who would arrive at the store and start "telling their story"—dutifully, as they are advised—when those stories would be all about the successful business they ran or high-paid job they once had and how they ditched it all to move to the country for the love of cheese. No matter how they put it, it just seemed somehow odd to me—as if they were pushing out the real rural cheesemakers. I even questioned myself. Do I find it easier to talk to the presentation-ready ex-urban/suburban folks who now make cheese rather than the slower-talking folks who are more awkward in a big-city store? Didn't their urban roots just give an automatic leg up to the newcomers, helping to further marginalize the always-rural folks?

Well, the answer—in truth—is probably yes, to some degree. This country has a large cultural divide. Old-school farmers are less likely to have an updated website, much less an Instagram account. In my early days of cheese, before I had met many cheesemakers—before anyone knew our store outside of our neighborhood—calling up a cheesemaker to ask a question felt like the cold-calling temp work I had done, and hated, before I got into cheese. Back then, though, almost every monger at every retail store was in the same boat. There were no websites to look for or foodie blogs to cultivate or curate. I know how they feel. Recently even I have had to deal with hip, urban companies who won't talk on the phone and don't even have publicly listed phone numbers. When I asked via e-mail if I could call someone to work out an issue I was told, jokingly—but also kind of not-jokingly—that "no one uses the phone anymore, Old Man."

In fact—and I try not to really feel this way, thus bringing in my own pastoral myths—I sometimes find myself assuming that the less I can find out about a cheese online, the more authentic it must be. I know in my heart, though, that the idea of a lack of computer literacy as somehow noble is a romantic zero-sum game, one that doesn't really serve anyone in the end.

And maybe I am the one that's guilty of even grander mythologizing here, envisioning a time when small-scale farmers and cheesemakers could just harvest a crop or finish a cheese and not have to soil themselves with the marketing side of the job. Today's society is probably more alienated from the land than any generation that has come before. I mean, why *wouldn't* it be? We are at the climax of an era that has seen rural populations diminish, farming become more and more consolidated, and food being produced in factories far away from the people who eat it.

The most popular narrative-driven cheese book in recent memory is *The Telling Room*, by Michael Paterniti. The real story in the book is that the author gets so caught up in the myth of the cheesemaker he is writing about that it stymies him. He cannot finish—he cannot take the steps he knows he needs to take in order to be a responsible writer because he is so enamored. Ultimately, years after his book was originally due, he comes to terms with the conflicts between what he wants to believe and what he has witnessed, but this passage tells us a lot about the myth-making trap one can fall into as people who see loss in the way contemporary agriculture has evolved:

> I'd let myself live in the stupor of belief—that Ambrosio [the cheesemaker] was so heroic and principled that he could never be tied to venal concerns, that, aside from being magical, from being a cheese of lost memories, Paramo de Guzman [the cheese] symbolized a kind of lost purity that needed to be protected at all costs, that only Ambrosio could have made, nurtured, and guarded a cheese such as this. How many times, in how many drafts, had I written it so?[3]

Taking this devotion to the myth of the noble artisan another couple of steps further, if only the most pure and magical food savants are the ones we should seek out, what is to become of Jane Doe Farmer who is just trying to pay for her kid's college?

I parodied this kind of myth-making myself when I was asked to help create a promotional video for the 2014 American Cheese Society Conference in Sacramento. At one point we talked about the idea of interspersing faux-documentary interviews in the style of *The Office* or *Modern Family* between informative scenes of the video, and I promised to write some dialogue for them. I ran with this. In fact, I ran so far with it I ran out of contention.

Since I have given up on filming it, here is my script:

(Subject will be in looking-at-the-camera interviews with the character acting as if they are answering a question.)

ON *TERROIR*:

"I find most Americans really do not understand the concept of *terroir* [pronounced Tare-waaaaaaaaa]. To really taste the *Tare-waaaaaaaaaa* one has to source locally. One cannot mix milk. I would submit that to truly taste *Tare-waaaaaaaaaa* a cheesemaker can only use the milk from *one* cow. This cheese is the *Tare-waaaaaaaaaa* of Bessie, a three-year-old Holstein/ Jersey mix."

ON ARTISAN PRODUCTION:

"We are creating a truly artisan product. . . . We refuse to use any technology invented after 1850. Anyone using a truck rather than a horse and buggy to transport their cheese to market is insulting the tradition of hundreds of years of cheesemaking."

ON CHEESEMAKING:

"Cheesemaking is an art. People have told me that I should standardize my recipe, account for differing seasonal differences in Bessie's milk . . . but that would mean making my cheese taste the same every time. Did Picasso paint the same picture every day? We are not looking for cheese customers [said with disdain], we are looking for patrons."

ON RAW MILK:

"I am creating a living food. Of course I only use raw milk. I want to see the natural flora and fauna of Bessie's milk in every piece of cheese. My cheese is so alive that you can see it move. . . . [Looking at jar and then holding it up to camera] See, it just moved again. See?"

ON THE AMERICAN CHEESE SOCIETY:
"We will only sell to stores who appreciate us. If people ask how much it costs, we tell them it's not available. We are not looking for salesclerks, for mongers, or even for curators. We are looking for people who think of our cheese as a debutante for whom they are hosting a coming out party. We need some- one wanting to introduce it to cheese society."

The promo video went in another direction. Hey, the intended video was supposed to get cheese people to fly to Sacramento in the middle of summer; it wasn't supposed to be art. Among other reasons, there was some feeling that my mockumentary could easily be taken out of context as making fun of the cheesemakers instead of as a parody of what the extreme consumer asks for *from* cheesemakers. My script was a self-conscious version of the kind of mythical devotion Paterniti showed to Ambrosio's Paramo de Guzman cheese. The idea was that the person most extreme in the pursuit of purity is the person who demands public and moral support.

Heather Paxson, in her groundbreaking study of the new American artisan cheesemakers, shows that while some come into cheese well-off, there is a great diversity of (still mostly white) people making the new artisan cheese. In fact, according to Paxson, many of them are operating on the land of farms that were foreclosed on in the great farm crisis of the eighties. A crisis that in many ways was the culmination farm strategies that focused on making every farm a factory.[4]

Paxson describes these new cheesemakers as "post-pastoral," not mythologizing a past that never was but working with nature to create sell- able nonindustrial cheeses. While these new-era cheesemakers help rural economies, they are working, also, to create new tastes that bigger opera- tions are not set up to capitalize on. Many of the new cheesemakers—and I see this among many of the new California cheesemakers—are not new to land or dairy, just new to cheesemaking. Some might even be relatively large compared with farms in Wisconsin and Vermont, but even they are having a hard time making ends meet as dairies get larger and larger.

The cheese world is unique—and this is stunning to agricultural workers not involved in dairy—because so many younger people are getting involved in cheese these days. When representatives from government organizations come to make presentations at the American Cheese Society, they almost always, off the record, mention being shocked at how young the average age of attendees is. At a time when the average age of a principal operator of a farm in this country is fifty-seven and rising,[5] I have noticed I seemed to have eased into the older side of attendees at our annual cheese conferences. By the time this book is published I will still be only forty-eight years old.

Many of these folks are using the dairy and cheese science available to today's small-scale artisan cheesemakers, which did not exist in the 1850s, to create cheese that simply cannot be produced on an industrial scale. Indeed, these folks are pushing it forward—with excitement—in ways similar to the most involved pushers of the cheddar factory system in the late 1800s. Sharing best practices, visiting each other's dairies, detailing failures . . . this is what made the factory system of Williams and the cheese ideology of Harding work.

The creation of food trends and the associated buzzwords—local, sustainable, artisan—can set up farmers and cheesemakers to fail by setting unreasonably high expectations on them, that in their magical purity they can re-create an era (that never really existed) of small farm economic bounty and security. However, the current food movements also create an ability for farmers and cheesemakers to tell their stories to folks with little connection to the land. Farmers markets, Slow Food, food security organizations, and the others have all given us urban foodies a language that we can use to "police" rural people, if we so choose, but also one that can lead us to find common ground. To be sure many farmer/urbanite conversations are mutual, fun, and really, just people talking to other people. At their best these interactions are a sign of hope that an urban/rural cultural divide is not insurmountable.

The mockumentary-that-never-was points out the danger of linking food movements (or more desirably, farmer movements) to sales niches. Retail, including food retail, is helping to spawn a culture of entitlement that is dangerous to America.[6] Present-day commerce is creating a nation of whiners. As a cheesemonger, I am basically just a retail worker with a pretentious title I gave myself. I have to deal with the things that all retail workers need to deal with, including the occasional customer with entitlement issues.

During the first dot-com boom in San Francisco, I actually had customers *literally* time discussions and then tell me how much money I cost them by answering their questions and addressing their concerns. About a year ago, though, I had an incident that exemplified the worst aspects of a culture that caters to consumers over community. A customer came in and started fiddling with one of the cheeses we buy pre-cut and pre-sealed. We keep a few of these in stock because they fit certain niches. They arrive with barcodes and heavy plastic. After a while the customer came up to the counter with the cheese—no reason to name the brand here because what followed was not that company's fault—and said, "I bought some of this and it was bad. Can I exchange it?"

"Sure," I said.

"I actually bought quite a few. I didn't open them but they all look bad."

"You bought a few? Was this back when they were on sale?"

"Yes."

"Well, I have to check the cost back then. Obviously they cost more at regular price."

Wrong answer. This unleashed a stream of National Chain this and Other National Chain that. According to the customer, anywhere else he could just describe a problem and more accommodating stores would give him product in exchange, no questions asked, no matter what it now cost. During this onslaught, I started to think about timing.

"Wait," I said. "These haven't been on sale for months. When did you buy these?" I realized that, though the cheese was sold weeks before their expiration date, that date was surely long past by now.

Another onslaught was released. "Why does it matter?" "Don't you stand behind your product?" And then, the clincher, "Other stores return these to their distributors and get credit from them."

While our store is not always the best about customer service, some of the misunderstandings arise from our origins as a community store. Businesses can develop personalities based on their histories just like humans. For the first twenty-plus years, our store served mostly people in the immediate area whom workers would see on the street, at the demonstration, at shared spiritual centers, or at potlucks, not just on the other side of a register. We try to treat people as equals all the way down the line, including the people we buy from. Ethically, I am never going to go to a distributor and say, "I need full price credit for this perishable product that I bought on sale, which a customer says went bad sometime in the months since he purchased it and the expiration date passed. And no, I can't really say for certain it was kept refrigerated." I may authorize the return to the customer, but I'm not going to ask someone else to pay for it.

Increasingly, grocery (and other) stores have no-questions-asked return policies. Many customers expect this now. I understand that these policies benefit customer service relationships. Any restriction on returns—even one as simple as requiring a receipt—can lead to a potential argument with a customer. Win or lose, you never want to have arguments with customers because those kinds of interactions make customers not want to return and stress the workers. I get that concept, I really do. But I think there is a deeper issue here about the way we, all of us, view our day-to-day relationships.

I don't think this is just a San Francisco issue, though; I think it's a national one. Perhaps, as the wave of change hits this city like a hanging bag of draining chèvre to the face, we are feeling some of this more intensely than other parts of the country. In my youth, the city was seen by people like me—suburban, with ideas of how to live that weren't possible where I was growing up—as the place of refuge. The cities were depopulating, and there were many political reasons for that, but the city represented a cheaper lifestyle with community and lots of possibility.

Cities, at least on the coasts, are almost the opposite of that now. We are in the midst of a massive cultural change not unlike the scale in which cheddar factories changed life on the farm forever or the consolidation of agriculture changed rural geography. Many cities are repopulating now and have become the expensive, sometimes exclusive, places to live. People who have lived in a particular city their whole lives are being forced out or forced to deal with a neighborhood suddenly changing its values and priorities.

Emiliano Lee, a fellow cheesemonger who grew up in San Francisco—his dad actually used to deliver tofu to our store in the eighties—put it this way: "So much has changed. [I]t's become apparent that the city I knew and called home, where I grew up and embraced myself and my cultures . . . that city is dead or dying, transforming into something I don't recognize."

Much like the loss of rural farms and artisan cheesemakers we bemoan, the displacement of urban natives changes the culture of the land. Trying to find a way to survive in a new and changing environment, folks like Lee sound a lot like people describing the grazing lands that are now shopping malls or the Grange hall that now stands empty. Lee can describe the place his grandmother took him for his first *pan dulce*, the restaurant in "whose old back kitchen I ate and fell in love with my first *relleno*, sipped my first Mexican hot chocolate and *atole*. . . ." Those are not the kind of places where you would come back two months later and demand free food because you decided your dining experience wasn't up to your expectation of excellence.

Lee is actually more philosophical than I would be on the subject, but he concludes with thoughts that really call into question the way that we let efficiencies, progress, and a lack of history affect our environments:

> That being said, I understand and accept change. I embrace much of it myself, particularly as I see many beautiful peo-ple thriving from it. But there are injustices that cannot be ignored and should not be allowed to continue. This is a path that can very much be more softly tread and people honored correctly and respectfully along the way. These things are not happening.[7]

When I hear Lee speak, I am reminded so much of the way that farmers talk of being put off their land, whether it was during the Dust Bowl era or in the later 20th century with agricultural consolidation. The slower, more respectful pace Lee can imagine is one that also may have provided a little more breathing room, a little less uprooting.

Saying that the customer is not always right, sometimes demonstrably so, can be retail suicide. But continuing to pretend that the weight of these scales always needs to go in the same direction—privileging the consumer over other parts of the food system, privileging the people with the most money over longtime residents, privileging efficient, scaled-up models of business over traditional ones—may, on some small but insistent level, be societal suicide.

Let us contemplate this anecdote of cheese return because I think it is an important concept. The concept of "personal responsibility" has been politicized. The Right claims ownership of this term and uses it, often in racist ways, to bludgeon poor people. But there is truth to the actual concept. Customers, according to the mantra of retail, can never be wrong and thus never need to consider their own role in a given situation. It may be the changing demographics of the city combined with the fact that our store is so much larger now than when we started—as are the natural foods industry and the artisan cheese business—but it's enlightening to watch the behavioral trends emerge. Our old-school neighborhood customers feel desperately guilty asking for a return on anything, even when it is clearly a bad product. Sometimes they even refuse credit or exchange saying, "I just wanted to make sure you know." The new era of customers—not just in our city and not just in our store—are much more likely to demand the right to change their minds on whatever purchase they have made, for whatever reason. Whoever has to pay for it, it's not them.

Unlike the stereotype of the Right, however, the lack of personal responsibility is not usually a poor people scam. The people returning things, like the person mentioned above, tend to be young, male professionals. What is lacking is the bond to community. There is no trace of a similarity with the feeling of a grandson coming to a restaurant for years until he is an adult, knowing that both he and the business are creatures in the same environment.

It's very odd indeed, when it feels like the pinko-Commie worker-owned co-op is the only place left arguing for personal responsibility in the business world. We might not use that phrase "personal responsibility," but it's the real issue behind our internal debates on the subject. Lack of connection to the people around us is a societal problem.

I put myself in the shoes of the customer who wanted the exchange. I just cannot see myself coming to the same conclusion. I would think, "I bought too much of that perishable product. That was dumb," and compost the bad cheese. I wouldn't think, "Someone else must pay for my error in judgment."

Most people, of course, aren't like the type of customer I detailed above. I actually like and feel kinship with most of the customers I talk to on a daily basis. People with a lack of connection to the world around them, however, are a real problem, and they take up so much time and energy, and cause such annoyance, that it's easier to give in and just give them their money back rather than treat them as adults who made specific—and in this case, poor—choices. What does it cost us as a community when many retailers treat community members as if they were spoiled children? And following that logic, how can we ask a customer not to mythologize a view of food production that never was if we cannot ask them to have realistic, adult views in their other actions?

Interactions like the long-expired return are ones that make me find some reason to call up a cheesemaker somewhere and have a chat about a great recent batch of cheese or something, just to get the yuck out of my system. Lack of personal responsibility is not as common a trait among people in rural areas making food. But you know, you can't sell small-production, handmade cheese without customers.

As I mentioned above, the artisan food movements of the last couple of decades have tried a lot of strategies to link farmers and producers with the customers they need so they can survive the consolidation of the food business and prevent the elimination of the small farmer from the landscape. One of these strategies is to attack the very basic tenet of our food system, that cheap food is good food. We can see, looking at the history of cheddar from progressivism through the industrial food system, that the theory has been "If we want prosperity, the answer is to increase efficiency through technology so that we have cheap protein for all. This, in turn, will uplift us all."

Clearly, though, we are not all uplifted. The cost of food is the difficult part of the pro-artisan-food movement case to make. Social movements like Slow Food—started in Italy to support traditional producers—soon became a worldwide sensation with the "initial aim to defend regional traditions, good food, gastronomic pleasure, and a slow pace of life."[8] Indeed, many U.S. chapters incorporate the following language about the importance of food being "fair": "We believe that food is a universal right. Food that is fair should be accessible to all, regardless of income, and produced by people who are treated with dignity and justly compensated for their labor."[9]

I mean, I believe that, too. The question is how we get there. The main thrust of the argument for paying more for food is that corporate agriculture is subsidized, directly or indirectly. The little folks don't stand a chance unless we as consumers prioritize spending on food.

And a lot of people are also working on those issues. The term "food security"—defined by the World Health Organization in 1996 as "when all people at all times have access to sufficient, safe, nutritious food to maintain a healthy and active life"[10]—has become a much more widespread and well-understood concept. The Industrial Revolution created a mass exodus from country to city, but the devastation of rural America has created a lot of "food insecurity" in places that used to grow their own food. In addition, a "food justice" movement has formed across the country, made up mostly of urban people of color, to bring resources to those food-insecure places (often called "food deserts"), which are often just miles away from neighborhoods where "sustainable" food can be purchased at prices the poor and working classes can't afford. Like the $20 "shit tacos" down the street from the mac and cheese judging described in the first chapter.

What's the term needed to describe this continuing condition in our current food movements? "Contradiction"? "Irony"? "Systemic racism and classism"? At this moment in history, not unlike other moments in history (because that's how history rolls), there is a desire to enable small farmers and food producers to stay on, or repopulate, rural areas decimated by the consolidation of agriculture. At the same time, there exists at this moment in history, not unlike other moments in history, a desire to bring healthy, less-processed food to people who have no access to it.

People are working on bridging these desires every day—I make no claim to this as my personal revelation—but how it all comes together, *if* it can all come together, is a major problem of our time. Because the answers are not obvious. When the food movements become more market-driven niches, they leave out the commonality, and potential solidarity, between struggling people in different areas. If the movements don't consider markets, those rural producers won't be in business.

How does a food lover and champion of the underdog support small farmers and help them make a living? The issues are complicated and sometimes confusing, but the answer cannot simply be "pay more for food." Every few months a politically engaged article appears somewhere, written by some farmer as a call to action. In early 2015, my social media feeds were buzzing about Jaclyn Moyer's piece in *Salon*, "What Nobody Told Me About Small Farming: I Can't Make a Living," calling for real talk about how hard it is for small farmers to make a living farming. That fact is hardly a secret, but it still shocks people when they hear that 90 percent of farms in this country count on outside income or wealth to make ends meet.[11] Kurt Timmermeister's great book, *Growing a Farmer*, provides almost excruciating—in a political, not unreadable, sense—financial details about why he abandoned his attempt to make a living growing produce and turned to cheese production and other methods.

In the *New York Times*, shellfish farmer Bren Smith called for an independent farmers' movement to work on these issues:

> It's not the food movement's fault that we've been left behind. It has turned food into one of the defining issues of our generation. But now it's time for farmers to shape our own agenda. We need to fight for loan forgiveness for college grads who pursue agriculture; programs to turn farmers from tenants into landowners; guaranteed affordable health care; and shifting subsidies from factory farms to family farms. We need to take the lead in shaping a new food economy by building our own production hubs and distribution systems. And we need to support workers up and down the supply chain who are fighting for better wages so that their families can afford to buy the food we grow.[12]

But there is also an almost automatic resistance and counterattack from some readers to these types of pieces that imply farmers who speak up about these issues are in the wrong geographic area, have the wrong business plan, or that somehow these folks aren't real farmers. And sometimes that comes from other farmers or artisan food producers, too: ones who have figured out a way to make it work, who perhaps are relying on myths of the small farmer for their own marketing, or perhaps are simply unwilling to admit there is a national crisis that also affects them directly. The ground to organize on is unstable and hard when family farms have been decimated over the last century, yet multigenerational farming is what seems to give a farmer the most legitimacy. This kind of increasingly rare "legitimacy" is a new agrarian myth, or a new application of an old myth: one that is designed for our time, and one that often serves the interest of Big Ag and consolidated farming.

A dairy insider once told me, in an appreciative way, that "the average dairy professional in Wisconsin sees the world as divided into two types of people: real dairy farmers and super-fringe granolas." I can acknowledge which one I am in this configuration of the world and appreciate that. This kind of viewpoint is actually one of the things that makes me love Wisconsin dairy farmers: camaraderie and community. But the fact remains that small- to medium-scale farming is very hard to make work even if farmers together could be a powerful force. As shepherd and cheesemaker Rebecca King of Garden Variety Cheese asks, "In how many other professions do you have to have a second job to support your first job?"[13]

Another aspect to the struggle of small and medium producers, and one of the reasons that one part of a couple often has to have an outside-the-farm job, has historically been healthcare. In a conversation with Lissa Howe of Chiva Risa Ranch in Arizona, a farmstead artisanal goat cheese operation, she mentioned subsidies that farmers and food producers get in other countries. Food producers often invoke the idea of international subsidies—many of which no longer exist directly due to the World Trade Organization (WTO) and General Agreement on Tariffs and Trade (GATT)—to explain how sometimes foods from Europe can be sold more cheaply in the United States than similar, domestically produced versions. But then I realized Howe was talking about a much more personal benefit not often thought of as a farm subsidy, healthcare coverage and retirement security.

We all know that the United States pays more for healthcare and less for food than most industrialized countries. Our historic system is, in effect, a subsidy for the healthcare and insurance companies when it could be a subsidy—if one wants to look at it like Lissa Howe—for farmers and small businesses. I know that as a worker-owner of a cooperative I would love to have us get out of the health insurance business so we can concentrate on what we do as a store. For this reason, I have never understood the resistance from business people to healthcare reform.

In the end, I am more of a tourist to farmer issues than anything. I care about my food. I care about the landscape. I care about the environment. I care about all the small- to medium-scale farmers and cheese producers I have met, but I have never lived in a rural area and have never even gotten close to trying to make a go at farming or making cheese. I care about my wife's family's farm that, in a microcosm of the West Texas rural economy, has gone from cattle to sorghum to (mostly) the farming of old Coca-Cola signs from abandoned businesses to sell to people driving by on the highway.

There is as great temptation in this day and age . . . while writing a book in the first person . . . to try to be a know-it-all. To try to tell you what you should think about these issues, to give you the formula to help create a world were there is food security and where people can make a living farming. But I don't have that for you.

I'm not saying it's not possible. I am saying that no one can do it alone. We need to listen to and support people who work for a living in this country. That includes cheesemakers and people working the cheese assembly line at a Taylorized cheese factory. That means mongers and farmers. That means people in cities and people in the middle of nowhere.

Chapter 13

Mammoth Cheese and the Resurrection of Cheddar

I don't know why I saved California for the last part of my journey in search of cheddar, but I did. Sometimes the obvious examples are in your own backyard. Traveling around for a while can make you realize that.

There is really nothing about the approach to the Hilmar Cheese Company that would tell you that you are nearing the biggest cheesemaking plant in the world. Driving down the dusty road off California Highway 99, you pass orchards, cattle, dairy farms, and other industrial agricultural buildings like you'd expect. Hilmar actually has two plants—one in Dalhart, Texas, as well as this one in Hilmar, California—and between the two, they produce over 2 million pounds of cheese a day, but the original is the larger of the two.

I was looking for large-scale, giant bigness, so I noted the warehouse next door to the plant. It was the largest cheese (and whey product) warehouse I had ever seen. Trying not to crash, I lost count of the loading docks, but it looked more like a Safeway distribution center than any cheese warehouse I had ever been to. Upon arrival at the actual factory, it's hard to see how big the cheese plant is from outside. The aerial view of the entire plant—available on their website—tells a better story. Hilmar Cheese Company looks like a small town unto itself. If you ignore the scale and the adjacent farmland for a second, it looks like it has high-rises, apartment complexes, and churches. You could plop a cropped version of this picture on a map of a city and no one would know the difference. Heck, it's even got what look like swimming facilities. The self-guided tour inside does warn against swimming in dairy lagoons, though. Yuck.

Inside the visitor center you can see a display of how the cheese is made. The video wasn't working the day I visited, but there are displays downstairs with sectioned machinery, fake curds, and mannequin workers so you can get an idea of the process. Upstairs you can catch a glimpse of a tiny corner of the factory. That tiny corner subtly shows you something that you don't see every day, even if you are a cheese professional: a cheese tower with an explanation of how the 640-pound blocks are made. You are supposed to be able to watch what the workers are doing, but there was only someone with a hard hat and notebook during the time I was there. The contrast with Tillamook was notable. When I visited Tillamook, I was there at the same time of year (though on a weekend day) and the place was packed full of people eating, buying ice cream, and watching the cheesemaking. Pretty much every picture I took has someone in it.

I have it on good authority that the Hilmar visitor center is also usually pretty packed—there are large outdoor areas, picnic tables, and a fountain, so I am sure that is true. But the biggest difference was that at Tillamook the entire process of the cheesemaking was visible to visitors through multiple viewing stations. I was the only person upstairs in the cheese area at Hilmar, and only a tiny part of the process was visible. I'm not saying they were hiding anything; I'm just saying it made me appreciate Tillamook's openness even more.

But I'm not here to bash Hilmar. Heck, San Francisco 49ers quarterback Colin Kaepernick's dad was even vice president of operations for a while, and I have already stated that I am one of the Forty-Niner Faithful.[1] I'm here to see where the dream of the Williams factory has taken us.

I believe that the pioneers of the cheddar factory system had great vision. The early adopters created a way to make cheddar that enabled cheese-makers to make a good living in rural America at the time. The people who followed and who pushed the every-farm-a-factory system led us further away from farms as they were once known. Every advance in technology and science changed the way most cheese was made, sold, and seen. So much so that it's hard to picture Jesse Williams being transported into the present day and seeing a stainless steel fortress—no animals in sight . . . not even any milk in sight, shooting rindless cheddar blocks out of a conveyor belt—and feeling at home.

Mammoth cheeses were a source of pride to the people in cheese regions over the last couple of centuries. These giants were a huge community effort, taking the milk of many herds, and usually made for special events, fairs, or presidential inaugurations. Old pictures show them surrounded by the people who had hands in making them: ten, twenty, forty . . . some-times the entire community gathered for the photo op. And it is likewise hard to imagine them recognizing the 640-pound block of rindless cheese in the Hilmar factory—made in a closed tank and untouched by human hands—as the great-great-great-grandchild of their Cheddar Revolution. And yet, at Hilmar, they make cheddar in a size that once would have been an every-few-years cause for community celebration as their coin of the realm. They make mammoths by the minute.

I had always thought that "mammoth cheddar" just referred to the size of the cheese, but it turns out to be more interesting than that. The first recorded use of "mammoth" as an adjective for anything was for a 1,233-pound cheese—a Cheshire (a close relative of cheddar) delivered to President Jefferson in 1802. According to Elizabeth Kolbert, in her article attempting to restore the legacy of anatomist Frederic Culver, the spec-tacular unveiling of the skeleton of an American mastodon (at that point mistakenly thought to be a woolly mammoth) produced a fever of excite-ment across the Northeast.[2] This might sound like an odd occasion for a big cheese, but according to Kolbert this was "America's first blockbuster exhibit," and Americans simply needed to participate in their own way, whether it be baking "mammoth bread," "growing a mammoth parsnip," Cool-Hand-Luking a huge amount of eggs in order to proclaim oneself a "mammoth eater," or making a big cheese.

In fact, many important civic events have historically been celebrated with big cheese. Eunice Stamm's *The History of Cheese Making in New York State* has index entries for "Big Cheese" listing 1835, 1871, 1908, 1909, 1913, 1915, 1918, 1920, 1921, 1926, 1929, 1933, 1937, 1938, and 1957.[3] Almost all were made for state fairs or larger events. The "World's Largest Cheddar" that I tried to see before I even knew I was on a cheddar jour-ney? That 34,951-pound "Golden Giant" was created for the 1964 World's Fair (and since that fair was held in New York, probably also created for sticking a finger in the face of New York dairy by its Wisconsin makers).

As I mentioned, not even the fake box exists from that giant cheese anymore, but it is not the only cheese attraction wiped off the highway signs. According to the Roadside America website—the source where I first learned of the Neillsville cheese and that turns out to be an amazing font of knowledge for large cheese attractions—also gone is something billed as "largest wheel of cheese known" in Berlin, Ohio. That was actually a cheese, size unknown, that was either eaten or went bad, depending on the source you consult.⁴ Why, oh why, are we losing our treasured national monuments?

Other information on big cheese from Roadside America: "In fall of 1995, a Quebec, Canada, cheesemaker produced a behemoth 57,518-pound cheddar cheese, the largest ever. For several years before that, the largest was reportedly the 'Belle of Wisconsin,' a 40,060-pound cheddar, at Simon's Specialty Cheese in Little Chute, WI." The Internet is trying to tell me that there was a 56,850-pound cheddar made in Oregon in 1989 that was the largest ever made in America but provides no traceable sources.⁵

There's a pageantry to big cheese. The best stanza that dreadful cheese poet James McIntyre ever wrote was about a 7,000-pound Canadian cheddar made in 1866:

We'rt thou suspended from balloon,
You'd caste a shade, even at noon;
Folks would think it was the moon
About to fall and crush them soon.⁶

Sarah Kaufmann, whom I believe carved that cheese head I bought to scare my friends, holds the crown for the world's largest cheese sculpture, according to Guinness World Records, at 925 pounds. "It took a total of 36 hours to carve into the final sculpture, which included a pig, cow, boy, sprite, and chicken riding on a rollercoaster and celebrated the 160th anniversary of the Wisconsin State Fair."⁷ The original cheese was a 1,000-pounder made by Henning's Wisconsin Cheese in Kiel, Wisconsin. How can you not love that?

I don't really want to tell you about my experience with mammoth cheddar. It is kind of embarrassing, even for me as someone who likes to re-appropriate my embarrassing moments as funny anecdotes and important moments of growth. A couple of years after I first started cheese buying, our store moved to a much bigger location. Our biggest cheese vendor kept suggesting we should buy a mammoth cheddar to celebrate. I was wary, mostly because the idea of selling that much cheddar at one time was a little daunting at that point in my buying career. I mean, the whole thing is that it is on display and out of refrigeration during store hours. Once you cut into it you cannot afford to mess around.

I was not embarrassed about the wheel itself. I like big things. I like showpieces. I liked the kitsch factor. I liked taking my turn in the part of American culture that has celebrated that mastodon/mammoth since it was discovered. I liked evoking the county fair aspect of it. You don't get a lot of "county fair" in the city. And heck, the standard "mammoth" these days is only 500 pounds.

When we moved into our new location and I realized that selling the cheese would be challenging but not impossible, I decided to go for it. I mean, what the heck, eh? What's the worst thing that could happen? We have to throw a little cheddar away? Besides, the mammoth came in a wooden barrel so at the very least we would get a display out of the deal. And indeed we did. Post-mammoth, we used that display for over fifteen years to hold our Parmigiano Reggianos! Sorry Wisconsin, parmesans hold up better outside the cooler than cheddars do.

Amusingly enough, back in those days, I didn't even ask who the producer of the cheddar was. It is hard for me to believe this—and I lived it—but pre-Internet and pre-cheeses trendiness, people really didn't care. In California, the names of Wisconsin master cheddar-makers—names that would grace a Cheese Hall of Fame if one were ever created—meant nothing back then. Furthermore, if I had heard any of the master cheesemaker names (Cook, Hook, Widmer, and so on) in 1996, I—with two years of buying experience and only one pre-cheesemonger drive-through trip to Wisconsin under my belt—would not have recognized them. I mean, they are not exactly household names to nonprofessionals even today, but a Wisconsin cheddar wing of that Hall of Fame would certainly include the name Henning.

Henning's Wisconsin Cheese, yet another multigenerational cheddar-maker in Wisconsin, started in 1914. Today they are mostly known for their big cheeses—like the mammoth in question—and their flavored cheddars, which often win awards at the U.S. and World Cheese Championships. They claim to be the last cheese company in the country making cheddar wheels (rather than blocks) that are over 75 pounds. While a mammoth cheddar was a super-big deal to me, Henning's is kind of casual about it. A 4,500-pound cheddar is available right now "on request"; the only real delay being the time it takes to age it.

Still, I can't be embarrassed about not knowing the Hennings in 1996. Buying the mammoth was part of the road to learning about cheddar and the Wisconsin stars of the cheese world.

———————

I remember the day the mammoth came in. I was doing all the cheese receiving in those days. And the cheese truck driver was not looking at me fondly since there was an extra 500-pound crated cheese on my order. My sales rep and the owner of the distribution company showed up to help since 500 pounds of cheese is no joke and they wanted to make sure I didn't refuse it. The mammoth came on its own pallet so getting it off the truck was no problem; getting it off the pallet, however, was.

We rolled and pulled and levered and, finally, lifted the 500-pound monster on top of its barrel. I can think of a hundred different ways to do this more easily now. In fact, Henning's website now explains how to do it very easily. But back then we were just the equivalent of dudes pretending they knew how to work on their car. Wisconsin mongers can feel free to laugh at us. Handling a mammoth cheddar is probably explained on the first day of training for you folks. I'm sure you learn how to do it right after you learn how to say, "California may produce the most milk, but Wisconsin produces the most cheese," or "California cows aren't really that happy."

I don't know how many people we fit around the cheese to lift it, but when we got it in place I suddenly realized I had a question. How do we cut this thing?

At that point we were using the custom cheese cutting board I detailed at the end of chapter 3, "Of Bandages and Blocks," mostly to take care of all of our cheddars. That board was too small by about five feet to be of any use here. We had gotten one of those cheese wire garrotes (aka hand wires) to do Gruyères, so I figured I would use that. I was worried about cutting in a straight line since we needed to cut out a section and continue putting the top piece back on top to protect the rest of the cheese. Plus, the wire couldn't get through the cheese on its own.

The cheese itself was covered in a yellowy wax. Black grit was worn into the wax from sitting for a while in someone's warehouse, most likely the warehouse of the company so eagerly trying to sell me this cheese for years. Still, those distributor folks were helping as best they could. They were even actually touching cheese for once.

The cheese did look very impressive. It reminded me of the huge annual fall pumpkin that one farmer always brought us to put on display at the front of the store. Every year he's grown one big enough to cover almost our entire customer service desk from October until we put it out of its misery in January or so.

The mammoth was an oddly serious cheese. Maybe because of the ticking-clock aspect of cutting it, maybe because of the thick yellow wax coating and cheesecloth bandage underneath daring us to try and break through. The mammoth spoke of stature, of special occasions, of many farms and many cows, of special cheesemaking skill . . . of the history of large cheddar. Our new cheddar may not have been presidentially "mammoth," but it was mammoth enough to be a showpiece: to show that our department must be something to be taken seriously; that we knew what we were doing.

Except we didn't. We had no idea what we were doing with this cheese. I had taken a knife to score the cheese in order to get the wire in, but the cheesecloth-and-thick-wax combo was hard to penetrate. My lines were not neat. I was in danger of butchering 500 pounds of cheese like an amateur. The owner of the distribution company had a solution, though.

We had come a long way in the grocery and cheese worlds in a very short time. I feel lucky to have spanned the old-school and new-school cheese worlds. I think something that best describes the change is a video that many cheesemongers were passing around the Internet and mocking a few years ago. The video was of a cheese guy at an old Italian deli showing how to crack open a wheel of Parmigiano Reggiano. With "this is the way you do it" resignation and enthusiasm, he went at the poor Parm with a chisel and a hammer. If memory serves, the chisel was chipped and the hammer was rusty.

Even twenty years ago when I started working in cheese, the "correct" tools were not available. While a present-day shop would probably launch a Kickstarter campaign to buy a set of Parm knives before they would even open the doors, we cut Parm with a hot, flat cheese knife for years because, not only did we not have anything else, we had never *seen* anything else. A cheese importer gifted us a set and it—to this day—is the most special present anyone has ever given the department. Back then, even knowing someone who could get you these knives showed you had risen a notch in the world of cheese.

So I get it. I see no shame in that video. I did not laugh at it. You make do with what you have and you move on. For many of us in food, our workplaces were not started with venture capital, and a set of Parm knives for the cheese department would never be as high on the list as day-to-day repairs or saving for a new cooler or register system.

On the day of the mammoth's arrival, the owner of the distribution company said, "Do you have a big piece of wood and some nails?"

We went to the maintenance shop. As a worker co-op we pride ourselves in making and maintaining a lot of our fixtures, and we have a shop on premises. In order to get at this cheddar, it was good that we did. Under the worried eyes of our main woodworker, the cheese distributor got a thin three-foot piece of wood and pounded two long nails in it about four inches apart. Yes, we're getting to the part I am embarrassed about.

We went back to the cheese. The distributor grabbed the cheese-cutting weapon and, placing the top nail on top of the cheese, cut a groove all the way around the cheese with the lower nail, taking as much care as possible to just cut wax and not cheese. When that was done he repeated the process with the top nail in the fresh groove and the lower nail breaking new ground four inches below. "You probably want to bleach this off between uses," he said. I got the hand wire and cut out the four-inch-high cross section of mammoth cheese.

I can tell you right now, there is no way in 2015 that using an illegal street weapon to cut through the wax and cheesecloth on a cheese is considered a "best practice." That's probably the worst thing I have ever done to a cheese. Mongers today get a much more serious lesson in food safety thanks to the efforts of trade organizations and an increased knowledge of the cheese world in general.

May the spirit of Jesse Williams forgive me.

We are in a funny time in the food world right now. It's almost impossible to address the issue of food safety and hope that the words will mean anything in a couple of years. As I write this the Food Safety and Modernization Act (FSMA, pronounced "fis-ma" if you want to say it and sound like an expert) is being codified and implemented. FSMA is the biggest change in the laws that govern our food system since the Progressive Era, allowing for federal standards and oversight over many aspects of food growing, production, distribution, and selling. Some of the impetus behind it came from the September 11 attacks and the desire to make the food supply safer from terrorism; more push came from a concern for food safety in a system that was increasingly complicated, creaky, and hard to manage. But the changes that come from it are so sweeping and—at this point—such a moving target that in writing about specifics I run the risk of being out of date before the ink on your e-reader is dry.

The 2012 American Cheese Society Conference was so focused on food safety issues that when I got home and my coworkers asked me about it, I just responded, "THE THEME IS FEAR." Artisan cheesemakers, while trying to influence the process of FSMA implementation, are scared. In early 2014, the Food and Drug Administration seemed to be outlawing the use of wooden boards for cheese aging. After a huge uproar, they clarified their position, but this sums up the anxiety of the artisan cheese world at the moment. Practices used safely every day in cheese plants—big and small—around the country (and the world) may be forced to change as regulations are written with industrial food in mind. The history of cheddar tells us that the biggest companies and the biggest interests view eliminating traditional practices as safer than creating interesting flavor, that regional "eccentricity" is not an attribute, and that "science" is prone to pressure from political interests.

Further, the issue of wooden boards is one that an audience beyond professionals can get behind. The image plays on romantic notions of cheesemaking, but there are reasons cheese agers do it. Plus, many of the biggest producers in the world age on wooden boards in Europe, so there is some clout from those interests as well. Raw milk cheesemakers—feeling under threat for well into a second decade at this point—also worry that regulations that allow cheese to be sold after (among other specified conditions) sixty days of aging will be altered.

Artisan cheesemakers worry that the next attack on traditional cheesemaking, in the name of safety, will be through regulations on things like nonpathogenic bacteria and coliform counts (themselves not actually evidence of existing food-borne pathogens), which are a lot more obscure—and scary sounding—to someone not intimately involved in cheese science, and thus harder to organize consumer support around.

Distribution and retail regulations on tracking—remember that the FSMA is in part a reaction to 9/11—are much more easily handled by large companies that can devote full-time jobs to wading through the regulations and making sure they are up to code. So at the same time that "artisan" is commanding a higher price at the register, it is becoming much harder to supply "artisan" food if one is not a large corporation.

Some of this oversight is good, don't get me wrong. Having best practices and standards in place is essential for minimizing risk and creating
good food. The earliest proponents of factory cheddar production saw that,
in fact, as one of their biggest accomplishments and strengths. The worry
is that the laws written for the industrial-style food factories will not fit
with safe small-scale cheesemaking; that inspectors with little experience
in nonindustrial food production—rather than the current system in many
states where safety plans are worked out with dairy scientists who are
experts in cheesemaking—will cite things they do not understand; and
that traditional methods directly related to the distinct flavor and quality
of certain cheeses will be outlawed step by step.

Stepping back, that potential lack of understanding by future regulators
is quite understandable, at least in a historical sense. Every advance of
scientific method and technology in dairy has lead to plants like Hilmar
instead of the family farm. Large-production, untouched, standardized
640-pound cheeses are the nonprocessed culmination of the desire for
maximum sellable yield from a gallon of milk, the most "food-safe" version of natural cheddar imaginable, the maximum efficiency of the make
process accomplished. Large, automated food factories produce the most
food, so of course the regulations are geared to that scale of operation.

Hilmar efficiency doesn't stop there, of course. A whole division of Hilmar is about transforming whey protein and lactose into raw ingredients
for foods. I don't know if employees had been borrowing from the museum
for lunch breaks, but at the Hilmar factory, a slightly haphazard display
proclaims the existence of Hilmar ingredients in Toblerone, a Pillsbury
cookie mix, and a box of "Pocky," a 1990s hipster favorite chocolate-cov-
ered cookie stick from Japan. Hilmar's brochure brags, "Whey protein from
Hilmar Ingredients may be found in protein-fortified noodles in China,
infant formula in Vietnam, sports drinks and energy bars in the USA,
yogurt in Mexico, and egg-free mayonnaise in Russia."[8] This is the ultimate
reach of turning the farm into a factory, using every resource to work for
maximum profit.

Hilmar—though it now employs twelve hundred people in its two
locations—was started in 1984 by a dozen longtime dairy farmers in
California's Central Valley whom wanted to take advantage of the higher
butterfat content of the milk from the Jersey herds they owned. There
is nothing more traditional in the post-1851 American setting than this

type of business model in terms of cheddar. In a classic[9] article published in 1875 by *Harper's New Monthly Magazine,* the author described the basics of the "associated dairying" system: "As the fundamental idea of the American cheese-factory is association, the early factories were generally built with capital subscribed by a neighborhood of dairy-men, who become stockholders in the property of buildings and apparatus."[10] Hilmar is "associated dairying," just on a scale unimaginable by 1850s standards when mostly folks were trying hard just to get their cheddars not to rot before they could sell them.

Within thirty miles or so from Hilmar is Fiscalini Farms. In many ways, the cheese of Fiscalini, a farmstead dairy, is the best modern-day American version of the "independent dairy" that was the norm before 1851. Not totally surprising since the farm was started by the Fiscalini family in 1912[11] from a family that traces their dairy lineage back to 1705. Though most of the milk from the family farm's fifteen hundred cows is sold as fluid milk, they started making cheese in 2000. Who is in charge of the cheese operations now? The man who pretty much brought clothbound cheddar back to the United States: Mariano Gonzalez.

The Fiscalini 18 Month Bandage Wrapped, since Gonzalez started to work there, is probably the most decorated American cheddar. The first non-British cheddar to win the Wyke Farms Trophy awarded for best mature bandaged cheddar, the Fiscalini clothbound also won gold at the World Cheese Awards three times and first at the American Cheese Society competition at least five times.

Gonzalez uses the milk from only a select three hundred of the Fiscalini cows for cheesemaking, and indeed, not always that much if the fluid milk price is on the upswing. His cheese put the Fiscalini name on the map outside of Modesto. Many people consumed the high-quality Fiscalini milk, but because it was not packaged under their name and pooled with the milk of other dairies, they never knew it. Still, even though it is one of the most ribbon-awarded cheeses made in the United States, there's not a lot to be had. The yearly production of clothbound cheddar made at Fiscalini is a little over one-tenth of *one day's* production of cheese down the road at Hilmar.

However, Gonzalez didn't start his cheese career at Fiscalini, nor was the Fiscalini 18 Month Bandage Wrapped the first bandage-wrapped farmstead cheddar brought back to the United States. But how it came back is the story of the new artisan cheese movement.

The story of the resurgence of American cheesemaking has been told elsewhere,[12] but I have to talk about the achievements of the new American cheese movement of the last four decades here for the story of the return of aged clothbound cheddar to be told. From the seventies forward, the scale of cheese made in the United States has changed tremendously . . . in both directions. While we now have the Hilmars that can produce a million pounds of cheese a day, we also have an increasing amount of folks making cheese outside of the maximum-efficiency commodity cheese realm. Some of these people were multigenerational cheesemakers who were holdouts from the massive consolidation of the cheese business—people like Ig Vella, Sid Cook, and Franklin Peluso, who continued to work in small-scale cheesemaking despite the obstacles—but others were new to cheese. One of the features that distinguished these newcomers? A lot of them were women.

Gonzalez said that it was Zingerman's Deli owner Ari Weinzweig who first put the bug in his ear—at an American Cheese Society workshop on cheddar in 1993—about making a more traditional clothbound style. But it was—to borrow Paxson's phrase—this post-pastoral cheese movement that nurtured the idea, helped make it possible with logistical support, and created the market for it, the market that had dried up probably decades before.

I'd actually been unable, in this trip across the United States of Cheddar, to figure out who was the last producer of clothbound cheddar in the country before demand and supply dried up. I've heard rumors here and there—someone in Massachusetts . . . a farmstead dairy in Vermont—but nothing solid enough to put into print.

A discussion with Sid Cook helped me refine the question when he noted that makers like himself *never* stopped making the bandaged-wrapped wheels; they were just waxed instead of larded, and only aged for a few months, to be sold as 24-pound daisy wheels. The style of cheesemaking never went away; "the thing that went away was the cave aging," according to Cook.

Cook, in fact, says he was still making 72-pound mammoth clothbounds at the time Gonzalez started experimenting, but just for a few customers. What is now Carr Valley Cheese Company had been making these large clothbounds—waxed—since the 1980s and started making larded versions in the early nineties. Not too many of them, though: "That's a big piece of cheese, a big pain in the ass to work with."

Despite this continuing cheese method, American-made, larded, cloth-bound cheddar had fallen off the radar of cheese buyers, even at the stores that were trying to seek out the best American producers. When Campbell's Soup stopped buying unwaxed clothbounds in the sixties—if you are old enough to have had Campbell's Cheese Soup in the sixties and wonder if it tastes different now, well there's your answer—much of the market for this style of cheddar and its particular aging went away.

Mongers like Weinzweig were going to great lengths to get traditional clothbounds from England, working with cheese people there who selected wheels from farmstead producers: first the Quickes, then the Montgomerys and Keens. But none was to be had from the United States that he knew about. Availability of any larded clothbound cheddar was so rare that—even in 1964—the writers of one American cheese book concluded that it must have been banned from import at the behest of "our congressmen from the dairy states who act as minutemen for their constituents, defending the lucrative American Cheddar market against the redcoats."[13] I love a good conspiracy theory, but the truth is that in both England and the United States, traditional producers were hard to find.

What is clear, though, is when American-made clothbound cheddar returned to the mongers and most of the public. It was when Gonzalez was working at Shelburne Farms in Vermont in the nineties.

With the bug put into Gonzalez's ear, he sought out the methods forgotten in the United States for making clothbound cheddar. Once the state of the art, this cheese had, of course, given way to the waxed, then plastic-wrapped rindless blocks, and to the 640-pound ones like those produced at Hilmar. At first there were no recipes at hand, no hoops to make the cheese in, and no place to age it.

In the experimental stage, the burgeoning new cheese community came through. Ricki Carroll of New England Cheesemaking Supply Company provided historical recipes and cheesecloth; Cindy Major agreed to let the experimental wheels live in the Major Farms caves; and Debra Dickerson helped provide contacts with Randolph Hodgson at Neal's Yard Dairy. Hodgson eventually connected Gonzalez with the cheesemakers at Montgomery Farm and Keen's Dairy, two of the only remaining producers of the clothbound West Country Farmhouse Cheddar that is name controlled and made near Cheddar.

That many of the people who helped Gonzalez create a once-extinct-in-America cheese were women is no accident. Though women were usually the cheesemakers in pre-factory times, and though some hung on as cheese-makers through the 1800s, most were gone from the cheese scene until the comeback of artisan cheese in the 1980s. I feel thankful to have started my cheese career in California, where much of the goat cheese revolution happened. Why goat cheese was predominantly the domain of women is another question for another day, but almost all the cheese people I met in my early years, aside from the legendary Ig Vella and Franklin Peluso, were women, including many of the cheesemakers, most of the cheese buyers from other stores, and my most influential mentors.

I was West Coast based and didn't travel a lot in those early years, so I hadn't yet met women like Major or Carroll, but I wasn't surprised when I started going to cheese conferences that many women were helping to drive the movement. In fact, I felt like I had to relearn history when I began looking at the more commercial cheese world and saw that women, displaced as cheesemakers by the factory movement begun in the 1850s, were few and far between. As Carroll puts it, "Perhaps we had to move out of the way for a while for the men to move in but we're back in full force and I don't think we will see this trend reversing anytime soon." It is only fitting, then, that women like Carroll, Major, and Dickerson helped bring a modern version of pre-industrial cheesemaking back from the dead.

Weinzweig hadn't known Gonzalez had been working on the cheddar for a while, but does remember Gonzalez approaching him at cheese event years after the initial discussion and saying, "I have a surprise for you!" Indeed, the traditional clothbound cheddar surprised everyone with its reemergence. Gonzalez perfected the recipe with some help from the dairy scientist he calls his cheese mentor, Paul Kindstedt, who suggested, according to Gonzalez, that "my cheese needed a little science." In 1996 it was sent to Neal's Yard Dairy as part of an American cheese promotion highlighting some of America's best producers. According to Gonzalez and Shelburne Farms, a panel of English cheese experts and cheddar-makers considered it on par with the best English farmhouse cheddars.

Gonzalez eventually moved on from Shelburne Farms, back to his native Paraguay—where he made cheese until the political situation made it impossible—and then came back to the United States in 2001 to work at Fiscalini in the nonsnowy San Joaquin Valley of California. His cheddar is the most traditionally English of all the American clothbounds. It's less sweet and more crumbly, more dank and earthy, more mineral and sharp.

The Fiscalini 18 Month Bandage Wrapped cheddar is a piece of cheese that allows you to dream of what cheese can be. Once it was grasses, grain, silage, and water. Then a cow transformed it into milk. Then a cheesemaker created something so amazing that, even as we now can scientifically explain the texture and individual flavors, the cheese defies textbook definition. A cheese like a well-matured, bandaged-wrapped cheddar, a testament to the power of human ingenuity, somehow also retains an air of alchemy to the person who eats it. The process can be explained again and again, but to anyone but the most hardcore cheese-maker or chemistry-cruncher, one of the biggest fascinations of cheese is the way it metamorphosizes from grass to chunk. The Fiscalini cheddar is proof that there are values beyond efficiency and yield (though those are still important to any cheesemaker). Flavor counts, and coaxing that complexity out of a liquid (milk) that is usually taken for granted is a true combination of nature, skill, and the ability to see something that is not yet there. To achieve the future.

Since Shelburne Farms and Fiscalini began producing clothbound ched-dars, many others have as well. In fact, it is almost unbelievable that a cheese that almost died in England and pretty much did die in the United States has come back with such a vengeance. Cabot Clothbound Aged in the Cellars at Jasper Hill, Grafton Clothbound and Queen of Quality in Vermont, Flory's Truckle in Missouri, Flagship Reserve and FlagSheep in Seattle and New York, Avalanche (made with goat milk) in Colorado, Geor-gia Gold Clothbound in the South, Roelli Kingsley and Carr Valley cheeses in Wisconsin, and so on—you can get one close to local almost anywhere you go in the United States. Clothbound cheddars have managed to carve out followings despite costing a lot more than what people expect to pay for cheddar. Why is the price higher? In an article from *Culture Magazine* in 2009, Kate Arding writes, "Recent figures, for example, show that a pound of cheddar made at a large-scale U.S. facility costs between nineteen and twenty-one cents to produce, whereas a cloth-wrapped, American farm-stead cheddar, mature at one year, costs approximately four dollars per pound to produce."[14]

Though this shows the huge demand for a cheddar whose flavor had been lost to "progress" a generation or more earlier, most of today's new cheesemakers do not make cheddar, or if they do, they might even call it something else. But Jasper Hill depends on it. I didn't go into great detail about the noncheddar Jasper Hill cheeses when I visited them earlier on this journey, but they make some of the best cheeses in the country as well as aging some made by other cheesemakers, like the Cabot Clothbound. Their Winnimere is a raw milk seasonal, washed-rind, bark-wrapped cheese that stands with the best of the world. Harbison is my favorite oozy, pasteurized, soft-ripened cheese; their Bayley Hazen Blue and alpine-style Alpha Tolman represent some of the best made in this country. But it's unclear if any of these would exist without the cheddar.

While Jasper Hill briefly made a clothbound cheddar-ish cheese called "Aspenhurst," that didn't sell well and few remember it.[15] Jasper was paying the bills at their new aging facility in part by storing the cheese that would later be known for on a national level, Cabot Clothbound. A cheese originally developed by May Leach at Cabot, Jasper was storing it because Cabot's modern factory didn't allow for things like cheese mites and mold that come along with a bandaged cheddar. When this clothbound was aged and ready, Cabot realized they couldn't sell that cheese to their regular grocery store customers—after 150 years of moving away from traditional cheddar methods, those currents of "progress" could not be overcome so easily. So Jasper Hill stepped in and sold it all using their connections to the new cheese world that was embracing the older styles. A lasting cheese partnership was formed.

At the beginning, about 85 percent of the cheese Jasper Hill was aging in their cellars was Cabot Clothbound. Those hundreds of pounds of cheddar were necessary for Jasper Hill to make it during those early days. The clothbounds still take up a good portion of the caves—a little more than half at this point—and enable Jasper Hill to be sustainable enough as a business to continue making other amazing cheeses that, frankly, even though they have been with us less than a decade, I cannot imagine being without as a monger.

The Cabot Clothbound cheddar, aged in the Cellars at Jasper Hill, helped popularize, or more accurately repopularize, this amazing style of cheese and, like Gonzalez's reanimation at Shelburne Farms, was done while collaborating with other cheesemakers, much like the pioneers of the cheese factory back in the 1850s. Jasper's Andy Kehler says, "[Aging the clothbound cheddar] has brought us closer to Cabot, Grafton, Shelburne Farms, but something that is unique to Vermont is the community of cheesemakers that exists. We feel part of a very tight-knit community of cheesemakers, whether they are cheddar producers or Vermont Creamery making goat cheese." Indeed, much like how Jesse and Amanda Williams took a year off from cheesemaking just to visit other cheesemakers and compare notes, Jasper Hill folks and people from Vermont Creamery are planning on mutual visits to compare onsite labs, safety plans, and the beginning of open-book management. The whole concept of the Cabot Clothbound, that the state's largest producer, Cabot, is collaborating with an under-fifty-cow dairy to produce a cheese, shows a true spirit of cooperation.

Like Rogue Creamery in Oregon and many other artisan cheese producers, Jasper Hill has become the leading employer in their community, helping rebuild, albeit on a small scale so far, the devastated rural economy of their area. Andy Kehler explains:

> When you think about all these farms started in last ten to fifteen years . . . I'm not sure I would do this if I knew how complicated it was. It's not a get-rich-quick scheme. It's really a labor of love. Cheese is the means—a cool and tasty means [he laughs]—to achieve other ends. [Those ends are] preservation of Vermont's working landscape, ensuring agriculture is the highest and best use of land, keeping this community from turning into Anywhere USA.[16]

Jasper Hill even went so American one year for the Fourth of July that they made a poster.[17] An old-timey, tough-looking bald eagle clutches a clothbound cheddar in one set of talons while safeguarding a field of grazing Ayrshire cows. The banner reads FREEDOM, UNITY, AND CHEESE.

Clothbound cheddar came back to life. American-made versions, once unattainable at any price anywhere in the United States, are now sold in every store that deals in high-quality cheese. Traditional cheddar's resurgence mirrors all American, nonindustrial cheesemaking. In denying efficiency, yield, and cost as the ultimate measures, the comeback of the clothbound cheddar shows that the 640-pound block is not the destiny of all cheese. In the same way, those who view the farm as more than just a factory have helped create a much-needed economic alternative for those who want to live a rural life and make good food.

I left my apartment in San Francisco at 7:30 a.m. to visit Hilmar and Fiscalini. I was back in the city at 3:00 p.m. That's how close the past, present, and future of cheddar can be.

Chapter 14

Saturday Night's Alright for . . . Cheddar

Working a Saturday night shift is one of my favorite things about working in a grocery store. Now that I am older and don't care so much about what is going on socially on a Saturday night, I love the energy of the busy day, the need of many customers to have philosophical cheese discussions, and the desperate, near-closing-time, I'm-going-to-a-party-fill-my-cart-with-good-things customers, especially when they come back the next week to say they felt we steered them right.

Because cheese is just food. Sometimes it's bought for survival, sometimes for community and sharing, sometimes for showing off. Saturday also brings visitors from out of town, including touristing cheese professionals. These folks are usually my favorite customers, but occasionally we have professional disagreements.

"I want to buy the best cheeses you have for my hosts," said the visiting cheese person from the Very Well-Known and Important Cheese Shop.

"Any particular types you are looking for?"

"No, just the best ones. I only have one rule. No cheddar."

I looked at her. I expected to see her smiling. I thought we would laugh together—merrily, as cheesemongers do—about the foibles of customers, about the weird demands we get, about people's weird and arbitrary rules. But no. She was serious.

Anyone who considers themselves a cheese lover, let alone a cheese professional, who dismisses a whole class of cheese out of hand is missing out on something. But for an American cheese worker—who works at one of the few cheese companies that is known nationally—to have a blanket personal ban on this country's most iconic cheese just struck me as sad. Mostly because I understand it on a personal level.

I mean, a customer's "no-cheddar" rule isn't really my business. People can choose to eat or not eat whatever they want, cheese-wise, and it doesn't really matter to me. But this one-person boycott seemed misplaced. As if, to prove you are a cheese expert, you have to draw that line for friends and family. You are saying, I am better than cheddar. I am better than the common people who don't know any better than to eat America's most popular cheese for 150 years.

American cheesemongers—and I recognize this in myself—can have an inferiority complex. This complex is well earned. As we travel from cheese curious to cheese committed, mongers can feel the sins of our collective American history. When you rub elbows with European *affineurs* (professional cheese agers); taste cheese with people whose families can trace their cheese history back to before there was a United States of America; visit impossibly small, cramped make-rooms where a fire is built to heat copper kettles because there simply is no power near the top of the mountains—well, you can feel something like guilt.

Not the kind of guilt like you personally did something, but the weight of being part of a culture that, for the most part, dismissed traditional practices in the name of progress, efficiency, food safety, and profit. As a cheesemonger today, you have a responsibility to put the new use of traditional practices in context, explain the pricing—and the value—of inefficiency. One of our many jobs is to share lasting images of the actual people who make small-batch cheeses.

So in some ways, we mongers get asked to stand in opposition to the most well-known of American cheeses. It's a small step to think that ignoring them, mocking them, or banning them from our lives can make us more pure and more in touch with a mythic ideal of "real" cheesemaking.

But what about all the clothbound monster-wheels and the lard-covered truckles? The bitter Vermonters and the smooth West Coast melters? The evocative Wisconsins and the trendy-sweet and crystalline 40-pounders? That's a lot of cheddar to deny.

I love cheddar too much to deny it. And really, I couldn't even if I wanted to. It's part of my inheritance as an American. Only someone with an agenda would deny that our inheritance is a mixed bag. The contradictions of our history are undeniable, but our responsibility, as humans, is to try to improve on the good that is possible in our contemporary lives. This responsibility applies to culture, political institutions, work, and everything else. It applies to the practices associated with producing food and to the quality of the food that we eat, as well.

Cheddar is part of who I am. I grew up on processed cheese—due to the societal forces that made it the ubiquitous choice—but I can seek out better types of the form today . . . better for health, better for workers, better for farmers, better for the environment, better for eaters, better for us all.

Walking home from the store that night, I thought about Rome, New York. I wondered if there was another rededication or community celebration in 2001 for the 150th anniversary of the Williams factory. A sesquicentennial would seem to be an obvious time to celebrate, a great historical reminder of Upstate New York's place in the history of cheddar.

Perhaps this time, instead of the Cold War hero that the town boosters tried to re-create Jesse Williams as in 1951, there would be a celebration of Williams's true admirable qualities, the aspects I like to remember more. The part of his 1865 eulogy that described his cooperative nature: "His was no narrow and contracted spirit that sought to cover up and hide the mysteries of his art for personal aggrandizement. He gave of his knowledge freely to all who came."[1]

I searched for the 150-year commemoration. I contacted the local historical society again. I asked everyone I could think of in that area if they had heard of any celebration. Nothing. If Williams was honored for his legacy in 2001, I couldn't find a trace.

I guess we'll have to hold the Williams cheddar legacy in our hearts. And honor it by seeking out the cheeses made by people who share a dedication to demystification, community, and real cooperative spirit.

NOTES

Chapter 1. Mac and Cheese, Class War, and the Many Meanings of Cheddar

1. A would-be urban editorialist? An ironist in the tradition of Ambrose Bierce? Herb Caen's ghost? The mystery remains. . . .
2. Undoubtedly by the time this book is published, drunken Ping-Pong will be just another nearly forgotten moment in the saga of hipster trends, but for now it is the most apt.
3. Interview with Jeannie Choe, 2/18/2013.
4. Pierre Boisard, trans. Richard Miller, *Camembert: A National Myth* (Berkeley: University of California Press, 2003).

Chapter 2. The Idea of Wisconsin and The Wisconsin Idea

1. As of the 2010 Wisconsin Milk Marketing Board Master Cheesemaker Directory.
2. Edward Jesse and David Wieckert, *The Dairy Industry of Wisconsin* (Madison: Babcock Institute, University of Wisconsin, 2007).
3. Interview with Jeanne Carpenter, 2015.
4. Promotional organizations tend to just say cheddar cheese has been made since the 1100s. Historians and dairy scientists tend to speak of the technical improvements that mark different eras of cheese made near Cheddar, enumerating the differences between the cheddar of different eras and what we eat today.
5. Clifford A. Wright, accessed from the website February 2015, http://www .cliffordawright.com/caw/about.html.
6. Patrick Rance, *The Great British Cheese Book* (London: Macmillan London Limited, 1982), 5.
7. John Squire, ed., *Cheddar Gorge, A Book of English Cheeses* (New York: Macmillan, 1938), 45.
8. Just a quick definitional note here since I use the words "farmhouse" and "farmstead" in close proximity. "Farmstead" means that cheese is made solely with the milk of the cheesemaker's own animals and on his or her own property. "Farmhouse" does not really mean anything in the United States, but it implies a traditional method of production and ingredients. In the case of West Country Farmhouse Cheddar, though, it is legally meaningful because it is part of a recognized Protected Designation of Origin (PDO) or "name control," which means that only cheese made in a particular region, using particular methods, can be labeled with those words. The "Farmhouse" in this PDO requires that the Cheddar age at the farm where the cheese is made, whereas the meaning will vary for non-PDO cheeses.
9. USDA Milk Production Report, February 2011, http://www.progressivedairy .com/downloads/2011/general/2011_pd_r_mw_stats_lowres.pdf.

10. Ibid.
11. Table 11, Cattle and Calves—Inventory and Sales, *2007 Census of Agriculture*, Vol. 1, National Agriculture Statistics Service, USDA, 381-398, http://datcp.wi .gov/uploads/Food/pdf/StateDairyStatsApril-30-2010.pdf.
12. Dan Simmons, "Scott Walker backtracks from striking 'truth,' 'human condition' from Wisconsin Idea," *Wisconsin State Journal*, 2/5/15, online version accessed February 2015.
13. Ibid.
14. Conversation with Jane Burns on social media, February 2015.
15. Not that there's anything wrong with that.
16. Edward Janus, *Creating Dairyland* (Madison: Wisconsin Historical Society Press, 2011), 7.
17. Janus, 9. I just had to include this because in today's day and age—when I can count the number of women I have seen managing herds of cows on two hands—this is just such a spectacular reversal.
18. Eric Lampard, *The Rise of the Dairy Industry in Wisconsin* (Madison: Wisconsin Historical Society, 1963), 113–14.
19. Janus, xii.
20. Janus, 20.
21. Things such as "filled milk cheese"—see chapter 5.
22. Phillips, at some live performances, gave credit to feminist Clare Spark for coining the term "long memory" in this context.
23. Interview with Andy Kehler, August 2014.
24. I should point out that this is not an equivalency because those opposed to the idea of climate change are actually elected officials, while those opposed to vaccines are relatively marginal (while still being able to do damage because of the math of herd immunity).
25. Janus, 20.

Chapter 3. Of Bandages and Blocks

1. Interview with Ari Weinzweig, February 2015.
2. Interview with Mariano Gonzalez, 2015.
3. It is pouring rain as I type this. I took a quick look at Facebook, and under the caption, "Some things at the Civic Center never change," someone had posted a picture of a plastic trash can set up inside the building to collect the rain.
4. Cheese triers are also called cheese irons or cheese testers. They are stainless steel tools that are sharp enough to stick into a cheese a few inches, twist, and come out with a nice, clean section of cheese to smell, examine, and taste for judging or grading. After judging the core part of the sample, the plug can be put back in and resealed (with a little spare cheese) so the cheese can continue aging.
5. A kilo, of course, is 2.2 pounds. In the United States, only drug dealers and cheese sellers are fluent in metric weights.

6. "Dermatitis caused by contact with mites found in grain, cheese, or dried foods," *Mosby's Medical Dictionary*, 8th ed. (St. Louis: Mosby, 2009).

7. This pooling of liquid can lead most often to the defect in flavor known as "whey taint," which is on one hand exactly what it sounds like and on the other hand totally *not* what it sounds like, depending on how much time you spend with dairy scientists or people who use words defined in the Urban Dictionary.

Chapter 4. Oh Geez, What Is Cheddar Anyway?

1. Dave Pierson, "Vegan mayonnaise maker sued by food giant Unilever," *Los Angeles Times*, 11/10/14, http://www.latimes.com/business/la-fi-just-mayo -20141110-story.html.

2. The image, or nonimage, of the egg on the label is another part of the issue bringing up existential questions of whether a representation is a representation of inclusion or absence, but that is beyond the scope of this book.

3. You can find lots of versions of this online. Personally, I love the Widmer's Cheese website because it's so old-timey, but there are many to choose from; https://www.widmerscheese.com/pages/Cheddar.html.

4. Frank Kosikowski, professor of food science at Cornell University and founder of the American Cheese Society, viewed the cheddaring step, introduced to the United States by Robert McAdam, as a crucial part of the historical improvement of cheddar made in this country. Piling slabs of curd on top of each other to exude more whey (which was then immediately separated from the curd because of McAdam's vat engineering skills) "permitted the unrefrigerated so-so quality milk of the period to be made into excellent cheese without concern for gassiness." Quoted in Robert Lake, "Cheddarland USA," Rome Historical Society, 1986, 7.

5. Conversation with Daniel Utano, May 2015.

6. Val Cheke, *The Story of Cheese-Making in Britain* (London: Routledge and Kegan Paul, 1959), 13–14.

7. Paul Kindstedt, *Cheese and Culture* (White River Jct, Vt.: Chelsea Green, 2012), 196–97.

8. Ibid.

9. Ibid., 171.

10. Ibid., 194.

11. Eunice Stamm, *The History of Cheese Making in New York State* (Endicott, N.Y.: E. R. Stamm, 1991), 89.

12. Kindstedt, 204.

13. Stamm, 89.

14. Frank V. Kosikowsi and Vikram V. Mistry, *Cheese and Fermented Milk Foods* (Westport, Conn.: F. V. Kosikowski LLC, 1997), 214.

15. *Code of Federal Regulations*, Title 21, Vol. 2, Revised as of April 1, 2014, CITE: 21CFR133.113.

16. Ibid.

Chapter 5. In Search of the First Cheese Factory

1. Hakim, Danny, "Is One Museum Honoring Cheese Really Enough?" *New York Times*, 5/10/2006, http://www.nytimes.com/2006/04/10/nyregion/10cheese.html?pagewanted=all&_r=0.
2. While that number is absolutely a guess based on no study whatsoever except personal anecdote, I should note that it would be smaller if not for the historical marker that all the Rome Fish Hatchery workers see every morning on their way to work.
3. E-mail correspondence with Nicki Sizemore, 8/26/14.
4. The only cheese I know that looks anything like the pictures and drawings I found is the Italian cheese called Grottone, which comes to the United States wrapped in a burlap sack and tastes like a cross between baby Swiss and a bitey Italian provolone. It's awesome, but good luck finding it.
5. "The Romance of Cheese," Kraft-Phenix Cheese Corporation, 1935.
6. Stamm, 45.
7. E. L. Resh, *Associated Dairying* (Lancaster, Pa.: S. H. Zahm and Company, 1879), 8.
8. Ibid., 8–9.
9. Ibid., 12.
10. Ibid., 15.
11. Alexis de Tocqueville, *Democracy in America* (New York: A. S. Barnes and Co., 1856 edition), 35–36.
12. In a passage that made me laugh over and over again, Fox News commentator Sean Hannity (according to factcheck.org and other sources) denounced President Obama for having "marginalized his own country by saying our sense of exceptionalism is no different than that of the British and the Greeks." Everyone should know our sense of exceptionalism is the best sense of exceptionalism in history!
13. All sources of this reference its original anonymous publication in 1864 in a newspaper or journal called *Ohio Farmer*. I could not confirm this, but I can confirm it was printed (as a reprint) in *The Kraftsman*, Kraft Foods Chicago, Vol. 9, No. 3, May–June 1951.
14. Not specifically about cheesemaking, but a great resource for further study of this question is Sally McMurry's *Transforming Rural Life: Dairying Families and Agricultural Change, 1820–1885* (Baltimore: Johns Hopkins University Press, 1995).
15. Robert Lake, *Cheddarland USA* (New York: New York State Historical Society, 1986), 4.
16. Erie Canal Village official website, accessed August 2014, http://www.eriecanalvillage.net.
17. Frederick A. Rahmer, *Jesse Williams: Cheesemaker* (Rome, N.Y.: Frederick A. Rahmer, 1971).
18. Welcome to the sentence that will make this book seem incredibly dated within just a few years.

19. Vermont State Board of Agriculture Annual Report, 1877, 19.
20. Kindstedt, 207.
21. Ibid., 164.
22. "Swiz" or "Swizz" is English slang for swindle or rip-off. It would have been a more appropriate name.
23. Filled milk cheese was effectively banned in the United States from the 1930s until President Nixon repealed the Filled Milk Ban in 1974. Immediately a few of the big companies jumped into the market with unsuccessful products that few remember today: "Golden Image," "Country Meadow," and "Cheezola."
24. *Hearing on Filled Milk Before the US House of Representatives Committee on Agriculture*, June 13, 1921, 18.
25. Ibid.
26. Squire, 45.
27. Stamm, 85–87.

Chapter 6. Vermont Is Not Wisconsin

1. Edward Jesse and David Wieckert, *The Dairy Industry of Wisconsin* (Madison: Babcock Institute, University of Wisconsin, 2007).
2. Though there was a Robert in the McCadam family, don't confuse this company with the Robert McAdam who was one of the people who popularized the cheddaring part of the cheddar process in the United States and whom I mention in chapter 4.
3. Correspondence with Dane Huebner, 9/8/2014.
4. Incidentally, Grafton is one of the only clothbound makers who—as of this writing—use butter on the outside of their clothbounds instead of lard.
5. Squire, 53.
6. It is really easy to get Vermont Farmstead mixed up with Vermont Creamery ever since the latter changed their name from Vermont Butter and Cheese Company. Don't do it! Vermont Creamery makes amazing goat cheeses and great butter, but they don't make cheddar.
7. This is the kind of thing one does when faced with repetitive work. I know that the Marley song is much more serious than our song, dealing with the courage of Black soldiers fighting racism while entrenched in a racist society. I also know that water buffalo are not bison. Lastly, I must credit Andreas Levi for the "refrigerate for survival" line that is the cleverest part of this doggerel.
8. What's up, Wisconsin? The community can own the Green Bay Packers but not save small-town cheese plants the same way?

Chapter 7. Eat My Wookey Hole

1. I was surprised when I looked it up, but "Wookiee" is the George Lucas–approved spelling. Since he made it up, we should probably defer to him on this.
2. Conversation with Mary Quicke, 2011.

3. The West Country Farmhouse Cheddar PDO definition is available here: https://www.gov.uk/government/uploads/system/uploads/attachment_data /file/271260/pfn-west-country-farmhouse-cheddar.pdf.

4. Again with the official George Lucas *Star Wars* spelling of Chewbacca's nickname . . .

5. Stamm, 76.

6. Rance, 9.

7. Ibid., vi.

8. Ibid., 6.

9. Ibid., 10.

10. Michael Raffael, *West Country Cheesemakers* (Edinburgh: Berlinn Limited, 2006), 74.

Chapter 8. Curds and Raines

1. Interview with Daniel Utano, January 2015.

2. Drake, Lopetcharat, Clark, Kwak, Lee, Drake, "Mapping Differences in Consumer Perception of Sharp Cheddar Cheese in the United States," *Journal of Food Science*, Vol. 74, No. 6, 2009, 277.

3. Michael Tunick, "The Biggest Cheese? Cheddar" *Boston Globe*, 2/23/2014.

4. It's actually a little more complicated than that, but for our purposes here this is the best way to think about it.

5. Interview with Neville McNaughton, May 2015.

6. Ibid.

7. "Taste Test: Artisanal Cheddar," *Cook's Illustrated*, July 2012.

8. Interview with Neville McNaughton, May 2015.

9. Ibid.

10. Correspondence with Paul Kindstedt, March 2015.

11. Interview with Neville McNaughton, May 2015.

12. Ibid.

13. No reason to bring any real names into this.

14. NPR, accessed on February 2015, http://www.npr.org/blogs/thesalt/2013 /11/07/243733126/ow-17th-century-fraud-gave-rise-to-bright-orange-cheese.

15. I should probably say that I have no idea if that company got the ad contract or not. All these conversations were on the phone, and I don't even remember the name of the person I talked to.

16. Kindstedt, 116.

17. Original quote is Maude Lacy, "A Neglected Side of the Labor Problem," *American Kitchen Magazine*, November 1899, 45, but I found it quoted in Charlotte Biltekoff, *Eating Right in America* (Durham, N.C.: Duke University Press, 2013), 20.

18. B. D. Gilbert, *The Cheese Industry of the State of New York* (Washington, D.C.: 1896).

19. William T. Stead, *If Christ Came to Chicago* (Chicago: Laird & Lee, 1894), 139.

Chapter 9. Velveeta: A Crowning Achievement of American Science

1. Harvey Levenstein, *Fear of Food* (Chicago: University of Chicago Press, 2012), 18.
2. Ibid.
3. Ibid., 21.
4. One might wonder if the eggs really wanted to be let out of prison just to be made into omelets, but let's agree not to dwell on that.
5. I did not quote from it, but I want to note my debt to her work for concise information about this time period in American food history.
6. Paul Kindstedt showed the incredible unlikeliness of this happening very thoroughly in his book *Cheese and Culture*. There is simply no excuse for telling this story anymore.
7. "The Romance of Cheese."
8. Are you actually looking for a source here?
9. There is a difference between "processed cheese" and "pasteurized processed cheese food," but I have already quoted the CFR for cheddar in this book and worry that quoting more CFRs will cause you, the reader, to give up in technical disgust. Basically, there is less cheese and more other stuff in the "cheese food."
10. All quotes about Soylent are from their website, accessed February 2015, http://www.soylent.me.
11. Cheke, 257.

Chapter 10. Boosting the Cheese Centennial

1. Sinclair Lewis, *Babbitt* (New York: Bantam Books, 1922).
2. *Rome (N.Y.) Daily Sentinel*, May 29, 1951.
3. *Rome (N.Y.) Daily Sentinel*, June 1, 1951, 18.
4. Ibid., 23.
5. Setting the mood in the week's editions of the *Daily Sentinel* was not only news of the Korean War, but also of a local union head dismissing a member who was accusing the union of insufficient anti-Communism, which resulted in the union leader losing his own job.
6. *Rome (N.Y.) Daily Sentinel*, June 1, 1951, 22.
7. Ibid., 19.
8. Stamm, 211.
9. William Nicholls, *Post-War Developments in the Marketing of Cheese* (Iowa State College of Agriculture and Mechanical Arts, Research Bulletin 261, June 1939).
10. Old-school Wisconsin cheesemakers would argue that it definitely wasn't Colby. Many are still annoyed at the recalibration of the Colby CFRs that happened more than a generation ago.
11. From video at tillamook.com, accessed February 2015. One issue I actually do have with Tillamook is the fact they do not use the .coop top-level domain, even as a redirect.

12. Archie Satterfield, *The Tillamook Way: A History of the Tillamook County Creamery Association, a Farmer-Owned Cooperative* (Tillamook County Creamery Association, 2000), 56.
13. To be clear, private label brands of cheese—ones labeled under your supermarket's name—are far and away the most popular. Also, calling Cabot third in name brand requires adding the two Cabot brands together. These numbers sourced from statista.com, accessed February 2015.

Chapter 11. The Cheddarpocalypse

1. Interview with Chris Roelli, 3/22/2011.
2. Deborah Fitzgerald, *Every Farm a Factory* (New Haven, Conn.: Yale University Press, 2003), 4–5.
3. Tami Parr briefly covers this in her terrific book, *Pacific Northwest Cheese: A History* (Oregon State University Press, 2013), and I am indebted to her for helping me find more mentions in *National Butter and Cheese Journal*.
4. "News of Food," *New York Times*, January 21, 1948.
5. "The Romance of Cheese," 24. I want to thank cheese consultant Marc Bates for pointing this out. I actually had read the pamphlet but missed that part the first time.
6. When "natural" is used to describe cheddar, it is to differentiate it from processed cheese and processed cheese food. It's the industry term, but it makes sense here.
7. Source for these three paragraphs is the USDA dairy products reports from various years, but I found it all put together nicely in Jorge M. Agüero and Brian W. Gould's paper, "Structural Change in U.S. Cheese Manufacturing: A Translog Cost Analysis of a Panel of Cheese Plants," presented at the Annual Meeting of the American Agricultural Economics Association in 2004.
8. Rachel Maines, "Rocky Landscape with Cheese Factory: The Stone Mills Union of LaFargeville, New York, 1896–1925" New York History, 2009.
9. **Four Principles of Scientific Management**

   Taylor's four principles are as follows:

   1. Replace working by "rule of thumb," or simple habit and common sense, and instead use the scientific method to study work and determine the most efficient way to perform specific tasks.
   2. Rather than simply assigning workers to just any job, match workers to their jobs based on capability and motivation, and train them to work at maximum efficiency.
   3. Monitor worker performance, and provide instructions and supervision to ensure that they're using the most efficient ways of working.
   4. Allocate the work between managers and workers so that the managers spend their time planning and training, allowing the workers to perform their tasks efficiently.

10. In about the most timely reference to work into this book before it gets published, Esther Kaplan's essay "The Spy Who Fired Me: The Human Costs of Workplace Monitoring," *Harper's Magazine*, Vol. 350, No. 1978, March 2015, is a fascinating article on current issues of increased scientific management enabled by new technologies.
11. Janus, 11.
12. See chapter 5.
13. My wife teaches college and has to spend an inordinate amount of time explaining what a "shirtwaist" is to her students before she can get to the meat of the story.
14. Janus, 100.
15. Interview with Sid Cook, February 2015.
16. All Arding quotes from an interview on 4/18/2011.
17. Interview with Chris Roelli, 3/22/2011.

Chapter 12. Cheddar-Making or Myth-Making?

1. Richard Hofstadter, *The Age of Reform* (Knopf Doubleday, 1955), 24.
2. I'm not saying that doesn't take skill. Just that the issues are different.
3. Michael Paterniti, *The Telling Room: A Tale of Love, Betrayal, Revenge, and the World's Greatest Piece of Cheese* (New York: Dial Trade Paperback, 2014), 297.
4. Heather Paxson, *The Life of Cheese* (University of California Press, 2012), 11–12.
5. U.S. Environmental Protection Agency website quoting the USDA farming census of 2007, accessed February 2015, http://www.epa.gov/agriculture /ag101/demographics.html.
6. Here is the disclaimer paragraph. Disclaimer paragraphs were not covered in my pre-Internet high school journalism class, but they are a new necessity in nonfiction writing. In this chapter, I am not trying to be all, "You kids get off my lawn!" In fact, I actually do not *have* a lawn, or even a small yard. When one writes about disappointing behavior these days, it often gets transformed by some readers or would-be nitpickers into something unrecognizable. So here it goes. . . . I am not talking about situations where customers have actually been wronged. Any reputable cheese person guarantees all their cheese not only for defect but for satisfaction. No, I am talking about situations where generosity is taken advantage of and where some customers consider themselves blameless while committing actions that are clearly their fault. This is the paragraph I am writing so that I can quote it later when the following is inevitably misinterpreted.
7. These quotes are used with permission from a nonpublic blog post written in 2014.
8. Slow Food website, accessed February 2015, http://www.slowfood.com /international/7/history.
9. Slow Food San Francisco website, accessed February 2015, http://www.slow foodsanfrancisco.com.

10. World Health Organization website, accessed February 2015, http://www .who.int/trade/glossary/story028/en.
11. Jaclyn Moyer, "What Nobody Told Me About Small Farming: I Can't Make a Living," accessed 2/9/2015, salon.com.
12. Bren Smith, "Don't Let Your Children Grow Up to Be Farmers," *New York Times Review*, 8/9/2014.
13. Conversation with Rebecca King, February 2015.

Chapter 13. Mammoth Cheese and the Resurrection of Cheddar

1. Gordon Edgar, *Cheesemonger, A Life on the Wedge* (White River Jct, Vt.: Chelsea Green, 2010), 90.
2. Elizabeth Kolbert, "The Lost World," *New Yorker*, 12/16/2013.
3. Stamm, 309.
4. Roadside America website, accessed February 2015, http://www.roadside america.com/tip/982.
5. I traced this back but am awaiting a confirmation response.
6. James McIntyre, "Ode on the Mammoth Cheese Weighing over 7,000 Pounds," accessed February 2015, http://en.wikisource.org/wiki/Ode_on_the _Mammoth_Cheese_Weighing_over_7,000_Pounds.
7. Guinness World Records website, accessed February 2015, http://www .guinnessworldrecords.com/world-records/largest-cheese-sculpture.
8. Hilmar brochure, February 2015.
9. Classic to the few hundred people in the world who obsess about old dairy history, at least.
10. "Butter and Cheese," *Harper's New Monthly Magazine*, 1875, 818.
11. This is likely an unnecessary footnote, but most articles and websites seem to list 1914 as the starting date. This information is from fiscalinicheese.com.
12. For an anthropological view, *The Life of Cheese* by Heather Paxson is an amazing study, but many books written within the last fifteen years—too many to name—tell parts of this amazing story.
13. Vivienne Marquis and Patricia Haskell, *The Cheese Book* (New York: Simon and Schuster, 1964), 84. I can find no evidence of any ban on English cheddar after looking through old quotas and tariff agreements and consulting English and American cheese people whom I thought might know. As far as I know the United States was importing almost 3 million pounds of cheddar a year, though mostly from Canada, not England.
14. Kate Arding, "Ask the Cheesemonger," *Culture Magazine*, Fall 2009.
15. Though, amusingly, it has spawned a "Bring Back the Aspenhurst" Facebook page.
16. Interview with Andy Kehler, 2014.
17. The artist was a Vermonter named Natalya Zahn.

Chapter 14. Saturday Night's Alright for . . . Cheddar

1. Xerxes Willard, quoted in Stamm, 136.

INDEX

ABOUT THE AUTHOR

Photo by Myleen Hollero

GORDON EDGAR loves cheese and worker-owned co-ops and has been combining both of these infatuations as the cheese buyer for San Francisco's Rainbow Grocery Cooperative since 1994. Edgar has been a judge at numerous national cheese competitions, a board member for the California Artisan Cheese Guild, and has had a blog since 2002, which can be found at www.gordonzola.net. Edgar is the author of *Cheesemonger: A Life on the Wedge* (Chelsea Green, 2010), and he enjoys mold in the right places, good cheese stink, and washing his hands upward of one hundred times a day.

green
press
INITIATIVE

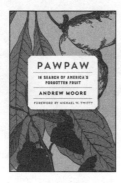

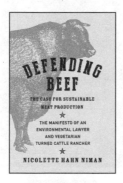

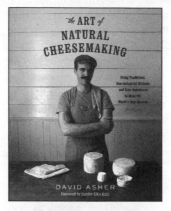

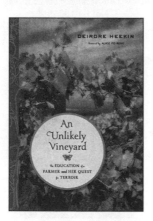
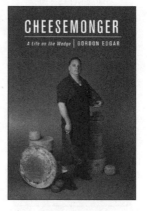